TRAINING MANUAL FOR GODS

Book One

Consciousness
and the
Unseen Universe

Chiron &
Sophia Ovidne

Training Manual for Gods, Book One
Consciousness and the Unseen Universe
Chiron and Sophia Ovidne

First published in Australia by Sophia Ovidne 2023
www.earthwithspirit.com

Copyright © Sophia Ovidne 2023
All Rights Reserved

A catalogue record for this
book is available from the
National Library of Australia

ISBN: 978-0-6457396-0-2 (pbk)
ISBN: 978-0-6457396-1-9 (ebk)

Typesetting and design by Publicious Book Publishing
Published in collaboration with Publicious Book Publishing
www.publicious.com.au

No part of this book may be reproduced in any form, by photocopying or by any electronic or mechanical means, including information storage or retrieval systems, without permission in writing from both the copyright owner and the publisher of this book.

*To my beloved Master and mentor, Chiron,
and all the gods and goddesses and angels
who are helping us humans.*

Also by Sophia Ovidne
Guide to Consciousness and the Unseen Universe
Training Manual for Gods, Book Two - Arrival of the Gods (Channelled from Chiron)
Training Manual for Gods, Book Three - Ingenuity of the Gods (Channelled from Chiron)
The Getting of Wisdom, Books One and Two (Channelled from El Morya)
Lady Sedna's Ascension Handbook (Channelled from Lady Sedna)

(Non-fiction, under her name '**Ovidne**')
Meet the Masters (including channellings from many Masters)
Ascended Masters Today, Vol 1, Love and Light (Channelled from many Masters)
Ascended Masters Today, Vol 2, Wisdom and Insight (Channelled from many Masters)
Ascended Masters Today, Vol 3, Power and Action (Channelled from many Masters)

(Fiction, under her name '**Paula Hartwood**')
The Celestial Crossroads
Secret in the Circle

*"Watch with glittering eyes the whole world around you
because the greatest secrets
are always hidden in the most unlikely places.
Those who don't believe in magic will never find it."*

Roald Dahl (1916-1990)
British author, spy, fighter pilot, chocolate
historian, and medical inventor.

CONTENTS

Preface i
Introduction by Sophia Ovidne iii

1. Genesis 1
2. Scientists vs gods 5
3. The fighting gods 9
4. Angels and Ego 13
5. What is consciousness? 17
6. Higher consciousness 21
7. The spirit world 26
8. Gifts of the gods 30
9. Love is consciousness 33
10. The screen of consciousness 36
11. Where is consciousness? 39
12. Healing through consciousness 43
13. Applying your magic wand 46
14. Be a fireball 50
15. Meanness 53
16. Consciousness as a tool 56
17. This unlimited universe 60
18. Juggling consciousness 63
19. Make a plan 67
20. Murderous intent 70
21. Ocean of emotion 73
22. Birthing consciousness 76
23. Symbolism 79
24. Jewels of consciousness 83
25. Your destiny 86
26. Exoplanets 89
27. Imagination 92
28. The past 95
29. The telescope of consciousness 98
30. Match-making 101
31. Fortitude 104
32. Your spirit-soul team 107

33. Pear-shaped society	110
34. Travel to the gods' world	113
35. Believe and you will see	116
36. Finding motivation	120
37. Educating children	123
38. Universe odyssey	126
39. Ghosts in the crypt	130
40. Keeping on track	134
41. What is reality?	137
42. Your spirit counterpart	140
43. Soul graduation	143
44. Raising yourself up	146
45. Seeing the signs	149
46. A trip to the New World	152
47. Spacecraft and UFOs	155
48. Disbelief	158
49. Desires	161
50. Falling from grace	164
51. Mercy	167
52. Your turbine power	170
53. Interjection of gods	173
54. The weather of your mind	176
55. Set yourself free	179
56. Are you lost?	182
57. Managing your crew	185
58. Explore your galaxy	189
59. Death	192
60. Reprogramming your consciousness	195
61. Wheels of the universe	198
62. The waves are coming	202
63. The Underworld	205
64. Ghost story	208
65. Pursue your dreams	211
66. A storm in your consciousness	214
67. Playing with Mother Nature	217
68. Your Source and healing	220
69. Design your death	223

70. Springtime in your mind	226
71. Love and not-love	229
72. The jump into godhood	232
73. Change those human minds	235
74. Our sun	238
75. Late for your destiny	241
76. In summary	244
Appendix 1 – About Sophia Ovidne	247

PREFACE
by Sophia Ovidne

In the first three books of the *Training Manual for Gods* series, Master Chiron takes us on an amazing journey which is targeted at those who are already gods (or Masters) on Earth, plus those humans who are in the process of transforming into gods, and those who are merely curious about what it takes to become a god.

In Book One of *Training Manual for Gods—Consciousness and the Unseen Universe*, Chiron describes the hidden dimensions of this universe, including consciousness, the worlds of the gods and the superpowers that gods can attain, and introduces the metaphysical foundations of our universe and reality. He explains in detail the journey we humans need to undertake to become gods, and how this is the ultimate mission of everyone on Earth. Our journey is not just a physical odyssey but an emotional, mental, and spiritual one too.

Because Book One contains much metaphysical knowledge that many people may find needs some extra explanation, I have written a companion book, *Guide to Consciousness and the Unseen Universe*, to describe these concepts in further detail and with many analogies from my own experiences and teachings. My guidebook covers only Book One of *Training Manual for Gods*. Books Two and Three by Chiron are more self-explanatory, but perhaps one day I shall write further guides to these volumes as well.

In Book Two of *Training Manual for Gods—Arrival of the Gods*, Chiron depicts what it will be like when humans are separated into two dimensions of First Earth and Second Earth, and how it will be to live on Second Earth as a human-turned-god, or as a divine god who has arrived on Second Earth from an even higher dimension. How will humans and divine gods interrelate? What will spark the Final Shift that causes our two Earths to split away from each other, and how can we prepare for this? What will happen to those left behind on the non-god First Earth?

In Book Three of *Training Manual for Gods—Ingenuity of the Gods*, Chiron deals solely with the training and operational needs of the gods on Second Earth. He describes how the gods can develop their superpowers and help build the fledgling all-god society on this new higher- dimensional earthly world. He also guides us in how to manage the transition from old world to new, revealing some of the incidents that will lead to the final event which separates our two Earths completely.

INTRODUCTION
by Sophia Ovidne

When Master Chiron (Chi is pronounced 'kye' to rhyme with 'rye') asked me to channel this book from him in August 2018, I felt a little aggrieved. I had been researching and working on a book about consciousness for many years, asking many of the Masters for their wisdom on this topic. It's a vast subject and I had boxes of input to sift through and make sense of and to weave together into some kind of comprehensible narrative. Perhaps Chiron looked at all this effort and felt sorry for me. He then proceeded to dictate this entire book to me in three short months, without any hesitation, rework, or editing, and illustrating for me quite clearly just how brilliant are the minds of these Masters of the unseen universe.

Who are these Masters, of which Chiron is but one? Some of us on Earth prefer to call them Ascended Masters, beings who were once upon Earth but who now live in an invisible higher dimension and who guide us mere mortals down below, if we are open to that guidance.

Many of the Masters utilise the term 'gods' to refer to themselves, and in *Consciousness and the Unseen Universe* Chiron explains exactly what a god is and how we humans can connect and communicate with them. In fact, the *unseen universe* of the title is the world of the gods, hidden dimensions that employ different physics from those of the earthly world. The gods' task is to make their presence known to us humans and to make the unknown known. So, perhaps the realm of science fiction is moving fatefully towards us?

Yet, Chiron explains that we are not going to see any alien invasion upon our soil any time soon. On the contrary, the gods are exceedingly careful not to expose their presence overtly, or too early, in order to maintain balance and harmony on this planet. They are working with those whose minds and hearts are open and who can cope with these ideas in mature and value-adding ways. The gods are connecting with us humans as our teachers, and they are working with our consciousnesses to help prepare us for our own transformation into gods one day.

Firstly, we will need to understand what consciousness truly is. It isn't something dull or dense, to be studied scientifically. It is the entire universe; exciting, mystical, and metaphysical. Once we learn to apply the magic wand of our consciousness and get results, we will never look back or look at our life in the same way again. And consciousness is certainly not just the brain inside a human. Take away the brain at death, and consciousness lives on. It lives on in invisible worlds in hidden dimensions of existence, alongside the consciousnesses of the gods and other souls not in physical bodies.

But it is not only after death that our consciousness comes into its own. Even while we are alive in human form, our human consciousness can connect with its spirit counterpart in a higher dimension, like two partners Skyping each other across time and space. Our spirit has sent us, its human partner, to Earth to play a role for this particular lifetime, like some sleeper agent that needs to be woken up at some opportune time to fulfil its mission. Chiron tells us that some agents never achieve this, and their whole lifetime is a wasted journey, and that most people maintain their car better than they do their consciousness and body.

We may have often wondered, "Do we have a soul, and what might it be like?" Chiron informs us that our soul is our divine guide in this lifetime, and this relationship is well-covered in his teachings, along with how to communicate with this guide and interpret its often mystical and incomprehensible clues for living according to the map of our destiny.

One of the main themes of this book is that our consciousness is the force behind manifesting the world around us. Whatever we are thinking eventually manifests as something physical or as a situation. Chiron introduces us to the 'toolbox' within our consciousness whereby we can create a better and more loving world for ourselves and others. We do not have to sit there languishing in pain or fearfulness or poverty or failure. We might have wondered if gods or angels can weave magic or miracles for us and change our lives, and indeed they can, but we learn that we all have the capability to be a magician; it is not denied to anyone.

Chiron explores the metaphysics of this universe and how things are not what they seem. But it will be necessary to adopt the view of 'I'll believe it and then I'll see it' rather than most people's view of 'I'll believe it when I see it". For the gods do not reveal their kingdom to cynics and non-believers. It is only when humans begin to want to walk and talk with divine beings that life becomes more divine and wondrous events start to unfold for them. We humans tend to embark upon this path only once we've had some personal inexplicable, transcendental experiences, and the scientific community cannot provide the answers we are seeking. Therefore, we go seeking for answers on our own. This book will help to provide some of those answers.

You may be wondering, "Who is this Chiron and what are his credentials and qualifications?"

According to mythological legend, the god Chiron was the greatest of all the centaurs, who were half-man, half-horse. He was the god of healing and teaching, and is often known as the 'Wounded Healer', after Heracles accidentally wounded him whilst undertaking one of his Twelve Labours in pursuit of a wild boar. In the ancient tales, Chiron was gentle and intelligent, and had been taught archery, medicine, and music by the god Apollo. In turn, Chiron tutored Apollo's son Asclepius who later became the god of health and medicine.

Thus, in present day astrology, Chiron has come to represent the sign of Virgo and the 6th House, and the traits of health, well-being, naturalness, purity, cleanliness, orderliness, and steady hard work. Astrologically, he embodies a small cosmic body that sits in the solar system between the orbits of Saturn and Uranus and acts as a bridge between them, channelling our focus to either the conservative, foundation-building Saturn or the irrepressible and rebellious Uranus who wishes to change our consciousness to a higher level of thinking and loving.

Whether or not you believe in the legends of the gods and the astrological significances of the heavens, Chiron as a god today is not speaking with us as some mythological beast or from a large rock out in space, but he is a very real being inhabiting a higher dimension that can be contacted and conversed with. If you have ever wondered what it might be like to speak with a god (and not just Chiron but any of the gods), this book will reveal all these secrets and more.

Although this is not my first channelled book[1], it is my first major project in working with Chiron. I found him to be a very composed and constant and reliable god to relate to. Never ruffled or judgemental, he always took great care to consider my well-being as I channelled and typed his words daily over several months. His professionalism and outstanding wisdom were profound and awesome to witness every day, and he personally advised me when I queried something or other about his topic, until I had all the understanding I needed. In all those years that I had worked on my own book about consciousness, I never learnt anything like the knowledge that Chiron has provided in these pages. For instance, I was particularly interested to learn the gods' views about ghosts, poltergeists, aliens and UFOs. However, the chapters aren't only about things that go bump in the night; there is also much advice about handling our emotional and psychological issues, and how to discover our true destiny.

I have been working with the Masters, or gods, for over a quarter of a century. Before I started on this weird yet exciting journey, I was a very left-brained, rational computer professional in the IT industry. If you had told me what I would be up to years down the track, I would have laughed uproariously at the absurdity of it. I had no intention of ever following such a path. Yet, when metaphysical experiences started to happen to me, I couldn't deny them, even while not being able to make sense of them for many years (and still can't, sometimes!).

But if I hadn't followed the clues and signs and gone exploring into this mysterious world that quite frankly scared me at first, I would have missed opportunities for some of the most wondrous and magical events to ever happen in my life. Not only that, but I became a much improved and more loving person because of it all. (I hope my family and friends agree!)

There may be a degree of disbelief, or even cynicism, as you read these pages, but if you can approach Chiron's information with an open mind and heart, you will benefit remarkably in many ways, no matter what level of understanding you may be at currently. He, himself, suggests that you read this book over and over, and at random once you have completed a first pass, for you will garner new insights each time

---

1. See the list of my books at the front of this volume.

as you raise yourself to new levels of maturity in your awareness of how consciousness truly works.

This whole book is about metaphysics and gods, and is therefore considered by academia to be a mythology. Is it all a myth? Well, neither Chiron nor myself can assert that the contents are 'The Truth', for we can offer scant scientific evidence (as yet) for the existence of gods, hidden dimensions, or indeed even consciousness itself. And so, it is up to the reader to ascertain the wisdom and beliefs contained herein, and to utilise them or not. The gods' purpose, and my own, is to present a different world view and universe view that might be of benefit to mankind in some way.

Some people may be asking how I channelled this information from Master Chiron, a godly being from a higher dimension? It was only later in life that I discovered I had this ability to speak with higher beings. It is not the same as being a psychic, for I have little ability to speak with human people who have passed over. It seems my destiny was to be a messenger for these higher Masters, a voice-piece so that they could communicate with us down here on Earth and get their message heard.

When I channel, I see the Master in my mind, and I hear what they are saying to me. It's like watching a movie inside my head, but also one that I take part in at times. It took me many years to discern properly whether the voices were coming from my own soul or from some much wiser source, but this was all part of my training. Now, the Masters are a part of my everyday life and they flit in and out of my daily activities like good friends or members of my family. I do nothing special to invoke them, yet I show them appreciation and respect at all times. They are always there, watching over me and guiding me and monitoring my work and thoughts. It is nothing like Big Brother, but rather a feeling of being part of a fabulous, productive, caring, and compassionate team. Think of it instead as like astronauts being monitored by Mission Control when they go out into space.

I feel honoured that Chiron has given me this opportunity to bring forth his wisdom in order to enlighten us humans, especially those who are in training to become gods themselves. He tells me this won't be our last collaboration, and I look forward to again channelling the pearls of his great consciousness in future sequels.

May you enjoy this journey with Chiron as he delves into the hidden mysteries of consciousness and the invisible worlds of light and dark that reside within our universe, just out of sight to our human eyes. After reading this book, it is my hope that these hidden dimensions are more accessible, and that hearts will open that yearn for reconnection with their divine source.

Many blessings to you as your consciousness blossoms and you discover the unseen universe.

Sophia

❖ *All following chapters have been channelled* ❖
from Master Chiron by Sophia

Chapter 1 – GENESIS

Ah, Sophia, Sophia, Sophia! I thought this day would never come. And so, my gratitude abounds that you would take the time and make the effort to hear my wisdom that I wish to share with all the world. We will make great marks with this book, so do not feel hopeless about it. It will find its niche and it will sit on the bookshelves of all those who need to read it. So, without further ado, let us get into the making of this tome for there is much that needs to be said, much that needs to be distributed, much that needs to be understood by a world that is largely ignorant, ignorant of our part in all that is going on.

So, let the dreamers dream away but let us bring some practicality down into the Earth. We need steps. We need guidelines. We need advice like never before. There is much that is on the wrong track so let us endeavour to change the ways and divert the paths of people onto the right plane. We will do this over the following weeks and months, although, when that is said, we will not be finished by a long chalk. We could go on writing for eternity, but that is what makes this universe so mystical and magical. We will never be done with her; she will foster our curiosity forever.

So, let us start at the beginning if we can, for was there a beginning to this universe? Of course there was! But perhaps your idea of the beginning is a little different from mine. So, let me share my story, my view of things, and then you'll be able to see which version you wish to take on board, for I am not forcing these pearls upon you; I am presenting my case and I will leave it there.

In the beginning of this particular universe...for there are many; many in existence at this current time and many that are past and gone. Many too will be created in the future. So, in the beginning of this particular universe that we are living within now, there was at first nothing, just emptiness, just a void. This void then became filled with light.

Who placed this light here? you may ask.

The gods that created this universe pooled their light and placed it within the greater domain, which is the universe that encapsulates all universes, and here they proceeded to create their playground. You may ask why I speak about gods in the plural rather than the One God? This is because the One God does not create universes alone. The One God has created son and daughter gods, whom we shall refer to as creator gods from now on, who are given the tasks, the projects, of creating universes in whichever way is their hearts' delight.

And so, we have *our* universe, created by ten creator gods a very long time ago. And they began with their light and, using their consciousnesses, they used their light to develop a universe consisting of physical and non-physical elements alike.

Did these creator gods know what they were doing? For the most part, they did not, for all was experimentation, and they allowed things to flow and bloom and birth and die, retaining those things that delighted them and discarding those things that did not fit their ideal. It was much the same as a child let loose inside an artist's studio with free rein as to what to create. It is not that the creator gods were childish but they were child-like in their creativity and enthusiasm. The One God was letting its progeny loose to play and learn. This was not the first universe that these creator gods had created, so there was an underlying understanding of the mechanics and the consequences. The creator gods were building upon their past experiences, much as we do in our lives today.

And so, the world you see around you today, and the other worlds that make up this universe, have come about by the creator gods allowing things to play out and grow. They have pinched out a few buds along the way, massaged this and that, corrected the ill-formed, and done away with the downright terrible. The human race and everything that consists of this universe have all evolved from the minds, hearts, and hands of these creator gods. At first, it was direct creation by they themselves. These days, things are created not directly by them but indirectly, by the entities that they have created. And so, humans are creating the world on planet Earth as it stands today; it is no longer a manifestation of the creator gods. The creator gods take pains not to interfere but, if it is requested of them, they will turn their wisdom upon the scene, and if their interjection is warranted, they may turn events around.

So, when humans speak with God, they are speaking with a rather larger entity than they expect. For the consciousness of God encapsulates all the creator gods, too, and all their further manifestations of other beings who could be termed as gods. So, when we speak of God or gods, I am referring to the united consciousness of beings who exist in a higher and unseen dimension of this universe. Later in our story we will get onto describing these gods and these dimensions in greater detail.

So, let us come back to our origins now. So, in the beginning, the universe was like paint in the paint pots, and it was all brought together upon a background and gradually a picture began to emerge. That picture is still evolving today. More and more has been added and the background canvas has grown and grown.

You yourself have been part of this picture from the beginning, for your consciousness has evolved out of the consciousness of these creator gods. Imagine a cloud, and a little part of that cloud is scooped away and becomes an individual consciousness. And then a little part of *that* cloud is scooped away and a new individual consciousness formed. And these little, tiny cloud balls do not remain pure in their lineage from the original cloud, but these clouds merge with other clouds, not just one but many others. And so new clouds of consciousness are perpetually forming—and you are descended from this.

And so, your lineage is not straight up and down as you would see from a human's genealogical chart. Your lineage of consciousness comes from all over the place, and you are descended from many more people than you could ever imagine.

And you might have some flickering memories of this lifetime or that upon this planet or elsewhere in the universe. We try to shade you from all these lives for it would be overwhelming for you to remember all these experiences while you try to focus on this life. But know that you did not come here as a newborn, fresh and pure without memories.

Your consciousness has access to a storehouse that contains the records of all your lives. And you may access these records when you are deemed to be mature enough to handle and assimilate them. As your consciousness becomes more and more stable, then more and more doors will be opened for you to reach into the vastness of the universe and your consciousness' travels throughout it.

Will this universe come to an end one day? Yes, it will. And we will pack up our bags and our consciousnesses and we will reunite as one consciousness again until we are provided with the task of creating our next new universe.

So, let us ponder on who we are and where we find ourselves now, in the thick of a universe that has been designed for us and by us. What will we make of it now?

Chapter 2 – SCIENTISTS VS GODS

You might be mesmerised by the very start of this universe. It is too big an event for the human mind to wrap itself around. We can only begin to imagine what might have happened there. And your scientists play games as they try to use their imaginations as to what really occurred at the moment that the universe came into being. It will not be understood from the platform of where scientists stand today. There needs to be a higher degree of understanding the finer concepts of consciousness and dimensions. For all is not just physical. There is a non-physical world too, and that is even harder to imagine.

And so, we are pushing the boundaries for today's scientists, and those who might believe along this path would be hard-pressed to make their beliefs known publicly, for there is shame in being too far outside the present mould. Scientists can only take innovation in small degrees, little, tiny steps at moving the known world outwards. We have all had to suffer the indignation of this to some extent in many of our lifetimes, the shame of being rejected by our fraternity for daring to think outside the nine dots. But someone has to do it, and those who have done it have paid the price.

So, do not judge your fellow man and his inklings and innovations, for you too may be placed in this situation one day where no one will listen to you, even though you have the lowdown on the next great breakthrough in scientific or mathematical endeavours. So, those who know about these things, or think they know, will tend to keep this information to themselves, for they do not wish to be targeted or branded as heretics or rebels. And yet, from this 'nonsense' that they espouse, will come the cracks in your scientific fault lines which will lead you to the truth.

So, dear humans who are on the pioneering edge, I doff my hat to you and I ask you to keep facing forwards, for it is tricky to keep one's balance when one is perched precariously on the very edge. And yet it is you who can see the clearest, for you are at the very edge of the horizon and you can see beyond, whilst the naysayers are looking back and patting each other on the back instead of facing forwards.

It must be allowed that scientists experiment and are free to voice their findings. Not all will find favour or result in the truths being heard. But that should not stop anyone, nor should they be stopped by others. It is necessary that all findings are voiced so that everyone can pick over the bones of these and take from them what they need. Your secretive ways are hampering evolution and revolution. If you could all harness your wisdom and knowledge and experimentation techniques, then this Earth would be further down the road than it is right now. You have cliques here and cliques there. You have countries which covet their information and success. Are you not one world that wishes to blast off now to other worlds? Yet you cannot come together for the benefit of cosmic travel.

So, I would like to say to you all at the outset of this book, that if my words are to have any meaning for you, you will need to open your minds and your hearts and cherish the notion that you are one human race and not a cabal of countries. It is astonishing that you have worked against one another for so long. And so, as the spirit of sharing rises within you, so shall we gods begin to share our secrets with you all. For we will not share what we know for the benefit of one group who uses it against another. The magic of our imaginations is for the use of all. So, let us have an overarching aim for humanity, and let my words and wisdom feed this whole entire arch. Let no one be refused its depth and breadth, for what we giveth we can also taketh away.

So, who are we gods and who am I specifically? I'm sure you want to know. We are the descendants of the creator gods, just as you humans are as well. We are gods in that we are not in human form. We have been so in many incarnations. But we exist now in another dimension which is adjacent to yours and which is ruled by different rules of physics than your own. The result is that we gods and our world are invisible to you on Earth. And yet we are interconnected and woven through your world. And what you do can affect us, and what we do can certainly affect you.

We have the advantage in our godly world in that we can see right across yours. And you humans are at a disadvantage, or so you think, for you imagine that you are alone in this universe when nothing could be further from the truth. We gods are helping you humans with all the abilities that we can muster. We are not perfect, for we are learning and rising to higher levels too. Yet we have much to offer you, if only you would believe that we exist.

And so, our task is to make our presence known. There are many among you who do believe, even though there is not much empirical evidence. For it is the consciousness that knows these things, and the consciousness has memories of worlds it has visited when you are not being consciously human. You do not need to die to visit these other worlds. Your consciousness is soaring off at many times during the night and day.

Your consciousness indeed has a life of its own. It is presently concerned with running your physical body and reading or hearing these words. But in other moments your consciousness is not in your world at all. It is travelling and learning and experiencing other ways of living. You are not aware of this for the most part. But sometimes you will recall your dreams, and sometimes you will have weird events happening to you that make you question the reality of this world. So, don't deny your experiences; they are guiding lights on your journey through the greater universe.

I am inspired that so many of you have inklings that this world upon Earth is not all that there is to be seen. Yet the shutters remain closed on the vast majority of the population. And why they would want to deny the most exciting part of their lives, we cannot comprehend. So, it falls to us who have seen the chink of light through the fault lines of this Earth, those who know that something more lies beyond, it falls to us to make the unknown known. It falls to us to explain the unknowable and to make inroads into consciousnesses that have been programmed against this path.

We weep for those who cannot see. We weep even more for those who refuse to see. We weep even more for those who teach that we are not here, for that is heresy, for we patently exist. Short of dropping in on you and exposing ourselves on the rooftops and on your TVs, we must somehow ingratiate ourselves into your lives, become household names, and be the movement behind social transformation that brings about a purer world. How do we do this, my friends? For if we appeared in spacecraft, you would shoot us down. If we appeared in person, you would deem us to be ghosts. If we interfered with your affairs, we would be taking away your free will. And so, we must languish here until you call for us and pave the way for us to visit.

We are working with some of your ambassadors now. It is not that you have rejected us, but we have been invited by very few. And so, we must get the word out, that you may wish to invite us to your party. We have no intentions of invading and taking over. We come as teachers but only when you call us to this post. So, we are not threatening; we are waiting in the wings. There needs to be a groundswell before you will see our faces on this Earth. But the time is coming, and this book is to help you to prepare.

Chapter 3 – THE FIGHTING GODS

Bear in mind that we are tackling the subject of consciousness, and that is what a god is, pure consciousness. It is not a thing of this planet or any other planet. The consciousness of a god rides above it all. It is a non-physical entity, and so, scientists searching for the physical evidence of gods will not find it. We, and you as your consciousness, are in a band above physicality. And this is a mystery yet to be understood and it will not be understood for many a year. And, first of all, your scientists must allow for the fact that there is such a thing as non-physicality. Then, with this acknowledgement, steps can be taken forward.

So, let us return to the gods as consciousness. What do I mean by this? There is much that has been written about gods, and much that has been written about consciousness, but not so much has been written about gods as consciousness. So, let me fill you in with some details.

The consciousness of gods swirls around this universe. It has no form and yet it can take many forms, any form at all. And so, you may see a god who seems physical, that appears as a mortal, or a god may appear as an animal or insect or bird or tree. A god can mimic any form. And so, a god can be the waves of an ocean, or electronic waves, or X-rays, or radio or TV broadcasts. A god can climb into anything and make it work, or interfere with its abilities to work. A god can interject themselves into any atom or subatomic particle, or between them. There is nowhere that a god cannot go or be. And yet we advise our gods not to interfere with the human world for it can be dangerous to both humans and to gods, for there are always consequences from interference.

And so, it is only when our help is requested that we will put in an appearance and dedicate ourselves to the issue at hand. Our advice is not always heeded. But that is okay, for we wish you to learn at your own pace and in your own way. We are not hard taskmasters here. And yet, if you undertake to complete a task for us, we would steer you to see it through, for we don't like to be let down. And if you negotiate with us and make a promise to us, then we would like to see you keep your end of the bargain. It does not go down well with us if you renege on a deal. And yet there is no punishment from us. You more often than not punish yourselves, and the consequences of your actions will visit you regardless of what we gods say or do.

So, with our consciousnesses, we gods travel all over this universe. But that is not to say that all gods will visit upon Earth. We generally have gods allocated to different departments and different locales. And so, there are gods and their consciousnesses who monitor the Earth and the human race and other beings who live upon her. So, you all belong to one company, as it were, and you are managed by a Board of Directors. And it is not so much that you are our employees, but you are our trainees. And we are training you up to take over our positions one day. So, at present you are human, but one day you will be a god.

And so, Earth is a school, or a university if you like, and we are skilling you up to take your places as responsible citizens who will then be allowed to travel the universe as we do. You are confined to campus for now, but soon some of the fledgling directors will be allowed to fly off and begin pioneering in other parts of the universe, for, some of you have evolved that far.

For the most part, humans do not understand that they are part of this training school. They think they are on Earth for other purposes. They do not realise there is a whole universe out there to which they belong and to which they will gain entry one day. For the most part, humans do not even realise they have a consciousness. They know they have a mind and they equate this with a brain. And too often in schools they are taught this, that there is nothing beyond their brain, that this is all they are. This is a terrible mistake, and I hope it is one that will be amended soon, and that your schools and institutions will begin to teach that beyond the brain lies consciousness, and that all that you are as a human remains under the control of your consciousness.

Your consciousness is just playing a part for this lifetime. When you die it will go on to play another role, maybe on this world, maybe not. For there are many other places in the universe that your consciousness can play out a life. But it is rare that humans will go off exploring the universe until they have got their humanness under control. For human nature is base and petty and this personality does not go down well with the other exotic travellers of this universe. So, humans tend to reincarnate on Earth over and over until they have reached a certain level of refined consciousness and then the barriers to travelling the cosmos are opened to them somewhat.

So, in the meantime, these mean and petty humans are being trained up in the earthly environment by the gods; the human consciousness versus god consciousness. There is a lot to learn. Many humans, most humans, do not like the idea of gods monitoring them and judging them and taking them to task. They do not like the idea of being under their control. And so, most humans abandon the idea of gods altogether and usually the whole idea of consciousness too. They like to think their own brains are in control, that they have free will and that they are free to pursue it.

I would like to set the record straight here, that we gods are not a controlling master race who seek to take over all human consciousness. We value every individual person, and we seek only to bring each person to their fullest potential and that is to become like a god. We have the same DNA, gods and humans, for the human race was created by the gods, not the creator gods themselves but descendants of those gods. And so, the gods are looking after what they have created, good or bad. They are responsible for these creations, and it is their everlasting job to take each creation and mould it into the best that it can be. There will be no creation left unmoulded.

So, you can see that the gods' job on Earth may take quite a while yet and it could be many generations before we make the breakthrough that we desire. And yet we are hopeful, for many humans have indeed progressed up the ladder and taken their place as gods. It is not the physical body that changes; it is the consciousness. The human consciousness evolves into god consciousness.

And so now we come to the nub of our problem. The gods are having to fight human consciousness, for it is selfish and ego-driven and will not surrender easily without a fight. The gods do not go in with weapons and boxing gloves or any manner of force. But the gods do have to fight in godly ways to make inroads into the human miasma and make some sense of it that will encourage humans to turn away from the way that they have been and reach toward a more palatable goal. You cannot say that the Earth is working very well right now. Humans have wrecked it. And if it wasn't for the efforts of a few stalwarts, the Earth would be in even worse shape than she is now. And what is coming soon—more climate change, more waste, including plastic debris and nuclear waste, more drought, more floods, more economic disaster, more homelessness, more tragedy. No human can be assured a good life anymore. These are uncertain times. There is no security of tenure on this planet.

And so, will it only be in your last desperate throes, as the clock ticks towards midnight, that eyes and hearts will open and look to the gods for merciful saving? Let us intervene before it is too late. Request our intervention and work beside us instead of fighting against us. Surrender your arrogance that you know how to take this planet forward, for at present you are only tipping it forward into the morass.

The gods are fighting, fighting to save you and this planet. They are not fighting against you but for you. When will you realise this and join their side?

Chapter 4 – ANGELS AND EGO

Angels are dear to our heart. They have a special place in the hearts of humans but also in the hearts of gods. Angels are not gods per se; they are pure consciousness and their minds come directly from the One God. They have taken a track through the universe that has not been bent and battered as it has been with the gods. The angels retain their clarity and purity. They are unsullied by the ego that taints gods and men alike. Yet, even though they are pure consciousness, they are still able to travel the physical world, and, like the gods, they are able to manifest themselves into any place or point and make a difference there.

Angels are like the helpers of the universe. They do not have an agenda of their own. It is their job to smooth things over and make things right. Yet it is not their job to clear up after us, to clear up our mess. It is their job to keep the universe on the right trajectory, and they will do whatever it takes to keep the path ahead clear.

Do not misuse angels, for they have lofty goals and targets, and it is not for them to become your slaves and servants. But when you are in true strife and cannot get yourself out of a situation then by all means call upon the angels and they will be there to help you out. You can speak with angels, and they will speak back to you. Do not be afraid of them but nonetheless treat them with respect. They are the closest thing to the One True God that you will get to meet.

You would do well to heed the angels' warnings, for, as I have said, their job is to keep the universe on the straight and narrow. And if you are in danger of causing the universe to tilt otherwise, then the angels will drop you a clue that you are bordering on misadventure. They usually don't shout it in your ear, so you will need to be attuned to their little whispers, their dainty clues. Be aware of their presence and, as you pick up more and more on their energies, they will declare their presence more and more for you.

Angels do not react with emotion or fear. They are quite stoic and matter-of-fact, yet compassion is high on their agenda. However, they are not a pushover and you cannot wheedle them with your charms or pleas. Work with angels as if with a friend. Do not use them or abuse them but respect their counsel and heed their advice. They are wise in the ways of this universe and can see the greater picture and help you to travel it more safely.

Angels are invisible, for you will never be able to see pure consciousness. And yet, if an angel wishes for you to see them, they will project an image onto themselves and it is this form that you will see, and it will be a form that you expect so that you recognise this angel. Yet, know that this angel is not this form. It is something else entirely, a consciousness that travels and weaves itself throughout this universe.

How many angels are there? More than you could ever count in this universe. And they exist in other universes too. But the ones allocated to this universe will remain within its boundaries, so they do not desert us for other climes.

The boundaries of this universe are fixed yet not fixed. By that I mean that nothing can escape from this universe. All is contained within its walls, and this will be so until the day when this universe is dissolved. And yet the boundaries are not fixed as if they were set in stone. The boundaries are movable and moving all the time. So, the universe is like a bubble that is getting bigger and bigger, and all that we are and all that we do is contained within the walls of this bubble. One day the bubble will pop and all its contents will be reconvened and redistributed into new universes. So, just because we have all been together in this universe for billions of years, does not mean we will find ourselves together in the next one.

And it is the consciousness of the creator gods that will create these new universes. So, who can say what will be created then. That is the fun of creativity. You never know what will happen and what will be the result. Now, you yourselves as little humans, will one day become creator gods yourselves. Granted, this is a long way off, but this is your trajectory, from human to minor god to major god to creator god. And there your progress will stop, for there is nothing but the One God above the level of creator god. But indeed, I am wrong, for progress never stops and creator gods will carry on creating until the end of eternity, if there is ever such a thing.

And angels will be on hand again in the new universes too.

Can a human get to become an angel? Well, no, but a human can certainly attempt to become more angelic. Angels are pure and egoless and there is much benefit in becoming like this. And yet we would not have all the ego taken out of you, for it is ego that drives you and propels you on the journey towards your goal. Without ego you would just want to be of service to others always. Of course, this might be your goal this lifetime around, but ego, when it is used positively, has its rightful place. The trouble for most humans is that ego is used wilfully and negatively to a large extent. And so, the gods and the angels are working with humans to temper that ego and mould it in the right way and use it for the right causes. It is possible to have a magnificent ego, one that drives you in all the right ways to pursue the right outcomes. So, do not vilify your ego but modify it.

Placating your ego will lead you down troublesome paths. You will need to learn how to get on top of your ego, to be higher than it, to take the higher ground and control it from up there. The ego likes to wallow, in praise and self-pity, in anger, in gloating, in judgement, in self-destruction and self-denial. It is a beast and can act bestially. And so, we must tame this ego and make it our puppet. But a puppet it does not want to be, and so we must teach it, that if it is our servant, the road ahead will be glorious. But this our ego cannot see, for it is caught up in the short-term manifestations of its desires. It does not care about tomorrow or others that might share our path.

So, just like a child that is having tantrums, we must teach our ego to share, to love, to consider, and to serve. We know how good it feels inside our hearts when we are able to share and love and consider and serve. It produces a warm glow within us. Imagine if our whole lives could feel like that.

So, there is a tussle going on within our consciousness between the high road and the low road, between the higher state of mind and the lower state of mind. And we see glimpses of both in everyone. What we gods and angels are teaching is that it is necessary to move out of the lower state of mind and into those higher quarters, making decisions from that higher place and finding that the whole of life can be turned around and made more melodious.

Too many humans are swimming in the pigswill of human misery. We are offering ways upwards, staircases to reach that higher place. Many are not taking us up on this opportunity. They refuse to see the staircase that is offered to them. They refuse to hear the marketing that will allow them to find this staircase. And so, many are playing in this pigswill and finding themselves drowning there. We are not allowed to go in after you and rescue you. We advertise our staircases, and you must find them for yourself. Only then can we offer a hand up. We are not 'Search and Rescue' gods. You must first determine that you wish to be rescued and then the staircase will be presented in front of you, and it is your choice whether you climb up it or not.

There are good reasons why we don't save everyone on this planet, for being saved does not change your consciousness in the way that it needs to be transformed. But when you save yourself, you develop all kinds of admirable traits, and your consciousness benefits and you grow in stature and esteem. If we were to keep saving you, you would never develop the traits you need to save yourself. So, it is tough love that we use, and we do not apologise for it. It is the only way, the only way that works. We are developing the next generation of gods. We cannot namby-pamby them. They must be strong and vigorous and know the right way to move. It is just like parents raising their children. We wish our children to grow up into great adults. We wish for our humans to grow up into great gods.

Chapter 5 – WHAT IS CONSCIOUSNESS?

Let us speak about the specific nature of consciousness, for when we say it is a non-physical entity, what do we mean by this? Yes, we are delving into the science of this. And, as I have stated before, it may not be comprehensible to your scientists but, nevertheless, we can describe its attributes and characteristics even if we have no scientific terms to describe what consciousness truly is.

So, first of all, let us look at physicality and what that is, and it will give us a better idea then of what non-physicality is.

Physicality is about materiality, things that we can see and touch and feel and hear, the stuff that we are made of, the stuff that things are made of, the stuff that planets are made of, and even stars. Everything is made up of microscopic bits which we call atoms, and these atoms are broken down again into smaller particles. So, in truth, everything in physicality is made up of microscopic dots.

And then there are other things in physicality that cannot be seen, things like electricity and electro-magnetic waves, magnetism, soundwaves, light and all the various spectrums of light. Light is indeed a physical entity made from a particle called a photon. So, not all of physicality can be seen or felt, or makes known its presence, but that does not make it non-physical; there is still evidence of it in our physical world. Electricity, although it cannot be seen, makes itself felt and we can utilise its presence. The same with magnetism; we can watch its force in action but we cannot see the magnetic waves themselves.

Consciousness is not physical at all. It does not consist of atoms or subatomic particles. And yet it is a force, and we feel its effects in every moment. And so, we might imagine it could be something like electricity or magnetism or even gravity, an invisible force that makes its presence known. And yet it is a force that can make decisions. It can think for itself, direct itself and others. It has memory, astonishing memory, and all those memories must be stored somewhere in its data banks. Consciousness seems to flow like water, or drift like the wind. And yet it is made from neither water nor air, nor any liquid substance at all. And yet consciousness is everywhere, flowing in between every physical particle and inside it too, just like air and space are around and inside every particle of this universe.

So, is consciousness the air of space itself? Well, you would be getting closer to the answer with this. But again we must remember it is not a physical substance. It cannot be measured or identified, not by your scientists on Earth. There are other scientists in the universe who have begun to crack what consciousness truly is. Humans are a long way off this knowledge at this present time. Yet, not knowing what it is does not mean that it doesn't exist. For a long time on your planet Earth, mankind felt the forces of electricity yet didn't know its makeup. So, we must be content to know that consciousness abides around us and within us. It is the driving force of this universe. And when we acknowledge this then paths shall begin to open towards discovering its constituents.

All gods and angels and creator gods have consciousness. All humans have consciousness, as do all animals and sentient beings. You may be surprised to know that all inanimate objects have an element of consciousness, too, that a stone has consciousness, and the rocks of your planet Earth. Water has consciousness, and so does the sun. There is nothing in the universe that does not have consciousness, albeit limited in many cases. Even the little bacteria and viruses that thrive within you and within the Earth, these too have consciousness.

And your consciousness can connect with any other consciousness and negotiate and come to agreement. You might be reluctant to be seen to be speaking to a stone, but let me tell you that that stone might have plenty to say back to you, especially if it is a crystal, for these are legion in storing knowledge and memories.

Consciousness does not operate like a single personality here and another one over there. Consciousness is one fluid substance, if I may use that term. Consciousness is like an ocean, and all that exists in the universe with its consciousness are like droplets within that ocean. And the ocean knows at any time what is going on with that droplet or this droplet. Every droplet is connected, and what is felt and experienced by one droplet is felt and experienced by the whole ocean.

The whole ocean of consciousness belongs to the One God. And yet it is sectionalised for easier manageability into the consciousness for our universe alone, and broken down again into the consciousness that belongs to each creator god, and broken down again into the consciousness that belongs to each god and angel, and broken down again into the consciousness that belongs to each human and animal and plant and so forth. So, we each have our bubble of consciousness within which we play.

But our little bubble is connected to all the other bubbles within our higher consciousness, and all the bubbles for higher consciousness are collected together into the higher consciousness above them. And so, it goes on until all the consciousnesses are collected together under the one umbrella. Take some time to ponder on this diagram for it will benefit you no end.

Consciousness is not static. It is not filled in the beginning with a set of rules, a set of systems, and a library of data. Consciousness is ever-changing. And everything that is ever experienced is stored in consciousness and can be accessed and replayed. But we do not wish to clog up the wheels, so we store experiences that belong to the past in areas that will not thwart the progress of the present. We need our wheels to keep on turning. We do not wish to be mired in the tracks of our past.

So, as humans, you can sit in your bubble of consciousness and it will provide you with all you need to survive. But know that your bubble can expand and grow, and greater areas are available for you to access. You may tap into the consciousness of others, with their permission, and you may learn many great things in this way. And you may tap into the storage banks of your own past if your experiences may give you greater leverage for your present. You may tap into your future too, but that is an explanation for another day, for in the arena where consciousness plays out, there is no time. Time is a physical concept; it does not exist in non-physicality.

I am in danger of bending your consciousnesses too far with all these concepts and explanations, but I hope you will enjoy having the lid lifted on this subject. Humans cannot deny the existence of consciousness any longer. It is pivotal to your existence. It is pivotal to this universe. How can you make sense of anything at all until you acknowledge the existence of consciousness?

Consciousness is not driven by the One God. Consciousness is driven by all the parts of consciousness working together, working as one mind. Just as all the cells in your human body have their own little bit of consciousness, they all work together to provide you with life and to help you live that life in the best possible manner. Your head does not work against your foot, your fingers do not work against your heart. Your whole body tries to work as one entity, to make sure that you are healthy and fit to do your work. It is true that at times parts of your consciousness do work against one another but that is part of your challenge in being a human, to bring all your parts of consciousness to work in harmony, to work as one well-oiled machine.

And once we manage this for our own body, then we can try to do this with other bodies, too, until we have every body on a planet working as one and in unison. And then our challenge will be to get every planet working as one, and every galaxy, and every part of the universe, until we have one consciousness all in harmony and singing in tune.

This is consciousness as best as I can describe.

Chapter 6 – HIGHER CONSCIOUSNESS

Let us rise on the energies today and let us speak about how we may raise our consciousness. We often speak about higher consciousness, so let us examine what this is and how we can arrive at it.

Take the position of most people, which is at a lower level of consciousness. They are not very aware. They are not aware of how they think, or what is going on in their consciousness. And they are certainly not aware of consciousnesses of people around them, and how they are affecting others, and how others are affecting them. So, people in lower consciousness, to all intents and purposes, live within their own little bubble, never questioning what is going on and never looking or exploring outside of their bubble. They are a world unto themselves.

And so, a higher consciousness must be the opposite of that, where people are well-informed of what is going on inside their bubble of consciousness. They are aware of the consequences of their thoughts and actions, and they are aware that there is a greater world out there. And they are considerate of other people's consciousnesses and aware that they are affected by them too.

Is it of benefit to have a higher consciousness? Yes, indeed, for then you are not at the mercy of it. You are not a puppet controlled by your programming, having no other way but to obey its commands and to react in the way that you have been programmed. When you begin to lift your consciousness and become more aware, then you begin to take control over yourself and modify your reactions and your thinking. In effect, you reprogram yourself to a more refined way of being. You do not get so upset, so cantankerous, so vengeful, so needy. You begin to make yourself more self-reliant, self-dependable, self-contained. You become stronger and more on purpose, and that purpose is set by yourself and not by others. You begin to take into consideration the effect of your actions, not only upon others but upon yourself. You begin to value consequences, you begin to take responsibility. You begin to act from a higher place, a higher mind.

And bit by bit you will raise yourself above the mire of general thinking. You will become kinder, more loving, more thoughtful, more reflective, and less reactive. You will have a plan and put that plan in place, rather than allowing life to happen to you. You begin to mould your life into what you want it to be. You make life happen instead of letting it happen. So, you can see the benefits of a life lived like this.

So, what kind of things can we do to raise our consciousness out of the mire?

First of all, we must desire to do so. The intention must be there. We cannot force anyone to do this. They must want to raise themselves up as a deep desire from within their own heart. Many times, people are placed on rehabilitation programs, and these often do not work because the participant is not willing and does not have the motivation to make it a success. So, consciousness can only start rising when the participant is willing and motivated to go the distance and to practise changes in their life, changes for the most part that will be neither simple nor easy, because changing one's program is not a walk in the park.

First, you must identify your programming, those habitual thoughts that make you act and react in certain ways. This programming has been installed in you from your very first days upon Earth. It comes from the way your parents speak to you and treat you, from how your family interacts. It comes from your schools, your teachers, and your school friends. These days it comes a great deal from social media, from televisions and movies, and the great broadcasting phenomenon that sits upon smart phones and computers. You undergo a hail of programming in your time. You cannot but be affected by it on every level.

And so, by the time you are a teenager you have been moulded by the world, and very little of it comes from your own input. And it is only in your late teens and your twenties that you begin to have ideas for yourself. And sometimes these ideas do not match with your programming, and then comes confrontation and internal conflict as you battle your inner demons. Some people never cultivate their own ideas, and they are blissfully unaware and go through entire lives never questioning their programming and just playing out their part, and only confronting others who do not match with their own programming.

So, first of all, you must know that your own programming is not always cracked up to be what it should be. You need to question your programming, you need to change it. It has been installed by other people who do not know what is best for you or the part that you are here to play. So, you need to crack open your programming and remove all those bits that do not benefit you. This alone will raise your consciousness a hundred degrees.

Often you do not know how your consciousness should be, how your programming should be written. And so, you will need to ponder upon your ideals. How is it you would like to be? How is it you would like to act in this world? What is it you would like to become? And with these ideals as your guidelines then you will better know what programming fits with your ideals and what doesn't. This is not some overnight job. This task of sorting out your programming will take the majority of your life. But do not despair and feel hopeless, for with every bad bit of programming that you jettison, your consciousness will be raised up one more rung. And every time you raise yourself up another rung of the ladder, you are moving away from the dark mire of humanity's baseness.

As you remove old programming you will need to replace it with new thoughts, new motivations, new ideals. And it takes time to break the habits of a lifetime, so be kind to yourself as you break yourself in and train yourself to move in different ways. Loving yourself is the basis of higher consciousness. So, learn this aspect first and the going will be easier for you down the road.

Take yourself to places, physically or in your mind, that bring succour to you and serenity. If your life is busy or full of irritations, come to this place often, as often as you need to, to calm yourself down and bathe in peace and harmony. Think good thoughts. Think positively and with love. Dream of good things. Even if they are impossible at this present time, dreaming sets up the vibrations for you to attract these things into your life down the track.

I have mentioned the word 'vibrations' and this is a word you will hear often from me from now on. For everything vibrates at a certain wavelength. Wavelengths are frequencies, and you can have low frequencies and high frequencies. Therefore, you can have low vibrations and high vibrations. Low vibrations move slowly, and they are, in effect, more human-like. High vibrations move quickly, and they are, in effect, more god-like.

So, in raising your consciousness you are, in fact, raising your vibrations. You will be causing your body and your consciousness to vibrate more quickly, and this higher wavelength that you will be on will connect you with other high wavelengths that the gods and angels and other high-vibrational beings exist on. You'll find yourself connecting to a different world all together. The higher you raise your consciousness and vibrations, the more you will be able to connect to these different and invisible worlds. For the higher worlds are vibrating so fast that they are invisible to you, just like the blades of an electric fan are invisible to you when they move very fast on high speed.

When the atoms of a material object move very quickly, then the human eye cannot see that object. It has moved too fast for it to be registered within the human brain. And so, there is much upon planet Earth that moves too quickly for humans to register it and view it. It exists, all the same. Gods and angels are part of this higher vibrational world. They are there but they cannot be seen. You too, as a human, if you raised your vibrations high enough, would also become invisible to this world.

Is this not an interesting and captivating way to be?

So, raise your consciousness, take it to new heights. Unhitch your anchors that keep you stuck in the lower world. Be more aware of how you are acting and reacting. What are the words that are coming out of your mouth? What are the thoughts that are flowing through your mind? What are the feelings that are coursing through your body? All these things dictate what vibrational wavelength you are existing at right now. Can you stop what you are thinking and readjust your attitude and take a different course? Yes, you can, but it is not always easy to stop a raging bull or a speeding locomotive. So, it will take time to readjust your attitudes and demeanours. You must work at changing your behaviours. Nothing, not even hypnosis, will change you overnight.

So, set your intention to work on one aspect of yourself at a time. Do not overwhelm yourself by taking on too much at once. Slow and steady wins the race. But just get started, is my advice to you today, for every little success is one step further towards life as a divine being. I cannot tell you what joy you will feel then. It is worth every ounce of effort and tears.

When this is a planet of higher consciousness, then we shall truly have Heaven upon Earth.

Chapter 7 – THE SPIRIT WORLD

We are speaking about consciousness and the unseen worlds. What do we mean by unseen worlds? Well, this consists of all manner of things. For there is much more out there than you would give credit for. It is not just one scenario but many; many different kinds of worlds, some like yours upon Earth, many more that are quite different, nothing that you could imagine in your wildest dreams.

So, let us stick with the ones that would be more familiar to you if you were to visit them. And visit them you can, but more about that later.

Imagine you took the Earth and duplicated it so that there was a second Earth sitting behind the first one. Imagine that you took this second Earth and gently placed it over the first one so that it was just millimetres away at every point. This would be the closest world that is invisible to you but only inches away. It is interwoven with your world. And so, where there is a tree, there is an invisible tree next to it. Where there is a rock, there is an invisible rock next to it. Where there is an ocean, there is an invisible ocean next to it and through it. Difficult to imagine, I know, but it is there, alright.

And you could move, if you knew how, from your world into that invisible world with just the tiniest of jumps. But it is not a physical jump that you need to make. It is a jump within your consciousness. And this will have many scratching their head, for how do you make a jump in consciousness into an invisible world?

To explain this I must backtrack a little. For not only is there an invisible world next to your physical world but there is an invisible you next to your physical self. And that invisible you is part of your consciousness. It is your spirit self, if you would like to use that term. And it is your spirit self who jumps into this invisible world. How do you make it do so?

Well, you do so every night when you go to sleep. You shut down your physical consciousness and you slip into another part of your consciousness that belongs to your spirit self. And this part of your consciousness can go travelling anywhere in the universe if it has that permission. But it certainly has permission to jump into your nearest invisible world, for that is its playground. That is where it resides. That is its true home. In truth, your human self is just visiting temporarily upon this Earth. When you die you will close down that part of your consciousness that has managed your human self, and you will become just your spirit self and go back home.

Now, most people have no control, no conscious control, over what their spirit self does and where it goes. Most people don't even know they have a spirit self as part of their consciousness. And so, part of raising your consciousness to a higher vibration, will be to learn about your spirit self; what it is and how it travels. Many people will wake up in the mornings and remember their dreams. What they are remembering is what their spirit self was doing and where it travelled. This is not just some fantasy you have made up in your mind. This is a world that you have travelled to, and experiences you have undergone. I grant that these experiences can sometimes seem weird; that is the nature of this invisible world. Many things can be created here that cannot be manifested upon Earth.

And so, as you raise your consciousness to a higher level, you will begin to connect with your spirit self, a higher part of your consciousness. And you will begin to converse as if you were two different people. In truth, you are all one consciousness but each part of you is acting out a role. You get this in your human mind too, where you can take on two different personas, where you say that you are in two minds; one part of you wants to do one thing, another part of you wants to do a different thing. In your consciousness there can be many parts to you, all playing out different aspects of yourself. You know yourself that you can have quite different personalities when you are with this person or that person. So, having a human part of your consciousness and a spirit part of your consciousness should not come as too much of a surprise to you.

Your spirit self is more knowledgeable and wiser than you. It can see things from a greater advantage point. It is wise to heed its advice.

And its advice will often come to you as intuition or gut feel. It does not necessarily come to you as words.

So, once you are aware that you have a spirit self that abides in this invisible dimension, you can become more conscious of it, and eventually you will become more conscious of it as it travels in that other invisible world. Your human consciousness will be more linked to it, and you will remember better what your spirit was doing and where it has been. This is what meditation will help you to do. It will help you to leave behind the human consciousness that governs this physical world, and you will pass your consciousness through the portal into the spirit side of your consciousness and into the spirit world that remains unseen with your human eyes. Your physical body does not travel here; your consciousness does, through the vehicle of your spirit self.

Once you are acquainted with your spirit consciousness you can travel to all kinds of places in that second Earth that is closest to you. But there are also other worlds beyond this. And when you are a more seasoned traveller, doors will open and allow you to travel further. It is an exciting thought, is it not?

And in these worlds you are not just a solo traveller. There are many like yourself in spirit form, and you will get to meet these beings, these spirits, and you can have conversations with them, and even relationships. Many of them will be beings that you have known before between your lives on Earth. You have families here. You have parents, and sisters and brothers, and children. There are houses and buildings and offices and places for leisure. Some of the ideas in your science fiction films come from spirits that have visited these places in the higher realms. There is nothing that you see upon Earth that has not already been designed and built in the heavens. So, do not think of yourself as brilliant or a genius. It has all been invented before. But it could be it has been invented by your spirit in its other world.

If you wish to contact your spirit self, get yourself mellow and in a space of peacefulness and calm. Ask to make contact with that spirit part of your consciousness and it will take place. Sometimes it will not happen immediately. More often or not, you will have to create a relationship with this part of you and this will take time, as it does when you are making any new friend. But put out the request for contact and connection, and your spirit will welcome the advance and make tracks towards you.

You will not see your spirit self with your human eyes, standing in front of you like some shimmering ghost. Your spirit self will make contact with you through your consciousness, so they can only be seen on the inner screen of your mind. So, it will require you to find a quiet space and close your eyes. Connecting with consciousness and divine beings cannot be done amidst the hubbub of a busy human life. It is not that you need to become like a monk or a nun, but you will need to get meditative and slow down your mind and make space for this connection to happen.

Your intention is the first step, so intend to meet your spirit self today and soon you will be travelling in the spirit world. Doors will open for you, and who knows what you might find there.

Chapter 8 – GIFTS OF THE GODS

A lot of my mind has gone into what I would like to explore today with these consciousnesses that are hearing or reading our words. It will be a mine of information, a mind of information. Let us delve into the mysteries of the mind today, into things that people know about but seldom speak about, for it seems that the mysteries of the mind are often quite unspeakable, especially by the scientists and the naysayers of our day. They do not like to think there might be hocus-pocus afoot, or that something spooky is going on in realms unknown to them, unfathomable to them. They like to think that everything is under their control, that their own consciousness has the breadth of things. How mistaken they are! For one's consciousness is only a tiny part of what is going on in this world, and there are many other worlds influencing you and bearing down upon you in every moment.

So, while you are not a puppet, you are certainly only one small cog in a very large machine. So, those who act from hubris will certainly have egg on their faces when they discover the true nature of things, and how they have no more control over their world than a baby does. So, we must know our status in the universe and where we stand. The universe is not our baby, but we are a baby of the universe. The Earth is not under the command of presidents and kings and queens. The Earth is under the command of the gods, and humans can either work with the gods or against them.

Now, when you decide to work with the gods and with the angels, a whole new dimension of living opens up for you. You are introduced to many facets of life that could not be revealed to you before. Many people do not know about these dimensions, for they are not open to their existence, and they deny that the gods have relevance in their world. It is your choice. Deny us and you deny your invitation into our dimension and the magic that we can weave. But if you are curious then our world is your oyster and we have many pearls to offer you.

The most magical gift that we train you in is that of creativity. We gods have created your world, and now we teach you to create your world. You need nothing more than the power of your mind. And when you train your mind, for it can be a bit like a puppy, all things will be available to you. You will not miss out on anything. But you must believe that you have this gift, and you must believe that you are capable of using it. It takes many years and often many lifetimes for people to understand this gift. But once you get the hang of it, then there is a rush of pleasure every time you use it and enjoy the result of your manifestation. There is nothing more fulfilling than creating something that you desire. The creator gods created this universe. Now you get to create your own little universe around you. There is nothing that is impossible, given the right focus and effort.

As you begin to climb up the ladder towards godhood, more and more gifts will be revealed to you. And you will need to ponder on which gifts you desire, for getting too many gifts given to you at once, you will not be able to make use of them all. So, take some time to meditate on what you really want and what you really want to be. As the power of your mind grows, so too will your power for creating things. And you will begin to notice that things pop into your life more often and more easily than you could have credited before.

Love is something that many people desire. And if you desire love to come to you then you must attract it to you by being love yourself. Wherever you stand in the love stakes, then this will be the love vibration that you send out. So, if you are not receiving all the love that you desire, then take a look at the cloak of love that you are wearing. Is it designed to attract what you want? There are many who fool themselves about love. They think they want it in this form or that, and yet, in truth, their heart is bending in another way, and so it is refracting or detracting from the love they are trying to manifest. Examine your deepest feelings and thoughts, for in here is harboured the programming that makes things happen. Even if your programming is just a little bit off, then the outcome you expect will not be forthcoming as you desire.

So, you really need to understand yourself and what signals you are putting out there, for every little thought and idea is broadcast on the wavelengths, bidden by you or not. So, you will need to be in control of what you broadcast. Not all that goes out on the wavelengths is conscious to you. Much of it rises up from the subconscious and wafts out into the universe without you knowing. So, it is important that you get into those little pirate stations and understand what is being putting out upon the waves. There is much sabotage underfoot when you start to investigate.

So, once you are across all your thoughts and ideas and feelings, then you will become a master of manifestation, and everything that you dream about can be dreamed up and brought into the physical. It is the magician's wand that we are giving you, but it is no more than mind power. Your consciousness is your wand.

The mind is really not so mysterious. You can go in and explore its every nook and cranny. It is not gated to you, but you may be required to open doors and look inside. And there will definitely be much to rummage through and throw out and delete. Just like living in a house, you are living within your consciousness, and it does require regular cleaning and big sort-outs every now and again. If you lived in the same house all your life and never threw anything away that came into that house, there would be no room to move and you would be drowning and suffocating under rubbish. It is the same with your consciousness, and yet some have never given a thought to taking a broom there and sweeping out the dirt.

Let go of things that no longer serve you, not just objects but memories and feelings too. Make space for new and more interesting things to visit upon you, and in this way you will keep your life fresh and alive. Do not do what you've always done, but find new ways to create and new ways to improve. Jazz up your life or you will be old before your time.

Is your consciousness like an old dusty, musty bookshop? Or is it like a new and trendy library, where all can be accessed at your fingertips, and there are portals to other worlds? Your consciousness is the best Internet that has ever been invented. Think how far the Internet has come in the last few decades. Think how much further it will go in the next one hundred years. Your consciousness will be a million times more excellent than this.

Chapter 9 – LOVE IS CONSCIOUSNESS

We are going to speak about love today. And you may be wondering how love connects with consciousness. How do the two bounce off one another? So, this is an interesting and useful thing to know.

Consciousness, as I have said before, is a non-physical thing. And so is love. Love may have symptoms and outcomes that are physical but love itself cannot be grasped. It is something that seems to sit in the air, something nebulous that on occasion entrances us, wraps us up within it, and transports us to other worlds. Is this not a little like your consciousness, something that can transport you to other worlds?

So, you may well ask, is love consciousness? And I would say yes to that, but not everyone's consciousness is love. So, love is consciousness, but consciousness is not necessarily love. What a conundrum to try and unravel!

Love is consciousness because it is everything that we are. Think about that; all that you are is love. However, there are parts of our consciousness that certainly are not love. Yet, all this means is that a layer of not-love has covered over the love that we really are. It is like a cheese that has gone mouldy. The cheese is still a cheese inside but it has a crust of mould on the top of it. So, if we can get rid of that crust of mould, get rid of all that is not-love that lies on top of us, then we will find that we are truly love underneath. We were spawned by the One God as love, and this love is still our makeup, still our foundation, and all we must do is dig down and find it once again, for in many many lifetimes we have encrusted ourselves with mould and all that constitutes not-love.

We have erred in many ways, as humans and other entities, since we were first birthed into this universe. But that's not to say we need to sit within this pigswill any longer. With intention, you can begin to throw off these layers from this moment on. Let go all that does not serve you, or does not serve the world. Forgive all those you deem to have maligned you or crossed you in any way. Forget being negative and look for every asset in your life. These are the ways you will haul yourself out of the mire.

And, my goodness, when you begin to feel that hint of love again, when it starts to show itself through the morass, then comes hope. And this little glint will have you digging further, for, once tasted, love can never be put aside again.

And I am not speaking here of the general romantic love that humans experience. Certainly, it can be deep and devout, and there is nothing wrong with that and I encourage it. But there is a far far deeper love within you, one that transcends everything. And it comes as a love for yourself, from knowing that you are love itself and that nothing can ever push you off track again. For you will cling to this love like you have never valued anything before. This love outshines every other love. And from the love of yourself it will take you to the love for other people, and this will take you to the love of everything in this universe. And this love will make you shine and make the universe a brighter place. You know yourself that when you are in romantic love with someone the world seems a much rosier place. Imagine how it is when you are in love with yourself and everyone around you, then this universe will shine with your magnificent fire. There will be nothing you cannot achieve. All will be possible. And you shall add such value to the treasures that are already here.

Love is such a magnificent thing, it's a wonder we don't want more of it. And yet there are people who deny love and turn away from it, not just in rejecting a mate, but in rejecting their families, or friendship, or good human decency, or the offer of help. Look to yourself and how often you turn love away. The gods encourage you to invite love into your life. For with love, there will be harmony. With love, there will be music in your ears and heart. With love, you will feel like dancing. With love, you will help all those around you to accept love too.

Catch yourselves in moments of not-love. What is it that causes you to act in this way? Where are the seeds that have sprouted into this behaviour? What is missing in your life that makes you act this way?

What woundings have you collected that are making you act like a raging bull? And why will you not play the game with others? Why will you not share, or take part, or care? Are you difficult to live with, or to like? Can you not soften your demeanour and let people in and show them your true light?

When you are love you are given a key, and this key will open portals, portals to other worlds. We do not wish those who are not-love to visit us. But for those who are shining, or ready to shine, the key is yours and doors will open. So, if you have a mind to explore this universe, then you will have to fill that mind with love, for those who are dripping with darkness will never have access to our doors. So, come, scrub up and then we'll let you in. And the more light you bring, the higher you'll be allowed to go.

So, let us begin to think of consciousness and love as one thing. We are not a mind and a separate heart. The two are of one.

But love is not missing in anyone. It is there in the sub-strata to be discovered by all. Get out your spades and picks and dig deep. Be a miner for love. You may strike gold and diamonds along the way, but it is love which is the true treasure, and nothing is as valuable as that.

Love your consciousness and flood it with your love.

Chapter 10 – THE SCREEN OF CONSCIOUSNESS

You are wondering what more I may have to say about consciousness. Well, we have hardly started, let me assure you of that. For consciousness is everything, so how could we possibly run out of things to say?

Yes, consciousness is everything. Everything has consciousness within it. We have spoken of this before. So, let us speak about another facet of consciousness, a little-known facet but an important one, nevertheless.

Consciousness is the screen through which you view the world, and, like any screen, it can be composed in many ways. It could be a clear screen, and this would be the most valuable to you, for it would let you see things with great clarity. But usually your screen is cluttered up like the desktops on your computers. You have several thousand apps going all at once and you have messages pinging at you from all directions, every second of the day. Your consciousness is not static and is never still. There are always many applications running in the background, and several more at the forefront of your mind. How could you possibly know what is going on inside there? Your screen, your consciousness, will only allow you to view a very small number of things at a time. These are the things you are putting your attention upon. And you deal with these things and then more will come to the forefront. There is never a moment when you are not thinking.

The screen of your consciousness will work better if you could be rid of some of the clutter that prevents you from seeing clearly. Just as you need to structure things within your computer, so too do you need a kind of structure in your consciousness. What is important and a priority? What can be stored away for another day? But just as your computer tends to get bunged up with old emails and files, so too does your consciousness go this way. And you will need to have a sort out, a rearranging, a de-cluttering, so that things may work more efficiently within your mind.

Just as banks of old photos will take up much of the memory within your computer, so too will banks of old emotions and memories take up much of the space within your consciousness. Keep the good ones and eject the bad. Why would you want to file away old grudges and disappointments, past traumas and misfortunes? These are done with; you've had the experience, now move on.

Many folks carry their woundings like medals on their chests. They say to all, "Look at me and what I have been through. This is why I am the mess I am today." Or they are more cheerful and upbeat, but still they parade their war wounds and replay their part, but now they proudly maintain that they are a survivor. Yet still they are clinging to the old story that made them so. If you are still alive then you are a survivor of all that you have gone through, good and bad. I am not saying that you should not be happy to have survived, but let go of your stories for it perpetuates the event and prevents you from letting go.

Move on, I say, and feel your strength and motivation to take you through today and into a better future. Always place your consciousness in this present moment. Make it the best moment you can possibly have, and already it is in the past and a pleasant memory. Build your future by creating a happy platform right now.

Even though this moment may be filled with tragedy, when you are made from love the tragedy will not cut you so deep. You will ask, "What can be learnt from this experience?", and you will utilise this teaching and move on to the next moment and the next, which will take you further and further away from that tragic time. All of us will experience shocks to our system; it is the nature of human life, but we do not need to remain shocked or in stasis. We can pull ourselves back together and be working again as wholly love and one whole consciousness before very long.

The basic makeup of a god is to be able to take the curved balls of the universe, juggle with them, and throw them back. A god does not let the universe flatten them or stay down for very long. Would you not like this kind of consciousness too? This is what we seek to teach you so that humans are much more resilient and do not get squished by the vicissitudes of the times. Unfortunate things will happen, and even more so if you dwell upon the misfortune of life. For your consciousness will attract events that confirm whatever you believe. Change your beliefs and you can change your whole world.

I will take great pains in this book to ensure that by the time you finish it you will know without a shadow of a doubt that your consciousness creates your world. The world mirrors back to you whatever is in your thoughts. So, the screen that you are looking through is really just one big mirror. There is not a single thought or feeling that is not echoed back to you in some way. You are the creator of your world and of your life. If it is like some unpleasant movie, then you are the director and you must rewrite the script. Don't blame others for all your woes.

Of course, it gets complicated when everyone's movies are interwoven with one another, but you can extricate yourself by being more conscious of the part that you are playing and the script that you are playing out. Bring it back to its source; you are the storyteller. What is your story you are telling yourself and the world? You can design things differently from this very moment on. Take some time to come to grips with your movie. Rein it in, edit it, delete some scenes, incorporate new players and sack others. But most of all, rejig your own part in this play, for you are the central character of your own movie.

Let you be a star and let you shine your light. Do not wait for others to make you into a star. You are your own star. Just shine your starlight and you will be seen. Be the star of your screen.

Chapter 11 – WHERE IS CONSCIOUSNESS?

Today we shall go searching for consciousness. And what do I mean by that? Well, if people, for the most part, are not conscious, then they must go looking for their consciousness. Where is it? Where is it to be found?

If consciousness is who we are, as I have stated before, then consciousness is already in place within us. For we *are* consciousness. So, all that is required, in truth, is for us to become aware of our consciousness, aware that we have one, aware that we can utilise it, aware that it is here to work for us. If people think that they are managed only by their brain, then they are overlooking a major asset in their consciousness. For consciousness is a million times more intelligent than their brain. The brain is a tool of their consciousness. It is a physical bridge between consciousness and the human body. But the brain is created by consciousness, so the brain will have limitations according to what you carry in your consciousness as your thoughts and your ideals.

So, how do we become aware of our consciousness? How do we wake up to it? Well, indeed, books like this will alert you to the fact that your consciousness is more than you ever thought possible. And there are many other books like this one, and many workshops and many teachers who can share this knowledge with you.

Many become aware of their consciousness when they are given a wake-up call from their spirit. It will be at some advantageous time of your life, when you are ripe for opening, when you are ready to perhaps hear and learn that there is more to yourself outside of your brain. These wake-up calls are not always happy events. They are designed to shock you out of your miasma, out of your stultified life. The shock makes you reflect on things, for nothing can ever be the same again. You will have been changed by this event. It will have opened your eyes, your heart, and your mind.

Many do not come naturally to recognising their consciousness, so it requires a little help from the divine world. Some people, it is true, will go, "Oh, that is interesting!" and then close the door on their consciousness again and revert to their previous way of being. But, with luck, some will open the door onto their consciousness and it will grab their attention and they will remain curious enough to go exploring more.

Consciousness does not reveal all its secrets in one go. It will take many years and lifetimes to delve into its corridors and rooms. Yet do start exploring from the very first day. We encourage you to have experiences, and each room that you enter in your consciousness will provide you with that new experience or some reflection upon the past. There are thousands, if not hundreds of thousands, of these rooms. I can assure you, you will never become bored.

For some it might be a house of horrors, for it is true not every room is inviting and warm. There will be things there that are distasteful to us, but these things must be looked at all the same. You may come face to face with something that you have done in the past that you are not proud of, and this occurrence must be atoned for, must be forgiven. It is not that you are punished for things you might have done that could not be labelled as loving, yet you will need to find some way to make amends and make this situation come right. You might say the past is past and what has been done cannot be undone, and this is the truth, but you can move forwards, mitigating what you have done with good deeds and trying to smooth out the consequences of your actions.

If you have killed, you cannot unkill, but you can go forwards by saving someone else. If you have hurt, you could ask for forgiveness and do something that will mend that hurt. And you can try forgiving those who have hurt you in turn. If you have been ignoble, then foster noble plans and carry them out. If you have been fearful or too weak, then strive to strengthen yourself and make yourself enter the fray.

There are many things all of us have done in past lifetimes, and even within this life, that we are not proud of and wish we could do over again. In our consciousness we can redo these scenes. Let us wind the movie backwards in our mind and let us replay that scenario and take a different part. You might think this a waste of time, but in the heavenly dimensions there is no time. Consciousness stretches across it all, and so if you decide to replay a scene in some different way, then you will make a difference to what is being held in consciousness from now on. And this different outcome will filter through the byways, through all the consciousnesses involved, and the whole dynamic of that event will be changed and people will be affected quite differently from henceforth.

So, do not think you cannot change the past. It is held there in your consciousness for you to refine and retune. Turn everything in your consciousness into harmony and then there shall only be music where once there was clashing discord.

Delve into those rooms of your consciousness and face up to what you must look at, or get out your mops and pails and cleanse every corner and every cobweb. Go through your consciousness as if you were spring-cleaning your home, for your consciousness is your home. It is the home of your mind, of your thoughts and feelings, and the way that you create. You could not create merchandise in a messy and dirty warehouse. Neither can you create the details of your world from a messy and dirty consciousness. Allow yourself some time to do this, every day if possible but certainly every week. Do the housekeeping on your consciousness and then you shall feel fresher every day. Many of you feel spongy or under the weather as you go about your daily lives. This is a clear indication for you to do your housework on your mind. Do not take shortcuts or sweep the dirt under the mat. Really get to grips with what is contained in the halls of your consciousness, for you carry this around with you every day and it need not be so burdensome if it were lighter.

And where do you put all this muck that you collect? Intend for it to go into the waste bins of the universe. We have good recycling plants here. All your trash is regurgitated back into the light from which consciousness can be formed anew. Do not worry about the mechanism of this. There are swathes of the universe given over to taking the darkness and transforming it into light. Set your intention to move your rubbish and your darkness into one of these depots now.

We have angels who make sure you do not pollute our universe. It is kept in pristine condition for those gods whose consciousnesses are clear. There is a perimeter barrier around your Earth that does not permit human consciousness to destroy the atmosphere of the higher worlds. So, if you muddy your waters then you will have to swim in them. Clean up the oceans and the waters of your consciousness. We appreciate every effort that you make to do so.

When you are clean and clear, then you are invited to fly through our dimensions with alacrity.

Chapter 12 – HEALING THROUGH CONSCIOUSNESS

Sophia: I've just learnt that my sister, Tina, is in hospital having an operation this afternoon, so I am a little tearful.[1]

Chiron: Let us see how consciousness can make the way better. We cannot obviously completely divert the way that the universe needs to operate. We do not know, and cannot fathom, the lessons that the universe has in store for us and the experiences, yet we can react to these with horror or agitation or serenity. It is your choice within your consciousness how to react to events. Does it do any good to put yourself into the same emotional state as that which you are perceiving? Wouldn't a clear mind and a clear heart serve you better?

It is not that we wish you to be as cool as ice and aloof from the situation. On the contrary, we wish you to put your energies into it, but your healing energies, your blessings, and your love. If you dive into the horror or tragedy of something, then you will take these energies upon yourself. And they will unsettle you and upset you and then you will be no good to anyone, and no god to anyone either. We need our gods to stay strong and resolute and to keep on standing while all about them may be falling down. That is not to say that a god does not feel deep emotions that hurt and cut, yet they can pull themselves up from this wounding, heal themselves quickly, and then go about healing everyone else.

So, how does a god go about healing? Do they all have miraculous powers? Yes, all gods do have these astonishing powers to heal, for

---
[1] She made it through okay, in case you were wondering!

healing is only manifestation of the physical. And as we have learnt in previous chapters, gods are masters of manifestation. And this is what the gods are trying to teach humans. As you begin to master manifestation, you begin to master the healing arts as well. So, even if you are not that fussed at manifesting physical objects for your pleasure, then you might be more interested in healing the sick and the lame.

As with manifesting materiality, your consciousness needs to set its intention for what it wants to manifest in the way of healing. And so, it is not for you to focus on what is wrong with the body but for you to focus on projecting the outcome that you want. See the person as healed and well again. See them whole and fit for purpose. See them smiling, with all in harmony within their form. See the light coursing through them. And if it is their destiny to get well, then you will be helping them on their way much quicker than if they had been left alone.

But sometimes a person's illness, or medical diagnosis, or challenge for their physical body, is the wake-up call that the spirit has commanded. By our healing efforts we can make the way a little easier for that person, but we cannot take away the path that they must tread. So, do not think that it is always up to you to affect a healing solution for someone. If you can open their eyes to the source of their problem, even if you cannot heal their woes, then this is a job well done and commensurate with healing in the eyes of us gods. For waking up to your issues is a kind of healing in itself.

You are not responsible for the destiny of another; you can only be responsible for your own. So, heal what you can about yourself and give solace and succour where you can along the way to your fellow humans. Certainly, sometimes magic will seem to have been performed and miraculous outcomes acclaimed, and we all rejoice when this happens. But do not despair when the opposite occurs and nothing seems to be budging or clicking and the malady stays as it is or gets worse. Give everything your best energies and intention, and that is the part you need to play. If adverse outcomes ensue, it is not because you have failed. You have done what you could and the rest is in the lap of the gods. You cannot amend a person's trajectory for them, but you can help them to take a different tack which will bring them more on course. When you do this, this is the healing that they need.

We have spoken before about consciousness being a magic wand. It is this, for it does have miraculous and magical powers. What you believe will come about. So, believe with all your heart and know that the very best result will follow. You may question what is the very best result if it is not in line with what you had desired. But you will need to accept that the universe is cleverer than you, and all that eventuates is for the best at that time for everyone involved. So, do not shake your fist at the universe and the gods. There is more going on in the background than you can imagine, and what happens at the physical level is just a mere blip and blink compared to what is happening at your higher spirit level.

There are many things to be taken into account at the level of higher consciousness. You, at your human level, cannot see this far over the horizon. So, you must allow and accept that you have only a teeny view of things and that all is playing out as it should in the higher realms and filtering down to you.

It would be unfair to say that you should not get upset when things don't go your way, or when tragedy strikes, or upsets happen. Allow yourself to feel all the tumult of your emotions. Don't suppress them, for that will make it worse. But let these emotions drain through your body, and through your consciousness, and let them drain away. This does not make you hard-hearted, but it makes you resilient and able to cope. If you are a blubbering mess, who will come and clear up after you and set you back into harmony once again?

So, let yourself have the experience of emotionality but let it not cast you adrift like a raft on an ocean of tears. Hold onto your consciousness and your sanity. Anchor yourself to the knowledge that there is more playing out than just in this physical field. So, practise calming yourself when you feel that you have the wobbles. Take deep breaths and ask for your spirit consciousness to bring down its energies and bathe you and soothe you. A shaky consciousness will create a shaky world. See the very best in each moment, hang onto your harmony, and practise at being love. This life is a minefield of events and experiences. Set up your consciousness with light and you will be able to tread lightly through this field.

Heal yourself first and then you can become a healer of others.

Chapter 13 – APPLYING YOUR MAGIC WAND

The study of consciousness can seem a little morose. And it should not be this way at all for consciousness is exciting, is magical, is metaphysical. And so, I would like to take you down a more adventurous line today so that you may feel more enthusiasm for our subject. I have already told you that your consciousness is your magic wand, but this may not be exciting enough for you to merely know this, for you will need to apply it and get results and then you will never again look at your consciousness as dour or doleful or boring. When you begin to create your life through your conscious manipulations as you truly want it, then joy will bubble up inside you and you will be keen to carry on your manifestation practices. This is what gives the gods so much happiness and freedom, that they can create whatever they want whenever they want. And this is not a trick that is denied to you humans.

So, come, let us practise at being true magicians. Let us take our magic wand, our consciousness, and let it pay its way. Utilise it for all you've got, for wouldn't that be the most magnificent thing, if you could create whatever you cherish and dream? There, of course, may have to be a few blocks at first, while you find your feet, or should I say your magic hands. For not all the things that you desire are good for you or good for this universe. And so, you may find we gods dampen some of your enthusiasm if you are trying to create a world filled with chocolate or naked women, or money growing on trees. Your requests and desires will need to be reasonable and manageable and not tip the balance of this world.

And yet there is still much scope for your creativity, so put your mind to work. Dally on the sofa or on your bed, imagining and projecting all that you would like to see come about in your physical life. See yourself in that scene. Play the part to the hilt. Jump in with all your senses and have a good time and enjoy yourself. This world has been dire for far too long. So, let us lighten it up. Let us pull the shades from over our eyes and let us bring lightness.

Creating your world is such a fun thing to do. You do it well when you are a child. But something happens to us along the way, and we put aside our childishness and elect to think like adults in an adult world, and we ditch many of our creative aspirations. And many will willingly admit that they are not creative in any manner at all.

Creativity is not reserved for artists and dancers and writers and all that ilk. Creativity can also be performed in the boardroom, at your desk, in hospitals and in prisons, in sciences and other academic bents. Everything in this world was created, so see what you can create today. You can create a pie in the kitchen, or a pie chart on your computer. You can create a weather map or create a machine. You can create a work of art or a dance move. You can create some writing or a poem. You can create a plan or a healing. You can create an idea, a garden, or a home. You can create children or a field of wheat. You can create love at every turn. Every moment is an opportunity for your creation.

Sophia and I are creating this book. What is it that you are creating right now, apart from more wisdom in your consciousness?

Think of the joy that will spring from within your heart when you see your creation manifest before you. It does not, of course, appear out of the ethers like some conjuring trick, but there will be a turn of events that cause your manifestation to come about. For the universe is always busy in the background, planning and manoeuvring to make your dreams come true.

Now, if you have not had much success in manifesting your ideas, then think about your thoughts that you are sending out upon the wavelengths. Is there some confusion there? Have you muddled up your order? Have you presented it to the universe and then negated it again by dwelling on negative thoughts? And so you might say, "I wish to get this job", and then thoughts might creep in like, "Who am I to get this job? I'm not good enough. I don't think I'd be able to cope." And so, the universe does not know what to do with your request, so it is put on hold, for it would seem that your intention is that you are not worthy to win this job.

So, be careful of that small talk that goes on in the background of your consciousness. It is the saboteur of many a dream. And it is not only small talk that you must beware, for there will be indecisive feelings too which scupper your plans, feelings like fear and anxiety, sometimes feelings that you can't quite pin down but which negate your request nevertheless.

So, we come back to that issue of needing to be very aware of what is going on in our consciousness. What orders are going out there that we would like to manifest, and what thoughts are then going out there to rescind those initial requests? We need to be firm in our intention. We need to be consistent and focused and aligned. If we are indecisive or in procrastination mode, our creation abilities will be crippled.

We gods want nothing more than for humans to learn the trick of creativity. It is a salve for the heart and spirit, for without this power you will feel powerless. And when you feel powerless then rebellion begins to bubble up within your veins. We wish you to be powerful, but we wish you to be wise. Most of all, we wish you to be loving. And when all three cornerstones are in place, then we have a god who is worthy to strut this universe.

The power to create wisely and with love, this is the gift that we gods are teaching you. So, come, do not turn us away. Listen to our teachings and begin to practise and apply them. Your world could become different from this very moment. Utilise your consciousness and create your Heaven on Earth.

What is it that you want? Are you afraid to want it? Does it seem too impossible, too far-fetched, too much of a stretch? Well, there are those who have made their dreams come true. You all have the same apparatus in your consciousness. So, take a leaf out of their book and dream how you want your life to be, and hold that dream and do not cut away at it with your negative thoughts. But are you prepared to follow your dream, for in most cases it will take some effort and plenty of time? Will you do whatever is necessary to follow your destiny, or will you pass on it this time around in this lifetime? Don't waste your life, but believe in your dream and the ways that you can get there. And there will be many ways shown to you by the universe that you could not have imagined.

So, put your order out there and let it fly. Do not snatch it back or hobble it. And then when events start to happen that may point towards your dream, take the steps forward. Don't hesitate or run away. Know that the universe is holding you within its arms. It wants nothing else but for your dreams to become true. So, work with the universe and know that she has your back.

Do not fear your dreams. They are the out-picturing of your destiny that you came here to unfold. Take them seriously and value them, then use your consciousness to find your way.

Chapter 14 – BE A FIREBALL

There are rising temperatures in the household, so let us maintain an even keel. Let us maintain our balance. Let us maintain our own amplitude, our own wavelength, and do not be pulled down onto others. With that said, let us see how consciousness can help us here, for consciousness is our magic wand and can make everything better.

Consciousness can sort out many ills, for if we are creating good things with our consciousness, we can also take the bad things in our life and recreate them into something better. So, let us first identify what is going awry, what is out of balance and out of kilter, what is ill and threadbare, what is not working as it should. All these things can be brought into the fold and washed over with the energies in your consciousness, and it will be as if they are rejuvenated, renovated, or dissolved.

There is no reason to put up with non-working things in your life. You recognise that things are not working, and you put them right. Yet many people will remain for years in the same situation doing nothing about it, even letting it atrophy further. So, stop the rot right here, right now. Turn a new leaf and turn things over. You don't have to let life get the better of you, but you can have the better things in life.

The best way to modify your life is to raise your vibrations, and we have spoken of this before. So, do all you can to make yourself feel like a bright shining star. Cogitate on the nicer and finer things of life, people you love, favourite places you have been, situations you are delighted to find yourself in. Ramp up those energies and vibrations in your heart until you are feeling like a ball of fire; in truth, like a star. And then apply this feeling to the situations in your life that are making you feel down. Send out waves from your fireball. And these waves will not burn up or destroy the good in that situation but only the bad. It will burn away the dross and the darkness.

And you can do this for ill health in your own body, or the ill health in others, or ill health in your relationships or in the world. Set your intention for everything to be healthy, and health comes from balance. When you are in ill health it is because something is out of balance. When relationships are unhealthy it is because one side is pulling more than the other. So, get yourself on an even keel. Ponder on what it takes to maintain this balancing act. Send out your loving fiery vibrations from the star that is inside your heart. Cover everything that comes within your remit and let your vibrations flow on and out into the universe, for you never know what good it might do there.

Your energies are affecting others all the time. So, what is your energy like today? Are you someone that others would like to touch? Or are you someone that people will run away from? Are you a monster in disguise? Or are you a kind of angel whose vibrations are welcome everywhere? You cannot heal all that is around you until you have got yourself into a place and space of higher vibrations. So, work on yourself first and then watch the remarkable results around you.

If everyone were to take control over their own vibrational level, then it follows, and you can see, that the whole world would be healed within an instant. Yet most do not understand this process, so you will have to learn it and then you will need to teach it to others. The 'fireball effect' is a most remarkable healing tool and without it the gods would be nothing. So, learn how to turn yourself into a fireball, into a star, into a magnificent and magnanimous being, and allow your vibrations to spread their tentacles afar, and watch your own health improve too.

Your consciousness is capable of many things, all things, if truth be told. And yet you must work up to becoming a magician. It will not happen for you overnight. You will start with little tricks here and there, and as you gain in confidence and belief in yourself, so you will be able to take more and more magic on board. If you feel like a failure, you will be a failure. But as you build upon your successes then you will feel the success of your craft and you will feel fulfilled.

Every magician will tell you that they did not get to their level without plenty of work and practice. Magic is not a gift bestowed by God like some inheritance that just comes into your life and you can begin to use it. The magic of your consciousness is there alright from the very beginning, but you must develop it and you must learn how. It is a skill that is acquired.

So, you can choose to become a magician, or you can allow this trait to lie fallow within you; it is your choice. All have the capability. It is not denied to anyone. So, become a craftsperson and skill yourself up. And then you will have the wonderful ability of making your world lighter and brighter and flowing more copiously and capably. You will begin to attract magic from other quarters too, for as I have said, like attracts like. And as you begin to make your life more bountiful, then more bounty will come your way as well. The universe wishes for you to have all that you desire. It is not punishing you by taking things away. It does not wish for you to be impoverished in any way. So, stop thinking like a victim and begin to think like a victor. The world truly is your oyster and you can pick up the pearls at any time.

But most people have a very dejected view of life upon your world. They think it is all a struggle, and that it should be. They are not taught that there is another way. They follow their parents' example, and the same kind of consciousness is passed down from generation to generation, never moving on or moving beyond. So, will you be the one to break the chain now? Will you be the one who sees the obvious way before you? Will you take on board all that I have taught you so far about your consciousness and how it can pave your path with diamonds and gold and more love than you could ever dream of? Or will you slump back in your armchair and forget all my words, all my wisdom, and carry on with your life just as before? Hopefully there are some who will grab their wand and become a wizard.

It is never too late to change your life around. Even if you had only one minute until your death, that one minute is all you need to raise the fire within your heart and to catapult yourself to a higher vibrational level from which you will begin your new life. It is not all said and done for you, no matter what your age or condition. Everything can be improved. Everything can be lightened. You can bring yourself relief and help those around you too.

So, come, take charge of your life now. Instil that fiery star within your heart. Make like a fireball and set yourself and the world on fire.

Chapter 15 – MEANNESS

I am thinking about speaking about meanness in our consciousness, for everyone has a mean streak in them somewhere that will get triggered off by a certain someone at certain times. Even the best of saints can show a mean side on occasion. Perhaps they are ill and feeling under the weather or some such excuse, but really there is no excuse for being slightly tart in our answers or turning our back on people when we are needed.

So, let us examine where this mean streak may come from. Why is it there at all and why do we feel the need to bring it out and hurt others, even if it is only infrequently?

Consciousness holds all facets of our personality. And there will be times in any of our lives where we have been hurt by others, either physically or slighted with words. And we harbour a grudge or a resentment against this. And so, when someone in another lifetime, perhaps far removed from the original one where you were hurt, they perform the same deed or speak the same words against us, then shooting up from the darkness comes that old resentment which wishes to fire back. There is no better way to resolve this animosity than to clear the original wounding where we felt harmed. Forgive the person or people who did this to us and let go of those energies into the recycling depot of the universe.

If we did not harbour this residual resentment then people could try to slight us all day long and they would not trigger us off, for we would have no triggers remaining within us. So, do a good job in deleting and erasing those triggers and you will find that nothing can set you off again. You will find life much more harmonious and people will not need to walk on eggshells around you, fearing that something they say or do will set off your bleeding once again.

I am sure that you do not mean to be a mean person and it comes out of you at the wrong time, in unguarded moments, or when you are especially roused. So, do this work on yourself. Cleanse all these old grudges away. And then you will know that your reactions will always be kind and considerate and well-meaning.

No one is immune to the hurts of past lives and those within this lifetime too. But are you going to dwell within these woundings forever, never lifting yourself above them and always feeling hurt? Bring the joy back into your life by knowing that all your wavelengths are harmonious and filled with music that all will want to hear.

Sometimes we do not realise that our consciousness contains these old hurts, and it is only when someone sets us off that they come to light. This is why you have so many experiences on Earth and need to meet so many people, for they all contribute to the raising of your consciousness in some way or another.

Thoth has referred to this as discovering the snakes in your snake pits that have lain dormant for many years or even many lifetimes. You never know when they will come to the surface to bite you once again. You can go digging for these old snakes, go delving into your depths, or you can allow them to be made manifest at an appropriate time where you then acknowledge the issue and deal with it right away. Why would you want to live your life amongst poisonous, writhing snakes in your snake pit when you could be living a life of happiness and joy? If you are moody or cranky then it is for sure that these snakes are moving in your snake pit, that woundings are triggering you off. And you may not even be aware of what is happening to you.

This is why you must take charge of your consciousness and be aware. Do not just float along in life, letting things happen to you and having shocks coming out of left field and further worsening your situation and your temperament. Be on top of all that is going on around you, and more importantly, within you. Scan yourself daily for what is going on in your body, what is going on in your emotions, and what is going on in your mind. You want this physical vehicle of your self to work well in this physical world. You probably maintain your car better than you do your consciousness and your body.

So, be responsible for who you are. Do not take your poisonous venom out into the world, either by your words or your deeds or your thinking. Your energies flow out from you and affect your surroundings, and anyone caught within your energetic net will suffer the consequences of your toxins if you are not careful. You would not like to be poisoned by others, therefore clean up your own vehicle and take only your freshness out with you.

It is time for the whole world to clean up their act. This Earth has suffered enough from your poisonous energies that leak out. Purify your own world and the world around you. Let us have a new atmosphere filled with clean and clear cells. You will know, yourself, of the difference in air quality between a polluted city and a mountainous forest of pine trees. Which do you prefer?

So, do not contribute to the smog and make yourself ill in the process. Cleanse yourself of all grudges and triggers. Let you be a sparkling sphere that no one can ignite into a destructive mood. The gods are clearing and clearing, themselves, the planets, and the universe. You will help them greatly if you could concentrate on clearing yourself.

Consciousness is a complicated web, and it doesn't take much for things to go awry when just one person decides to have a bad day. You are not just putting your own self at risk, if you are this person attracting bad energies, but the entire warp and weft threads of the universe can be affected by what you decide to do and how you decide to react. You are sending damaging pulses down the lines, threatening the lives and harmony of others, and you will need to atone for this one day in the future. How many damaging pulses have you sent out down the line? And how many have you received back again from which you have felt smarted and hurt? You have a saying on your planet, "What goes around comes around," and this indeed is what I am speaking about.

So, clean up your act, my dear friends, for all of us wish to live in harmony and good health. We are all trampling on each other's carpets, messing things up, dirtying the path and leaving it soiled behind us. Think about everything that you can clean up within your lives; yourself, your homes, your gardens, your offices, your streets, your towns, your methods, your relationships, your behaviours, your speech, your attitudes. There is no shortage of tasks to be done. And as we complete these tasks and bring clarity and cleanliness into our worlds, so too will the meanness fall away, and we shall have a much more likeable and liveable planet to be living on.

Do you understand what I mean about meanness?

Chapter 16 – CONSCIOUSNESS AS A TOOL

Let us speak today about consciousness as an uplifting agent. We do not need to stay down in the doldrums when we can use our consciousness to get us out of there. Consciousness is such a fine and useful tool. It is like one of those Swiss army knives, only better, for it is a tool for every occasion. There is nothing that consciousness cannot lend a hand to. And so, when you have consciousness at your side, and within your heart, then you are able to overcome any manner of difficulties.

Why do we not teach this in schools? Why do parents not teach this to their children when they are young and amenable to these ideas? Well, it is the adults of this world that we must first get on board so that they may become the teachers of these wonderful and world-changing ideas.

Back to consciousness as our aid, as our can-opener to a better life.

So, things are not working out for you as it stands. Do not just sit there and let it all swill around you and think there is nothing to be done, and worse, think that this situation will last forever. You know that everything moves on, even in the next minute. So, begin to help your life to move on by applying your conscious thoughts to what you would like to have happen now. Do not think, "I will just dwell in this drizzly mood for a while yet." But rather tell yourself, "Why must I suffer? Why must I feel this pain, when if I work with my consciousness I can be up and laughing and loving once again?"

Secretly, I believe that many of you enjoy wallowing in your pain. You like to be seen as a victim. You like people to feel sorry for you and come running to support you and comfort you. Perhaps it is all the attention you ever get? But that said, if you genuinely wish to rise above your doldrums and your demise, then you must start to form images in your mind, scenes that you wish to play out in the next moments, in the next days. See yourself as overcoming your travails, of coping with your situation, of accepting with good grace where you find yourself right now. And then mustering all your strength and all your belief in yourself and taking yourself through the door to a new playing field, a new plane.

Disaster and tragedy will happen to each and every one of us. You cannot avoid it, for these are the lessons of life. But you do not need to be out for the count. You can bounce up again and get yourself on the road once more. You may not know how you will muster these resources that will get you going again, but when you believe this is possible, the universe will come in from every side and provide you with the ways and means that will see your dreaming come true.

You are not alone in your endeavours, even though it may seem like it at the time. Physically there may be no one else around you, but in the spirit world you are surrounded by helping hands and hearts. Feel the presence of these spirits. Let them envelop you and guide you through your world. They are your extra eyes and ears, your extra pair of hands. Do not dismiss them or reject them or cut them off without a word. These spirits are other parts of you. They reside in your greater consciousness. Do not deny who you are yourself, for the expanded version of you is always available to help. Listen to their voices which will come through to you as intuition or gut feel. Heed those urges that will take you onto your true path.

Now, many will ask, "How do I know if these are good voices or bad?" It depends on the base state you are in when you are hearing them. If you are highly emotional or in fear, then you may be attracting voices of another kind, ones that are in the same emotional state as you. But when you set your intention to only hear the voices of angels and god-like beings, and you truly wish to be downloaded with love, then the instructions you will be given will be enfolded in that love. And this advice will always be for your highest good.

Never forget that like attracts like. If you are in a shambolic way then you will attract shambolic beings into your aura and your life, either from the divine world or the physical world. You must set the timbre and the vibration that you wish to connect on. So, send out for true love and divine help and you will receive it. If you play at games with yourself and others, then you will attract other game-players who will trick and manipulate you, for that is their joy.

So, how is it that you would like to feel today? On top of the world, lying in a bed of roses, contented, fulfilled, in love, of brilliant mind, in glowing health? All these things are possible when you put out this order into the universe. But how many care to do this every day? They get out of bed and they accept things as they are, not taking a single moment to readjust their consciousness and bring in new and brighter vibrations. And so, their world will stay much the same. Yet others will enjoy growth and glory, and magical things will rain down upon them from the heavens. You too could benefit from a magic storm but only if you are game enough to order it in.

There is no danger of this magic running out. The treasure in Heaven's coffers is full to the brim and ever-replenishing. You can never ask for too much, but you will be given only what you can deal with. There are many jewels waiting here with your name on. Come and collect them, for your life will be brighter and more glorious when you do.

It is time now for everyone on Earth to realise what they are made of, how they are constructed, and how consciousness is at their heart. For too long you have been denied these facts. For too long humans have denied these facts. Now we are opening the whole book for you. There is nothing that is secret anymore. You now know what it takes to become like a god. We are giving you instructions. We are helping you find your way. There is no excuse now for dwelling as a human in the old human's world. We require you all to uplift yourselves. We require you all to raise your vibrations. We require you all to work from a higher consciousness, for the old days are coming to an end and we will not abide the dark and dour consciousnesses that have ruled this Earth ere long.

Why would you want to linger in that mouldy mousehole when we are offering you a divine new world? Many just think that it is not possible. I am here to tell you that it definitely exists. All it requires is for you to climb up the stairway. There are many steps, but you will get there in the end. Many people have done this already and they are experiencing the benefits of living from a higher place. It is not some other physical world that you move to. It is the same world but seen with new eyes and felt with new heart. Just as you would see this world differently if you fell blissfully in love, our new acolytes are also feeling that way as they bask in the glories of this new world. If you are not yet feeling these higher vibrations, then look to see how high you are on that stairway to Heaven. There may yet be a number of steps to complete. Don't give up now, for all is within your reach. Just use your consciousness to take you there, and one day you'll be living from Heaven.

Chapter 17 – THIS UNLIMITED UNIVERSE

Consciousness is not limited. It does not have a frugal amount of things to give us and then put a stop on it as if it were working to a budget. No, the universe is completely unlimited. As long as you go on asking, it can go on delivering. It will not come to an end of its supplies. That is not to say you can expect copious amounts of luxuries to begin appearing on your doorstep, for, as I have said before, you will need to be able to cope with everything that comes into your life. The universe does not over-deliver and swamp you with its bounty. But if you have need of something, then request it and your order can be fulfilled.

And this will include a little pleasure in your life as well. You are not limited in the amount of pleasure you can partake in, but bear in mind that the universe demands balance. And the balance for pleasure is work and effectiveness. The scales cannot be tilted, or not for long, in either of those directions. Balance must be maintained. For every effort that you put into this universe, you will receive commensurate rewards in return. So, do not think that you can get something for nothing. Add value to this universe and you will receive equal value in return. And so does society expect this of you, that you will receive fair pay for a good day's work.

Yet the universe does not dabble in money. Money is just an energy, a word of trust between two players. Money does not figure in the universe's dictionary, so don't speak to the universe of money. Don't request money or the monetary equivalent for objects. If you are in need of something then request the item itself, be it food, a car, a holiday, school fees, a house, or money to pay bills. You are not requesting the money itself, but that a car or a house be obtained, or that bills be paid off, or that you will find the means to take a vacation.

The universe understands money, of course, and how the system works upon this planet. And it will utilise its magical ways to make what you want available to you. It will rarely come in the form of money itself.

And so, there might be many interesting events that manifest the equivalent of money for you, but which do not derive from your own income or your own bank account. In fact, the universe seems to enjoy providing strange and unfathomable ways for your dream object or its monetary value to reach you. Competitions may be won, inheritances may be gained, a gift may come winging from someone. There may be special offers or discounts, and other startling ways that money may be gained or saved. But put your focus on what you want to achieve rather than the money that is needed to achieve it. Then the universe will find it easier to help you create your dream.

Because consciousness is a network, it has connections all over the place. There is nothing to which consciousness is not connected. You think you are well-connected if on social media you have millions of followers. Imagine, then, how it is to be the universe with billions upon billions of followers. Now, it is true that not everyone is tuned into their consciousness, but consciousness is tuned into them. Consciousness is aware of every thought, of every emotion. It is aware of the mood and the upcoming crises. It is aware of blossoming love even before the participants recognise it. It is aware of the weather in every quarter and inside your soul. So, it is easy for the universe to put two and two together. It has the ultimate big picture and knows what is going on and going down.

If you wish to create something, then it can pull all the strings together for you, and if you are listening out for its messages, you will hear where to go and what to do. You may find yourself unconsciously walking into a bookstore, staring at a shelf of books and wondering why. Then all of a sudden, your eye catches on a title, and you know darn well that you need to read this book and why you found yourself here. These types of things are happening for people in every moment across the Earth, people who are wondering why they walked over here, or why they said this thing, or why they had that idea. They are all creating their future with the help of this connected universe. They are being shuffled into the right place, at the right time, with the right people.

Yet, if you block out this connection to the universe at large and go along only with the consciousness of your human mind, you will be missing out on all these special deals. Certainly, you can make headway by utilising your own forces, your own willpower, but it will take some mighty effort from you, and you will not feel that starry glow that comes when you feel divinely guided.

The human mind is capable of many great things. Imagine how much greater if you were to allow the gifts of the gods to bless you. So, open yourself up to go beyond your mind. Your spirit's mind is there waiting for you, and behind them are many other souls too. The more you open your heart to the universe, the more can be gathered and downloaded into your world. Do not deny yourself the pleasure of working with this universe. Its resources and storehouses are vast. It holds a cornucopia of goods and goodness. Why would you limit yourself? Why would you run from this generous benevolence?

Get a grasp on this universe and do not perceive yourself as grasping. It is not greedy to want to share in this treasure house and all it can offer you. The gods are bountiful and the universe even more so. You know yourselves how good it feels to endow somebody with a gift. The universe feels the same way, for it has so much to give and it is blessed in the giving. So, do not be backwards in coming forwards, for the universe wants to grant you your wish. Believe that it is available to you. Don't feel guilty, for you are a child of the gods, and the gods are rich and wealthy indeed. It is what you are here to do, to create and manifest and add to this universe. How will you do this in a loving and enjoyable way? Spread your sparkle around the world and allow others to see how they may sparkle too.

Consciousness is the gift of creation. Create your world wisely and let others enjoy it too. We are all creators together. Let us create a Heaven for us to live in upon this Earth.

Chapter 18 – JUGGLING CONSCIOUSNESS

Today, let us speak about juggling and tumbling and let us see what that has to do with consciousness. You will know that juggling and tumbling are tricks. They are skills that have been practised over and over until the person is accomplished in this art. Your consciousness will need to learn such tricks, to be able to juggle many things at once, and to be able to roll with the tumbles that it will take. Your consciousness will need to be adept at this if it is to make any headway in this world. It will need to be avid and alive, agile and active and aware. You cannot be a consciousness that is asleep in this world, for then life will just flatten you and you will not be able to hold the reins to anything.

So, come, let us learn a few agility tricks for our consciousness, that you may ride with the rolls and fly with the fazes (phases). It is not that we wish you to become a trickster, but it is beneficial for you to learn a few tricks.

The first trick to learn is that nothing is as it seems. Yes, you will see things with your human eyes and touch things with your human hands, but even these things are not solid and are really quite unreal. If you were to see material things right down at their basic components, you might see an atom here and another atom right over there with plenty of space in between. All objects, even your own body, are loosely held together as a collection of atoms and even smaller particles. The atoms you might be able to see through a powerful microscope, but the subatomic particles that make up these atoms are moving in and out of existence all the time.

So, does that mean that the atom is there in front of you, or not there in front of you, in any particular moment? It is a conundrum that your scientists are working upon as we speak. Do we exist in the here and now, or don't we? For all intents and purposes, we humans and the rest of our planet are solid, and we can stake our claim that we are here. But if parts of us and the planet are sometimes not here, where do we and these items disappear to in the meantime?

Well, you can probably guess by now that we are moving in and out of the higher dimensions, the invisible part of the universe to us humans. We, and other things, are moving in and out of this earthly dimension all the time. So, physicality is not so solid as it would seem. And your subatomic particles are visiting temporarily and whisking off at lightning speed to other places in the universe and then returning to Earth before you have time to notice.

The science of quantum physics is exploring these alternate laws of the universe, and before too long it will be better understood and you will begin to teach these things in schools. But I do not want to make this too complex for you, so if you wish to know more about this subject then study quantum physics in your own time. But the message that I bring to you is that there is much much more going on behind the scenes, and your consciousness needs to be aware of this, that things are going on in this physical world and there are even more things going on in other alternate worlds, some of them not physical at all.

And you yourself as a human are here in this physical world and yet some of you, that is your consciousness, is traipsing around the universe meeting other challenges and having other adventures. You are juggling parallel lives. A part of you, a part of your consciousness, is here on Earth managing a physical body and physical life, and other parts of your consciousness are flying elsewhere and carrying out other tasks throughout this universe. It is an exciting concept, is it not?

So, your consciousness is not just living one life. It is juggling other lives too, maybe not even only one other life but several. And when you are a god you will be managing and juggling thousands of lives at the same time. Several of them could be on Earth within the same era. So, if you are having a hard time getting your head around just the one life you are living now, imagine how complex it is when you are a god running several thousand lives in parallel.

There is an overseer to all these lives, and that is your soul. Your soul is the central hub and pulls all things together and pulls all strings together. If you want to know what is going on in any of your alternate lives then just ask your soul. Your soul is a higher part of your consciousness, a very high part. Yet your soul does not sit still and stay at that level forever. It too is always learning and progressing and evolving to higher and higher levels. One day your soul will become a creator god and will take part in managing the whole of this universe. But for now, your soul is managing your own little universe around you.

So, know that you are not all that you think you are. You are not just this body and this brain. You stretch much further, out into the universe as your spirit and your soul. So, your consciousness is juggling far greater things than your everyday challenges on Earth.

And as for tumbling, you could learn a trick or two. In any lifetime you will need to learn to roll with the punches and how to fall gracefully so that you do not hurt yourself or break a limb. Those who are hurt when they take a big fall, are those who do not realise that consciousness can get them up again, dust them down, and help them on their way. They take their fall and they think that life has dealt them a severe blow from which they will never rise again. If you learn to tumble you will hit the deck more softly. You will roll out of it quickly, shake yourself off, and begin smiling again in the shortest time.

Falling to the ground does not need to result in brokenness. When you use your consciousness adeptly, then taking a tumble is more like just a bump in the road. You get over it quickly and you move swiftly forwards. Many is the time when you will take a tumble in your lives. Learn to roll out of it with the agility of an acrobat and you will survive this lifetime more healthily and with joy.

Let your full consciousness take control of your lives. Don't give all the power to your little human will. This is but one small part of your consciousness. You are so much much more. Become aware of the superior powers of your consciousness, especially when you allow the higher parts to take control. You will still have your say and you will not be side-lined or ignored. But work in cooperation with all parts of your blessed mind. You are a team, not a lone wolf. Bring in all the skills of the various parts of your consciousness and then you will be a very smart person indeed. Open yourself up to playing with your team. It will be very beneficial for you, for their wisdom, power, and love know no bounds. If you want magic to happen in your life then this is the way to create it, allowing the magnitude of your consciousness to come to the forefront of your mind.

The final trick I would like to teach you today is to use your magic wand in every moment. Whatever you are thinking becomes manifest in some way. So, take the trouble to adjust your thoughts, fine tune them to what you really want to do, and magic your desire into being. Most people run their lives on autopilot. They do not give their consciousness a moment's thought. But when you begin to work with your consciousness, to blend your will with its ideals, then magic can truly be performed and miracles can happen.

Begin to explore and meet with your consciousness today. There is much you will learn from it and many more tricks it can teach you.

Chapter 19 – MAKE A PLAN

I am wearing my magic hat today, my magician's hat, for I would like you all to know what magic I can weave, and it is not just because I am a god. All of you are gods-in-training and all of you have the same capacity for weaving this magic throughout your lives. I have said before, you are not denied this even though you are still in human form, for you have come from god stock and this means the magic is within you and just needs to be awoken and applied.

So, what is the magic that you would like to come into your life? Think about this carefully for you know now that your thoughts are creating your reality. Most people do not give a second thought as to how they would really like their lives to be lived. They accept the status quo and keep on running on the spot, never progressing very much and often going backwards. But when you sit for a while and give this some purposeful deliberation as to how you see your life playing out in this quarter or that, then you can make remarkable progress in chivvying up your life, sprucing it up and bringing in the joy once again.

You do not need divine guidance to do this, but if you were to connect with your spirit and soul, they could give you ideas as to how your life could be more masterful, more full of good and god. You will be required to put in some effort, it is true. You cannot just wave your wrist with your wand at the end of it and magic these things into being. Reality and physicality come from your consciousness, and the best kinds come from deliberate thought.

So, will you take some time to think about your goals, your ideals, your dreams and wish list? What would you like to achieve, today, this week, this month, this year, this lifetime? What is it you would like to have accomplished by the time you lie on your deathbed and make for Home? Not much will get done if you do not pursue it. So, do not continue to lie on the couch like a sack of potatoes, or tell yourself there is nothing can be done to change the course of your miserable life. I am here as your wizard, your fairy godmother, if you like, to grant you your wishes and help you to change your world.

If you do not want to change, well, that's another story and I wish you well with that one. But for those who are grumbling and know that all's not right, let us begin to climb up that stairway. Let us begin to know that we can take these steps and reach a higher place. All the misery and dire straits that we see upon your planet could be undone and unfolded the moment that you decide to take alternative choices. If you carry on doing what you've always done, you will stay in your quagmire and remain in stalemate.

Some button has to be pushed to release you to take your new journey. I am here today, as you read these words, pushing that button for you. I am offering you freedom. I am offering you a new world. I am offering you release from your prison. But I cannot drag you out of there. You must put one foot forward and move yourself along. We have found in the past that those released without effort will soon find themselves back in their dungeons again.

So, come, make your move before the doors clang shut on you again. Hop up onto that first step and you'll find the second is much easier. Leave all those trifles and pettiness behind. Leave all the deep shit, the travails and tragedies, the murders and the rapes. Leave all the distrust, the betrayals and the deaths. Raise yourself up into a brighter atmosphere, one where you feel clean and clear, where you are ready to work with the gods of this universe. You will be delighted to pitch up to work here every day.

Whatever is sparking within your consciousness is going to be reflected out in the wider world. It will be projected back to you. So, if merciless trauma is going on for you, what is it that is going on within your mind to unleash this upon you? Clean up your thinking and begin to think only with love.

Now, this is a difficult thing to attain when you have been used to thinking without love for most of your life. You get used to it, it is habitual, it is a way of life for you. Your reactions are spontaneous; your reproaches come subconsciously. But you are not a lost cause to be written off as evil. The programming has gone into you and it can come out of you just as easily once again. And we can replace that old programming with new thinking that is more lined with love. Catch yourself when your thinking is not love-aligned and begin to question if this is really how you wish to be. You must be aware of what is in your consciousness so that you can begin to transform it. Catch those little lies. Catch those catty or narky remarks. Catch that judgement, that putting down of others. Catch that spitefulness, that meanness, that cruel aside.

It *is* possible to clean yourself up. We may never get you whiter than white, but a semblance of white is acceptable. And you will feel better when you are not filled with these dark stains. You will love yourself more, and others will certainly love you in return. For how can you love yourself if you are such a grinch?

It is time for the whole world to look at themselves and who they are. Do they like what they see, and can they sleep with themselves at night? Are they attracting wonderful people into their lives, or mean-minded people like themselves?

So, cleanse this consciousness. Make a start on it today. With each little thought that is thrown out and banned, you will be climbing another step towards Heaven's realms. And as you climb higher, the magic will start swirling around you too. Every effort will beget a reward, and life will be sweeter, more generous, more filled with love. Who wouldn't want that on their wish list?

So, we come back to it, time and time again. It is your consciousness and your thinking that are causing all the faults. And it is your consciousness and your thinking that will raise you up into a magic place. Don't lie about, lying about your condition. You know jolly well the rot that is within you. You must face it and make it well again. If you had cancer, you would be sure to do your bit. Well, most people have cancer of the consciousness, and they sit in it and do nothing.

So, make a plan to follow your dreams today. Ponder on all the details of your new life, how you will live it with dignity and love. And cast aside the wreck of your old life, all the parts that have not worked, and decide today to go for transformation, and smarten up to be fit as a god. This is the day that the door is open. The field before you is green. The sun shines her brilliance on the path before you. Take up this offer before it is too late. The magic is there before you. Step into this kingdom and play your new role.

Chapter 20 – MURDEROUS INTENT

I am calling in help today for we are embarking on a subject that I am not the best expert in. So, I am tapping into the consciousnesses of others who will enlighten me and further both our learning today.

We are speaking on the subject of murderous intent. Now, you may want to shy away from this, but I can assure you it is implicit in many a human consciousness. And therefore, we need to bring this to the surface, examine it, and see what must be done with it. For, clearly, we do not want murderous intent to be a part of our consciousness in the higher realms.

It should be obvious what we mean by this phrase 'murderous intent'. Our television screens and movie theatres are filled with this subject, and I do wonder if it doesn't serve to stoke the fires within some human minds. We must acknowledge that murder has been on the minds of humans from the outset, from when they were first brought into this world. It has been a natural inclination to kill or be killed, and to kill so that one can covet his neighbour's goods.

Doing away with the enemy, or the competition, or with baggage that merely uses up resources, this has been the way of humans since time immemorial. Even in these days we are still seeing killing fields, even though the majority of the world would like to think they have moved on from these barbaric practices. There are still pockets of murderous intent upon your planet, more than you would think and realise. Even government agencies, some clandestine and some not, are going out there with murder on their minds. And we know all too well that some individuals, even within civilised society, will still end lives by their own hands.

Some take the action and perform the deed. There are many more who would like to do these things in their consciousness. Who hasn't wanted to murder someone at some time or other, even if in jest? So, we must own up to these feelings within us, for taking another's life is viewed very dimly in the realm of the gods. And it is not that the gods will punish you, for you will see your own actions rebounding onto you, and even if not in this life, you will get it in the next. No one gets away with any crime, not ever, not in any way. The universe balances and redresses all actions. So, if you have murdered, then you will be murdered too. It is your own deed finding its way back to you.

So, even though people may have done dreadful and terrible things to you, murder is not the answer. And, indeed, quite the opposite is called for, for you will need to find forgiveness and foster love. It can be done, folks. I have seen it done. It will take magnanimous grace from your heart to do it, but you are capable of it, so let you try and see.

Waging a war against someone in your consciousness is waging a war against the universe, and all that will happen is that war will come to you. So, forgive all the death threats, the murders, and the crimes. Send out your love to harmonise them. Let go of the emotion into the universe's depots. Swill away all animosity, cleanse the darkness and the stench. There are trails of blood accompanying your life line. Swish it all away and watch the stains come clean. Let good grace flow down the arteries of your lives. You have not been an angel; forgive others when they haven't been too.

Many are the arguments in this lifetime that have begun in lives long past. You come back again and again, and the old rage rages on. Many cannot even remember the original sin, but still the emotions bubble on the embers and are fired up again when you meet each other this time around. Ponder on why a person can raise your hackles. Ponder on why it can feel like you are being stabbed over and over again. Ponder on why this person has come into your life. And finally, ponder on how you can make it all good once more.

There will be many in your life towards whom you feel bad vibes. Some you will not entertain even for an instant. Some you have banished completely from your life. Others you are forced to put up with but can barely pass a word. And some you may be actively harming and carrying out scenes of vengeance in your mind. All of this will count against you, so clean up your vilification and replace it with more positive vibes.

Even if you are high up on the stairway to Heaven, there will be lingering lives that still need to be cleared away. Much of the hurt has been buried deeply so you can't feel it, so dig up this treasure to reveal these horror pasts. If these lifetimes remain interred, they will pollute all the environment around you, including your consciousness and those of whom you love. So, deal with this pollution to your lineage. Clean out all the skeletons in your cupboard. Pick over the bones from your past. You don't have to know exactly what went down there. Just cleanse it and sweep it and make it white again.

There will come a time when you can climb no further up the stairway for you will be blocked. You must deal with all your baggage and your past, and then you will be passed. New doors can only open for you when you have shut the old ones on cleansed and purified rooms. Your consciousness must be brilliantly shiny if you hope to walk in the dimensions of the gods. So, delve into all your backwaters. Get rid of the mud and the murders. Ask for forgiveness and wipe your slate clean.

We are offering you a pardon and the chance for a better life. Leave the old ways of the world behind. Adjust your consciousness and move into the clear. Let the horrors of the old days be a thing of the past.

Chapter 21 – OCEAN OF EMOTION

Let us speak about calmer things today, for the energies are more balanced and harmonious. Let us take a dive into the ocean today, and I mean the oceanic waters of consciousness, for that's what these energies can be likened to, swimming or drowning in water. You don't have to be a Neptunian or Piscean person to have experienced the waters of consciousness. You would call these your emotions.

Can you touch or feel an emotion? Can you grab it by the throat and cast it away? Can you bottle it? Can you save it for a rainy day? No, emotions are just as enigmatic as the rest of your consciousness in that they are non-physical entities but which result in you experiencing physical symptoms. The emotion of love cannot be caught; more's the pity. But you will feel certain symptoms in your body if you are in love, if you are feeling love on the wavelengths. The same too with sadness; you cannot identify it in any shape or form, and yet sadness takes a toll upon your body.

So, we can take all these emotions and call them, for want of a better word, an ocean. They are like waves; they come and go. They crash over us. They can support us and make us float. They can take us down into the depths and make us drown. They can be stormy, or glitter like diamonds on a bright summer's day. The ocean has many moods. And we can love the ocean at times, or we can feel its treachery in our waters. We must respect the ocean, and those who cooperate with her will have a smoother ride.

Your ocean is of your making. Calm, still waters, or racing waves. Doldrums, or hurricanes, or spirited crests. You can fly above it or beneath it, depending on which dimension you choose. As gods, we prefer to fly. Humans prefer to wallow.

So, are the waves of an ocean crashing inside your consciousness, or do you have idyllic, turquoise seas? As with everything, your ocean is governed by your thinking. So, if you think your ocean is not nice for you, then think again and readjust your thoughts. Think of the times when you are at your best and your nicest and recreate those conditions as often as you can. Get into the habit of being at your best and your nicest and then it will seem like you are on holiday every day. When you have a war zone for a consciousness these conditions will reflect around you. And while you may not be living in an official war zone, war will be raging in other ways and forms.

What is it you would like to see outside your window when you rise from your bed? How would you like your home to play out as you have breakfast in the morning? See your day unfolding with love and ease and flow. And enter your door when you have been away, and feel the soothing comfort there, surrounded by those you love and things that bring you joy.

There is only a lack of visualisation on the part of most people that causes their lives to be lost and loveless. They focus on what is, instead of viewing what will come to be. Every moment you are creating your reality, I will say this for the umpteenth time, so if you are focusing on lack and loss then this is exactly what will be projected back into your life.

So, sit down with pen and paper. Script out your life as you would want it to be in the future. Draw pictures, obtain images. Vision boards are a very good idea. There is nothing wrong with dreaming; in fact, it is very right. We encourage you to do so and make tracks towards those dreams. If you are here and your dreams are over there, then get yourself a ribbon and connect them. And begin to inch your way along, for with every bit of progress that you make, the universe will bring your dreams closer to you as well. You cannot just place your dreams upon a cloud and stare at them there and wish for the clouds to touch down upon your field. For, as you know, clouds remain up high, and it is you that must make your way towards them.

Don't give me excuses of why you can't take any steps. Even just changing your thinking is usually the first mighty step that gets you going on your path. Believe in your dreams and know they are there for a purpose. It is not coincidence that you have your dreams and no one else's. These seeds were sown in your consciousness long ago. They are beginning to grow now. They need nurturing, they need action, they need love. Don't let your dreams wither on the vine. It is the saddest thing to see when humans let go of their purpose.

Your dreams do not need to be world-changing, but they do need to be life-changing for you. One man's dreams may seem insignificant to another, but to you it is your journey, your destiny, the gift you have come here to develop. It is of great significance to you. Bear no mind what others may say and how they might seem to be transforming all around. You are required to transform only your own little world. And if that then spreads outwards, then that is added value and icing on the cake.

So, what kind of ocean is flowing within you today? Is it agreeable and as you want it? Or are there eddies and whirlpools or rip tides at certain times? The ocean can be gentle, fun, and richly rewarding when you work alongside it and are aware of its signs. But if you call up a tempest or a tidal wave and try to resist it or deny it, then you'll be in for a battering, and Heaven knows if you can be saved.

Get to grips with your ocean of emotion, for your waves crash not only upon you but upon your loved ones and neighbours too. Bring about peace and then you can enjoy the idyll of your mind.

Chapter 22 – BIRTHING CONSCIOUSNESS

We are getting into the midst of things now. We are delving into the science of con-science-ness. Where shall we start today? Let us start at the beginning and end at the end. Let us follow consciousness through on its trail. Let us weave with it wherever it goes.

Try as I might, I cannot let go of consciousness. That is because I *am* consciousness. And to let go of it would mean that I no longer exist. But you cannot kill off consciousness. That means I will exist forever. And I have existed for forever before this time. So, where did I come from? How did I come about if I have always been here?

This is the conundrum that scientists and theologians have argued about for centuries. Where indeed did we come from? Scientists will tell you we come from fish and apes. Theologians will tell you we come from the hand of God. And I have come to tell you that a blend of both these ideas is possible.

We have come not so much from the hand of God but from the mind of God. God's consciousness created other consciousnesses, which created yet more consciousnesses, which eventually created the consciousnesses of humans. And through the deftness of their hands, those consciousnesses in physical form created human forms. Those who created physical forms you would term as gods today. But you humans yourselves are also adept at creating physical forms, so would you term yourselves to be gods too?

You are in the process of creating physical forms that resemble yourselves, these things that you call robots. You are fitting them with artificial intelligence, and you are teaching these robots to think for themselves. So, when does the term *artificial* intelligence become *natural* intelligence? At what stage have you given birth to a human-like being?

And will these human-like beings be deemed to have consciousness? These are the ethics that your scientists are tussling with now.

We gods once tussled with this same issue when we first created the human form. It was based on the physical form that we had adopted as gods, a physical form that we grew and evolved over millennia. Humans did not pop out of our consciousness overnight. We had to work to develop them, and at first, like your robots, they had only a rudimentary consciousness.

With each year, the consciousness of humans is now tripling in its effect. What you are achieving with your consciousnesses today is vastly greater than could have been imagined a hundred years ago. In one hundred years from now, what will your robots be up to? They will have consciousnesses that you cannot imagine right now. What you have created will be something you'll need to manage. You think that will be easy, from the position you stand in today, but let me tell you, consciousness grows in ways that you cannot imagine or control.

Be careful what you are letting loose here, for these creations are your responsibility for evermore. We gods are still trying to train our humans after many hundreds of thousands of years. We lost the reins at one point. We are still trying to grab hold of them and master them once again. We understand your desire for robot consciousness; we gods had the same idea too. You perhaps cannot understand what you are unleashing. It is not just physical forms you are giving birth to, but new forms of consciousness that will go out into this universe.

You might think that the creator gods would have a handle on all this, that they will be able to pull the plug at any time if things got out of hand, but as I have said before, consciousness cannot be killed off. Once it comes into existence it exists for evermore.

When you create a baby, you take parts of consciousnesses, bring them together, and give life to that new entity. And that entity will develop its consciousness further. Why is the universe expanding? It is the nature of consciousness to expand. And all these billions of consciousnesses in the universe are expanding every day. The universe is the sum total of all consciousnesses. It is consciousness itself.

Where did the first consciousness come from? There is an answer which you will never understand. So, be content with my explanation, that your consciousness comes from several parts of consciousnesses cobbled together to manifest you. You are not one consciousness handed down whole and entire from incarnation to incarnation. When you die to this lifetime, your consciousness will return to the group consciousness, and it is from that great soup that you will be formed again as the basis for a future life.

So, Jesus or Leonardo do not come back again as a rehash of who they were. Some of that prior consciousness may be retained, but they will return to live out a quite different life, and although they may remember elements of their previous life, they are not the whole consciousness of that person. It is for them to have new experiences this time around. The consciousnesses of Jesus or Leonardo may be split over several thousand new consciousnesses over future centuries.

So, you cannot say, I was once this person or that person in history. An element of your consciousness may have been so, but that historic consciousness does not come to live again. It is dispersed through many new personalities, all with much to learn. So, when you return in your next incarnation, you will not come as the you that you are today. A thread of you may run in your veins, and there may be some remembrance of this lifetime, but you will be joined by threads from many other consciousnesses and past lives. So, who are you really? It will be very hard to say.

Consciousness is a shared asset. It is a living breathing thing that will go searching for experiences that will wish to explore many worlds. It will venture into places to learn things it needs the most. And it returns to the nest after its incarnation, bringing with it all the value it can add to the group consciousness and the universe. Consciousness seeks not only to inform itself; it seeks to inform the group and the whole. So, whatever is needed for the universe to develop and evolve, there a consciousness will be sent forth and provided with its destiny. It sounds a little like an ant in a colony, and you could perhaps compare it with that. The nest is all, and, for consciousness, the universe is all.

Your consciousness will live on, but not only as you, but as many threads of you, and these threads will be entwined with the consciousnesses of others. You will not be able to know where you stop and others start. You are a fluid, amorphous mass, a wave in an ocean. Where does one wave stop and another start? So, where will consciousness end and where did consciousness start? We have no way of telling, and that is the way it must be.

Chapter 23 – SYMBOLISM

Today let us speak about symbology, that is the study of symbols. There is nothing that our consciousness likes more than utilising symbols and imagery that represents something else. A picture says a thousand words, is one of your sayings on Earth. And so it is true of the universe too, that showing a picture, an image, or a symbol to someone can convey greater depths of meaning than merely words alone.

Think of some of your common symbols on Earth, like the Statue of Liberty, the Tower of London, the Sydney Harbour Bridge, Mount Fuji, or Christ the Redeemer Statue overlooking Rio de Janeiro. All of these things will trigger off multiple meanings in your mind, and they may very well be different meanings for different people. So, we can never be sure that a symbol or image means exactly this or that. The meaning will be unique for each individual and yet will contain a general theme for everyone involved.

So, we must be careful with our symbols and our images, that they are understood correctly and that what transpires is that the right message gets conveyed. For instance, if you were to see the symbol of a snake, what would that mean to you? For some it might be frightening and a warning. For others it may represent wisdom. For snake-lovers it might be a source of joy.

So, when you receive a symbol or image in your consciousness, conveyed by your spirit or other entities in higher realms, you must be circumspect about what you are receiving, and you will need to do some research and enquire more. Some people will intuit the right content every time, but you only need to be a little off track for the message to relay a different meaning.

And this is why we have so many misunderstandings in communications between Heaven and Earth. Humans will not receive written manifestos that give detailed instructions of what they need to do; spirit speaks with symbols. And just as if you were to learn Egyptian hieroglyphics, you must work with spirit to understand the language of the gods. As you practise this, all will become clearer, and before long you might understand that a bird might mean 'spirit' and not 'a bird'.

Humans tend to take many of the symbols that they see in their consciousness quite literally. We advise against this, for, as I have indicated before, things are not always as they seem. You will need to delve into your consciousness and understand all the ramifications of this symbol or this image. There will usually be multiple meanings which will play out at different levels of vibration. So, if a group of people were to see the same image or symbol, it may have one meaning for higher vibrational people and a different meaning for those at lower vibrational levels. And this is how the gods can speak with many people at the same time. It is an art form, is it not?

So, you must get clear in your mind what your symbols and images mean for you. And when you yourself create symbols and images, you must get clear in your mind what is the meaning they contain before you broadcast these out on the wavelengths to others. Then we will not so often be speaking at cross purposes. There will be more clarity and unison. As it is, the religions of your world have served to confuse the people greatly. There has been mismanagement in the identification and deciphering of symbols and iconography. Much of what you have been taught is not the message we have conveyed.

Your consciousness is filled constantly with symbols and images and words. Most of it just flashes past briefly on the screen of your mind, but your subconscious is taking it all in and digesting it and trying to make some sense of it, and acting upon it as if it understands. As you grow in awareness in your consciousness, you will come to realise that it is not beneficial to accept everything as it seems. You will need to question things more and interpret things differently, search for other meanings, and perhaps come to different conclusions. There is much flashing past you in every second. How much is influencing you? How much is directing your choice? You have little control over these subliminal messages that are flitting past your mind.

So, ask your subconscious to become more aware. Ask it to pick up on questionable images and signs. You are being programmed by society in every moment. Are you aware of that programming and do you like who you've become? Question your behaviours and your reactions. Have these come from your programming or from someone else's. There is much that is iniquitous going on behind the scenes, and your consciousness is being channelled this way and that by energies that are secretive and not always on your side.

Are you aware of the effect that advertising and marketing campaigns have upon yourself? Do they make you go out and do something you would normally not have done? Are you aware how newspapers and news programs can make you change your mind? Are you aware how your friends can put pressure upon you and make you change your ethics? Will you do things because your family wants it, things you wouldn't do if you were living on your own? You are being pushed and pressured from every side.

So, how do you know what you stand for? Are these your own ideas, or have you been formed by the minds of others? People are using symbols and imagery to change the very fabric of your mind. Is this how you want to be transformed, or will you think about it and mould yourself? Do you have any original thought, or have you been strung together from the thoughts of others?

I am not saying that you must be entirely original and individual, for there is a thread of Oneness that runs through us all, yet you will need to give some thought to what it is you stand for. For you have come here as an individual to add your unique value to this world. If you are just like a lemming, then what value do you bring?

So, begin to look around you at all the symbols and imagery that surround you in your life. Is it making you the you that you want to be? Or is it affecting you and distorting who you really are? We would have more authenticity amongst humans. Many are not being true to themselves. They see a boat going past and they hitch a ride, not questioning if this is the right boat for them and where they are being taken. There is a price to pay if you climb aboard the wrong boat. It may take you to a destination, but far away from your own destiny. Think long and hard before climbing aboard.

Symbols are magical and contain great power. They are not just a two-dimensional form. There is energy coming out from every angle.

There has been consciousness that has gone into the creation of this symbol, and that consciousness will be oozing out of every atom of that symbol.

So, take some time to really study the symbolism existing in your lives. Some of it will mean a great deal to you, and, for some of it you'll give no passing thought, yet the consciousness emanating from it will affect you all the same. Become aware of the energies of symbols. They are not some inert form. They are power grids that can affect you adversely if you do not take the precautions to protect yourself from their effect. Other symbols may have magnanimous energies, and fill yourself up with these. But you will need to know the difference between pure symbols and the tainted. You will need to become aware of what is good for you and what is bad.

So, begin to view symbols in a new light. They are the way the universe communicates, so understanding them is essential, like learning to read and write.

Chapter 24 – JEWELS OF CONSCIOUSNESS

Let us speak about the jewels of consciousness today, for there are plenty of these and they are not just baubles to ogle at, but they are beautiful, exquisite aspects of yourself that play a great and important part in your life.

The first of these jewels is your eyesight, not the sight of your human eyes but the sight of your third eye, your seeing eye, your psychic ability, some would say. This is a jewel that is wholly under-utilised by the majority of the population. Yet when you get it out and look through it, there are many marvels to be seen, many useful titbits of information and, most importantly, the directions for your destiny.

So, if you are not using your third eye, the intuitive part of yourself, then you are going through this life as a blind person. You are groping your way, not understanding what is around you and where you need to go. When you place this jewel up front in your consciousness and unveil it and put it to use, then a whole new world reveals itself to you and you will become much more capable of finding your way and finding solutions to your travails.

So, polish up this beautiful stone of yours. Clean away the dirt and debris. Set your intention to use this jewel. Place it prominently in your consciousness as a centrepiece and become very aware of what it has to show you and tell you. It is as useful as any television set, and the more you use it, the clearer the images will be, and the messages will have greater clarity and understanding for you. So, take this jewel out of its box and begin to use it today.

The next jewel of your consciousness is quite different from this. It is more like a sapphire or a blue topaz and definitely has a blue note to it.

And this jewel is a balancing stone. We have spoken about the waves of the ocean in previous chapters; this blue jewel will help everything become still and calm and serene. Tune into this jewel when things in your life have become tumultuous, upsetting, or like a roller coaster. These blue energies will settle through your body and bring things back to an even keel. Try it now and see if I am not wrong. Allow these blue energies to filter through your systems and feel the immediate relief and peacefulness.

(Pause to take in blue energies.)

Then we have a red jewel, not unlike a ruby, and this stone will have an opposite effect. Its energies will enliven you, activate you, motivate you, and bring you to the boil. So, when you are feeling a little lacklustre, bring to the forefront of your consciousness this red jewel and feel its fiery energies burn through your veins, helping you to feel a frisson of excitement, uplifting your passion, and bringing you to a place where you can take rightful action. Try it right now and see if I am not wrong. Feel the warmth in your blood, the eagerness to get going, the aliveness and awareness that overtakes the mugginess of before.

(Pause to take in red energies.)

And then we have a green jewel, not unlike an emerald. And with this stone you will feel freshness, cleanliness, and purification. It is a very translucent jewel and returns health and vitality when you bring forth its energies into your consciousness. With this jewel much healing can take place. Harmony will prevail. And where things have got out of kilter in your body or your life, these green energies will bring things back into balance once again, into harmony once again. It is a treat to bring these green energies through you, for you will feel refreshed and replenished afterwards, sparkling and anew.

(Pause to take in green energies.)

And finally, we have a yellow jewel, perhaps like a topaz or citrine. Within this jewel sits goodness and goldenness. It is as if the sun itself is inside it. And the sun is, of course, a star, so we are speaking of starlike energies here. When we bring this yellow jewel to the forefront of our consciousness, we are bringing the starlike qualities of ourselves into our mind. We are seeing our full potential. And with the love that this star brings to us we can see the ways we might fulfil this blazing potential.

So, if you are stuck as to what is your destiny, this would be the jewel to bring out and place at the forefront of your mind. Allow its energies to filter through your cells so that each atom of your body and your consciousness become like little stars themselves. Then what can you do but shine like a star yourself? And in this starlight all manner of things can be achieved and accomplished. Try it for yourself and see.

(Pause to take in yellow energies.)

There is much more magic within your consciousness but let us stick with these jewels for today. Practise using your third eye and the four coloured jewels that I have described here and see what a difference they will make in your life. It does not take long to grab a jewel, set it in place, and let it do its work. We will describe more of your toolbox in further chapters, but it would be excellent if you could play with these for now.

The more you practise, the faster they will come online for you as you use them in the future. Before long, you will only need to have a flash of the ruby jewel in your consciousness and your whole being will be filled with lively energies. And the more that you utilise your third eye, the more it will remain open and available to you at any time. Then you will be connected 24/7 to the world wide web of the universe. Think of the power that will garner for you.

Your consciousness is a powerhouse of energies and healing tools. Begin to become acquainted with them for this is the way of the gods.

Chapter 25 – YOUR DESTINY

So, let us turn our thoughts back again to our consciousness, to that which is at the heart of the matter. Our fortunes rise and fall, our emotions go left and right, and yet consciousness is always there for us, our bed and nest to come back to. Don't eschew it. Come back to the heart of yourself, to your consciousness, to your hub, your control centre, whenever things are not looking good for you outside.

Destinies spill, and yet we must keep walking on the road ahead and try to discern what our new path may be. For the path to our destiny is not carved in stone. It takes zigzags, shortcuts, and detours, and sometimes takes you right around the houses, down into the depths, through briar patches, and flooded creeks. You will need to be adaptable if you are to follow your destiny. It is a capricious fellow and yet it will lead you true.

For it is not one journey that you are on; it is a journey of many parts and there will be many milestones in the making. And when you have achieved one phase of your journey, it is on with the next. You will not be left idle in wonderment with no place to go, yet you may sit at your crossroads for many a while before you ascertain in which direction to go.

Your soul, sitting in your higher consciousness, will always know which is your next station to arrive at. Ask your soul, for they know the score. They know the itinerary. They know the best way to get there.

Some people float around on the same spot for most of their lives. They are hard put to drag their feet towards their destiny. They do not feel it, nor any urge to make towards it. These people are separated from the wisdom of their higher consciousness. Others will have seen peeks of their destiny through an open door. Even if the door has subsequently shut on them, they will remember what is behind that door and will make their way towards it. If you are wise, you can throw all the doors open and get a grand view. Your destiny will shine there in front of you, like some holy grail, like some spectre that draws you on.

Do not be afraid of your destiny. It is that part of you which you must become. It is true, it is not a doddle or a walk in the park. There will be challenges galore and setbacks and upsets and crazy days and weeping. We, all of us, including us gods, must taste these ways. Even the most senior of gods have destinies to fulfil.

As you tick off the checklist that moves you towards your destiny, you will find yourself feeling more aligned. You will feel stronger and brighter, more able to cope. So, don't resist your destiny for it is making a man or a woman out of you. More importantly, it is moving you closer to becoming like a god.

You know yourself, when you go on a journey, that there is pleasure in arriving at your destination. It is confusing, frustrating, and upsetting when you lose your way. It is the same with your spiritual adventure. We advise you to enjoy your journey along the way, but there is a marvellous feeling of achievement when you find yourself arriving at your goal. When you are not on track or on target to meet your destiny, then life will feel uncomfortable as if the pieces have been juxtaposed, as if some parts are missing. And when you cannot see where you are heading for, there is a malaise within your consciousness that breathes sadness and discontent.

Everyone needs a purpose, even if it is not world-changing and very small. Your higher consciousness knows your direction, yet your lower consciousness may live in a world of its own. And this little world may be constrained and limited, and of no purpose and no use at all. Your consciousness does not like to feel useless and purposeless. It knows what it is meant to be doing, and yet often is fighting this off. And that resistance takes up quite a lot of energy, and then there is no energy left to be doing the things that you love.

Resistance to one's destiny brings many consequences and usually pain, for you will be butting your head against the brick walls of obstacles. For these obstacles will be designed to get you back on track once again. Yet, we gods see how people congratulate themselves in overcoming all these obstacles. They do not see the signs before them that are pointing them the other way. We admire their perseverance and courage. We would admire their wisdom even more. For the way does not need to be so hard or tragic. When you work with the universe, the universe paves your way.

I have said that you will be beset by challenges, but challenges are different from disasters. So, face up to your challenges and make your way through, but question implacable obstacles, for this may not be the way for you to go. "How will I know?" I hear you ask. This is why you will need to be in communication with your soul, for your soul has all the answers and can set you straight. If you do not call upon your soul, you may find yourself floundering down many byways.

Your destiny is a fine thing. It is your compass, it is your grail. It will give you a reason to get up in the morning, a reason to smile, a reason to celebrate and feel good about yourself. Reaching for your destiny will make your soul come alive. You will feel their presence in your consciousness. You will experience their magic as they smooth the path for you. Working with your soul is the most delightful thing you'll know. They will be your companion on your journey. They will be your light at night. They will provide for you and protect you. They will comfort you and cheer you on.

Your soul is your future who you will step into one day. Your soul is paving the way for themselves for an incarnation to come. They are very invested in the outcome of your journey. They will need you to get the badge and win the medal. It will be a wasted lifetime if you do not make the mark.

So, you are being driven by your soul but, for many, they are not listening. Open up your channel, tune into your soul, and let them have control. Your destiny is awaiting you. Your soul will get you there.

Chapter 26 – EXOPLANETS

We are going to speak about exoplanets today, those planets that revolve around other stars, planets which our scientists hope may contain another Earth-like environment like ours. It wasn't so long ago that it was believed that no other planets existed except those within our own solar system, orbiting around our own star, the Sun. Now we know there are planets orbiting around almost every star. So much for being certain about things, hey?

What else are our scientists certain about right now, that will be burst apart in the future? So, never dismiss possibilities. You can never be certain about anything in this universe, for it delights in proving us wrong. There is always something hidden which will be revealed in the universe's own time. So, know that what we have right now, what we can see and touch, is but a temporary arrangement and things will move on and be replaced.

Exoplanets are the flavour of the day in astrophysics but, given time, they will become quite mundane, and you will be off exploring for other uncertain things that have yet to receive the light of day.

Will we ever get to visit any exoplanets? Not in the foreseeable future, for you haven't yet even been able to visit Mars, not as humans, at least. For there is some scientific ingenuity needed before you will invent the propulsion systems needed to get you to the orbit of other stars. We are not speaking of faster and more powerful rockets. We are speaking of an altogether different technology that will take you there. And this will only be revealed when you have stepped into the higher dimensions and learnt what we know up here.

So, your days are numbered in the lower vibrational dimension of Earth as it is today. Things are coming to an end there. All is being wiped away. It is not sustainable and is collapsing in every quarter. So, we encourage you to ride the waves into the higher dimensions. You could call that an exoplanet, if you like.

Yet, we do not orbit around a different star. We are next to your Earth, only millimetres away, and many of you are now jumping on board as you feel us and see us. Yet, many cannot see what is staring them in the face. So, a few millimetres is not a very big step up to take, and yet it will take many years for you to make this crossing. The vibrations are vastly different, and you would be electrocuted if you stepped up without having been trained. As it is, when you get here, you are electrified instead.

So, if you have not yet started on the journey between the old Earth and the new, then you had better get going, for time is running out. As the new higher vibrations nestle closer and closer into the old Earth, living conditions at the lower end will become quite intolerable and many will go mad.

And so, the answer is to stop running away. Do not bury your head in the sand and fear to look over your shoulder. Heaven is like a great bright moon behind you, shining its luminescence, but you don't want to know. Why would you not want to step into the light and prefer to cling onto your dark and shabby corners?

Many are hoping that the discovery of exoplanets will augur the survival of mankind. But it is not some distant star that we need to arrive at; it is the star in our own backyard. We have everything we need right here, on this planet, in this solar system, to bring our consciousness to its full potential. We go searching for something we think we might need in the future, but all we need is here, in our consciousness, in our higher levels.

We are, to all intents and purposes, evacuating the old Earth and moving ourselves to a new planet. Yet don't be fooled. Our feet will not be leaving terra firma, but our consciousness will cross the millimetres and cross the abyss that lies between Earth and Heaven. It is not so much a physical journey as a journey of the mind to higher vibrations.

From here, the planet will look very different indeed. People will behave as one heart, and the wheels of innovation will ride very well indeed. There will be a gloriousness that sits in the air. You will feel it, and it will strike you up and make you come alive. The travails and tragedies of the lower Earth will be forgotten and forgiven, and we shall move on to more lovely and sunnier days.

Are you across that bridge yet, experiencing the energies of Heaven? For you will know what I am saying, and you might want to spread the word. For those who are still making that crossing, I bid you god speed. May you be strong and loving in your choices. May you look behind you and look ahead, and know which place you would prefer. Don't give up but keep on coming every day. We are awaiting your arrival and we will celebrate it with great cheer.

You might want to help those who are stumbling to get up upon this bridge. For it cannot be seen with human eyes and it is being by-passed and we are losing many who do not see the door.

There is not a single person who wouldn't change something about their world. No one is completely satisfied with who they are and how they live. They think they want this or that or the other, and then everything will come right. But what they really need is to find this bridge and begin to take steps towards their true Heaven. Heaven can never be found on the lower Earth. It will have its moments, but they will dissipate fast and end. To find lasting happiness and everlasting joy, you will need to cross that bridge and enter the higher dimensions.

This place is no fable, like some Utopia or Shangri-la. It is a planet that we truly exist upon, where our lives are lived out in pure joy. So, let us abandon our desire to reach for other stars. Our star is here, within our consciousness. Cross over the bridge and begin to live in her light.

Chapter 27 – IMAGINATION

Let us see where we are taking ourselves today in the realms of consciousness, for I have an idea, and this is what I wish to speak about today, the realms of ideas, of notions, of inspiration and imagination.

(**Sophia:** *And I note that today is a Full Moon in Pisces, so it's a very good day for this particular subject.*)

Chiron: Yes, let us take flight with our imaginations. And where does this take us? Where do we fly to? Where does imagination come from? How is it born? It is not a question we often ask ourselves. We like to utilise our imaginations, but we don't often ask what it is or even how we can improve upon it.

Imagination comes from our consciousness. It is a hybrid of all our experiences mixed together to provide the synergy for something entirely new. A new entity is born, a new idea is given birth. And it is not only our own experiences that we tap into here. We are networking with the consciousnesses of others as well, and so their experiences filter through to us and we can utilise these or let them go.

And so, there is much swirling around our consciousness, and we can take a little bit of this and a little bit of that and cobble together a new idea. We can make use of the experiences that we've had and extrapolate them into different settings and environments with different personalities. And this is the basis of daydreaming, where we place ourselves and other people into new roles and new landscapes with new dialogues. And then we will receive new experiences and we call this imagination.

Some people are hard-pressed to conjure up these scenes. They cannot play 'let's pretend' or 'what if'. They can see things as they have already played out and they cannot take the pieces and rearrange them on a different board. It is not that they are incapable of doing this, but that they haven't been trained. And some people will be more fit for this role than others. While some are very visual and can see things happening within their mind's eye, others are more auditory and prefer to hear things, while yet others prefer to feel things and they utilise other senses.

Imagination is not only visual, for you can imagine yourself a symphony or perhaps a merry tune. You can imagine sensations in your body, feeling this, touching that. And if you can utilise all these aspects together, your vision, your hearing, and your other senses, then you will have one cracking imagination.

Practise sending your imagination out into new, unexplored fields. Have yourself smell a flower, touch a dog, hear yourself laughing, and see the ground beneath you as you walk across the land. Watch the clouds scud by in the sky, pretend the leaves are rustling in the wind. Jump over a fence, knowing you could not do this in your real life, and bound up a hill and holler loudly from the top.

There is a whole world open to you within your consciousness that you could never get to or experience in physical life upon Earth. Take some time to explore these realms for they will add much to your learning and attitudes. You will not be the sole participant, the only occupant of this world. There are many others bounding through their consciousness too, and you will meet these beings along the way. Stop and have a conversation with them. You never know what interesting people you might meet. There are all levels of society hanging around in consciousness.

You might think that you are making all this up. And indeed you are! For this is what your consciousness is all about. It is creating these imagined worlds for you as you move through them. So, of course you are making it up. That makes it no less real, for these are still experiences that you have. And other consciousnesses mixed with yours are contributing their experiences too. It is no different from your physical world upon Earth, except in the world of consciousness you flow more rapidly and easily. You manifest what you are focusing on, and all is possible in the world of your dreams.

If you never utilise your imagination, then your life will be very flat and dull. You will allow the consciousnesses of others to create your world for you, and you will just live that out and believe you have no other choices, that this is the way things are. As you will know by now,

I am here to tell you that things are not always as they are, and that your consciousness is a prime creator. It is your imagination, and it is your tool for manifesting a better world.

So, if you are sitting there and wondering why the world is not so kind around you, then jump into your consciousness and open up your toolbox. Dust off ideas that have rarely seen the light of day, and ponder awhile to bring many old ideas together so that they may create anew. Ask to get together with the consciousnesses of others, for they can contribute much to the scenario that you are dreaming about. They can offer you advice and viewpoints new.

So, you don't need to feel stuck and in the doldrums, for consciousness has many ideas to get you out of there. Tap into your consciousness and ask it to play the game, the game of 'what if I just did that?' and the game of 'I'm going to pretend my life is like this'.

There are many who give vent to their imaginations in superb and terrific ways. Many of you value their contributions, and you watch their movies, read their books, admire their artwork, enjoy their inventions, and benefit from their systems. What are you contributing to this world of great ideas? Do you have some dance steps or melodious music, words of counsel, or food that will nurture and grow? Every avenue of life is a developmental area for imagination. There is truly not a moment where things could not be improved or raised to a higher place. Every moment is an opportunity for a new notion, a grand idea. How many grand ideas have you yourself had today?

So, wake up your consciousness and get the wheels turning. It is a brilliant feeling to have brilliant gems of ideas. Don't just accept the status quo. If we all did that we would never have moved beyond prehistoric times. So, get excited about creating. It does not need to be about the next space mission to the Moon. Creation comes in little ways, often piggy-backing upon ideas you've had some time before. So, be persistent, keep persevering, build your momentum, and give your mind some time to dream the day away.

Imagine yourself in the New World, living in the higher dimensions. This is the ultimate idea. This is the destiny of your dreams.

Chapter 28 – THE PAST

There have been many shenanigans going on in the background these past few days. So, let us have a breather from them. Let us poke our heads up above the muddied waters. Let us bring in the love and the calm and the healing. These waves may be tumultuous, but they are waves that you can ride, and they will deliver you to shore unharmed. Whether you will still be together is another thing, but you are not going to drown through these events. But let me stay on track today as we speak about our consciousness, and let us see what we can find that will bear fruit for your own situation which has been centuries in the making and cannot, and will not, be undone overnight.

So, let us speak then about consciousness and the past. How do we harbour past memories, and how do we clear them out and bring in new and brighter memories to take their place? You are the sum total of all your experiences. You will have had many lifetimes, on this planet and in many other domains. Of course, you will have notched up a few successes in that time, and very many failures.

Not all relationships have been romantic and kind. There are many people still nursing their wounds, even after several generations have passed by. For consciousness forgets nothing. It is all stored away there; every look and word and nuance. It is as if a video has been capturing your every moment in every life. There is nothing escapes your consciousness. It is all there for you to review when you wish to bring it up once again.

Now, of course, it would be boring to have to sit through every detail of every video, so consciousness can bring us highlights. It can edit our videos to point out the salient issues and bring them to the fore. Nothing is cut out that would be important. Consciousness is not stupid in that regard. And yet you are kept away from the details, the knowing of which would not serve you. Perhaps these will come up at another time.

Is it necessary to review your past? Well, sometimes it is if it explains your present. For why are some of your relationships unbalanced and going awry? There is much water going on beneath the surface, antipathies that have bubbled and simmered there from times in ancient past. And so, you might want to know why you feel this way, or why another feels that way towards you. You have not come together with a clean slate. There are many issues written there that need to be redressed.

And so, you must go in there with the other consciousness. You must seek to view the situation from all sides. For, now you are standing from a better viewpoint; you are higher, more experienced, and you know your ideal is to love. This viewpoint was not available to you way back then, when you fought and attacked, defended and protected. It was your survival that you were serving. Now, you understand that you are serving love.

So, what can you do to bring love in? What can you do to smooth these troubled waters? Can you forgive and wipe clean the other's slate? Even our gods have much work to do in this regard, for we have had lives since time immemorial and we have garnered as much failure as we have victory. So, all of this must be put right. All the tables knocked over in skirmishes must be righted again and harmony reign. If there are loose ends floating off into the universe, these must be attended to and brought back to their rightful place.

The universe requests order and symmetry. Balance is its keyword. It cannot have its dimensions running amok. So, wherever there is imbalance you will be directed there, whether it be in this lifetime or many years ago.

As we move into the New World, we cannot bring our outstanding issues with us, so we must knuckle down and sort them out. It will not do for gods to be at each other's throats, or sulking in corners and avoiding another's presence. The gods' world is filled with clarity of love. Nothing can be allowed to diminish this. So, consciousnesses must be cleared and cleaned before they can abide in our Heaven.

So, if you are wondering why you haven't got further than you have, then you will know that your consciousness is blocking you, and you will need to deal with these energies that emanate from your past. Ask your consciousness to show you the scenes that offend. Become aware of what you are dealing with. What are the undercurrents, the hidden themes? Ask for it all to be brought out into the open. And, sure, it might wound you, but stay there and make a stand. You are consciousness and you cannot die. So, from this standpoint alone, you can enter the fray and know that you'll survive.

But now it is time to take control over your lower consciousness, the part of you that remembers what you did and what was done. Now, you get to replay that scene all over again. But play it wearing your new hat, the cap of your higher consciousness. Play that scene out as you would today with your brighter and higher heart. Be magnanimous, be forgiving, be unconditionally loving. Surrender with grace. Have you evolved enough now to bring a new ending to this old scene?

And this is all it takes, to change this present moment, is to clear away the old plays and replace them with new roles and scripts. These new energies will filter down the byways of time, and so now you'll be looking at new dynamics. Who said you cannot change the past? I am here to tell you that it *must* be transformed.

You will need to make some effort in taking out the old scenes and plugging in the new. It does not happen automatically or naturally. You will need to address these situations and bring them into the clear. For whilst there are still sharks bobbing about in your ocean, you will not be welcome to set up home on Heaven's side.

So, make it your mission to clean up unfruitful lives. The energies are still tainting your dimension. They pull you down and trip you up. They slice you in two. They take away hope. Get busy reducing all this baggage and come to our door with a clear and vivacious heart. Then you will be ready to act out as a god, and everyone around you will be gods and goodly and all life will shine with love.

So, if your day is not feeling so bright for you, what is scuttling your emotions that is rearing up from your deep past? Call out this interference and dive into your consciousness like a superhero saving your world. The sooner you do this, the sooner you'll be flying with gods.

Chapter 29 – THE TELESCOPE OF CONSCIOUSNESS

Let us speak about looking through a telescope today. What do we see if we look through a telescope? We might see the moon or planets, or the faint twinkling of other stars. What we don't see is all that which is in between, that great space out there that, in truth, is not space at all but filled with energies. That space is a matrix, and everything is connected together even though it may seem very far apart.

And you can hurtle through this space in a spacecraft and you will not be blocked in any way by any large physical objects, unless you happen to meet a passing asteroid. For although energies are made up of minute particles, your spacecraft will pass straight through these, or should I say these particles will pass straight through your spacecraft. And it is the same for you down on Earth. There are energies passing through you in every moment; many particles entering and exiting. You may feel them or you may not, depending on your sensitivity, but these particles of energies are unimpeded by your mass.

And so, there is much out there that cannot be seen by your telescope, no matter how powerful it is. And it may be a while yet before you get to see these energies that we are speaking about. Your telescopes will need to be very high vibrational. In truth, you have your very own high vibrational telescope within your consciousness, and it will be able to see things that cannot be seen with the human eye. So, perhaps humans need to cultivate this kind of technology instead of putting their faith in computers, mirrors, and steel.

Your consciousness' telescope can reach to the other side of the universe if you were practised in this field. Your consciousness can jump from moon to planet to star. There is no place that your consciousness cannot go except if it is barred by the rules of vibrational levels. You cannot journey to dimensions where the vibrations are higher than yours unless you have specific permission to be there. So, you are not barred from these higher places yet your presence there will be monitored, and you will be guided so that you cannot cause consternation there. The higher dimensions do not like their energies rippled by low vibrations.

Yet there are plenty of places for your consciousness to discover and explore. Look through your telescope and pick a spot and fly off there and have yourself an experience. You can fly further than any telescope on Earth can see. You are not limited or inhibited by distance, and it does not take you many light years to get there. In an instant you can be transported there. Teleportation is the magic of the day. You do not need special machines to teleport you anywhere. Your consciousness is your machine, your time travel vehicle, your sphere in which you travel around the universe.

These are not the fantasies of Jules Verne or H.G. Wells. Gods, and even humans, have been using their consciousness to travel the universe for billions of years. When you learn how to do this, who will need spacecraft?

In half a century, humans have gone from conquering the moon to flying out past Pluto. You are beginning now to conquer intergalactic space. What shall you find out there in those parts? You will find that you are but one small planet, in one small galaxy. Distances are vast to keep you well apart from your neighbours. For until the human race has evolved sufficiently well, we cannot allow you to play with your colleagues in the neighbourhood. You haven't been able to quell the revolutions on your home ground. How would you fare in meeting alien nations?

So, it will be a while yet before we open up the galaxy for you, for you to meet other next-of-kin. For, yes, there are other human-like races out there, whom you would recognise if you met them out in space. We are preparing you for these days to come, but it will be a while off yet before little green men will be sitting around your dining room tables, or you at theirs.

But your consciousness can make contact at any time. Try this and you might be amazed at your experiences. Don't dismiss them as ludicrous fantasies. Your consciousness can reach out to alien races, for they have consciousnesses just like yours too. You might not speak each other's tongues, but symbolism is the language of the universe, so if you speak with symbols then all can be revealed.

Some alien races are at higher vibrations than yourselves, therefore they will remain invisible to you until you reach that level too. But there are indeed other alien races who exist at vibrational levels equal to yours and even lower. But this will mean that you might never meet, for your knowledge of technology is not quite up to the mark. So, what this in fact means is that if you wish to become acquainted with your alien neighbours, you will need to move yourselves up to higher vibrational levels. And then much more than aliens will be revealed to you.

And if you need reminding once again how you raise your vibrational levels, let me say to you that it is through love, love, and love. While you are enmeshed and mired by the darkness of not-love, you hold yourselves down in the lower and muddy waters.

So, utilise your telescope, the telescope of your mind. See the stars there and reach for them. Go dancing amongst them, for you will be like one of them one day.

Chapter 30 – MATCH-MAKING

It is remarkable what consciousness can achieve in one night, so let us get back to consciousness and what it can achieve. We have already spoken about many of the remarkable things that consciousness can accomplish. Let us enumerate them again and then I shall add to this list.

Consciousness has a whole toolbox of tools for you to utilise. Like any workman, you have to get to know your tools. You have to practise with them and use them on a daily basis, and then you will become a craftsperson, producing works of art.

So, consciousness is a tool for healing, a tool for connection with others on Earth and beings in other dimensions. It is a tool for raising your vibrations through love. It is a tool for bringing up memories and for cleansing them away. It is a tool for projecting into the future; your dreams, your hopes, and discovering your destiny. It is a tool for networking with the group consciousness. It is a tool for travelling and teleporting yourself around the universe in other dimensions. It is a tool for cracking open barriers and blocks. It is a tool for dissolving those parts of yourself that no longer serve you. It is a tool for connecting with who you have been and who you are to become as your soul. And it is a tool for accessing all kinds of knowledge, for everything is stored away in the universe's archives.

How useful, then, is consciousness? So, what else can we apply from our consciousness, for it has many more tricks up its sleeve?

Consciousness can be like a bicycle. You can ride it and it can take you places. You can observe the landscape while you are riding, and you can make decisions to go this way or that. The only difference is that consciousness never stops and you cannot get off this bike. You are forever carried along on your consciousness. And while you might want to drift along for some time, eventually you will be forced to take one direction or another. Consciousness is like a treadmill and it will never let you go.

So, rather than allow the universe to make your choices for you, and you ending up in places you might not want to be, become more aware of what your consciousness is doing and then you will have more control over your handlebars and you can steer in the direction that you feel is best for you. Bear in mind, though, that you will have a passenger on the back of your bicycle; it is your soul. And so, whilst you may want to make choices of your own, listen to what your important passenger wants to say, for they have the map and they can guide you true.

So, your consciousness is a means of transportation through your life. It takes you to the next situation and the next. It brings you to the crossroads, to the stations. You are always being carried along by your consciousness. You cannot remain still. Even if your progress is imperceptible, you are still being moved along.

So, when you become aware of this and turn to work with your soul, you can manifest a great itinerary for yourself. Consciousness will always move you in a general direction, but you can decide on the details and what you would like to see along the way. Make towards the higher vibrations, for in these dimensions you will find exactly what you are looking for. Your soul knows the way; let them guide you.

I have spoken about the magic that your consciousness can perform. It can create and manifest all kinds of situations and material things. It can bring people into your life and also push them away. So, consciousness can be a kind of match-maker. When you are needing someone in particular in your life, your consciousness can pull the strings to get them there. No exorbitant fees to set you up for online dating! Your consciousness knows who the best match will be for you.

So, fill out your wish list and give it to your consciousness, and they will look through their database and see who would be the best fit. You may not like who they provide for you, but trust me, your consciousness knows who is best for you. For it is not only for you to have fun with these people, or to utilise their skills, for there are other undercurrents here that you will not be aware of. And it is these deep waters that need to be brought to the surface, examined and resolved.

So, do not disdain who your consciousness matches you up with, for there might be threads to be tied up with this person, or there might be new projects to be born. So, when you wonder why certain people have been brought into your sphere, know that it is no coincidence and your consciousness has brought them here.

Your consciousness is always dreaming, but you may not be aware of these dreams, and you are being urged on and guided towards a subject of this dream. It may not make much sense to you, but if you enquire of your soul you'll get the background. So, if you are feeling a little lost and confused about where you are feeling you are being moved to, tap into your consciousness and ask to be shown the bigger picture. Then you'll gain more clarity and feel more motivated to make that move.

Nothing is done without reason by your consciousness. It has a very clear idea about where it is heading. But you yourselves, at the lower level of your consciousness, may feel like a puppet and that you are being played. Your consciousness is certainly using you as a vehicle to get its dreams met, but see yourself as part of a team, and you will need to take the action that your consciousness is dreaming out. It is not that you will suffer by doing this, for all is for your benefit. You are being raised to higher places, and conditions will improve all the time.

But if you choose to resist your consciousness' movement, then you will be peddling hard against the flow. And why would you wish to go backwards when all your dreams and your future lie ahead? So, do not put the brakes on. Do not refuse to pedal. Do not cover over your eyes and act like a blind man, but come to the party and do your part. Consciousness is not your enemy. Rather, it is your best friend.

So, begin to feel the oneness with your consciousness and your soul, for together you are a unit. Together you are a remarkable team. You can never attain for yourself all you wish for if you work alone. But when you are part of this dynamic divine grouping, the universe lies at your feet and awaits your commands. Your consciousness will take you to the place of your dreams.

Chapter 31 – FORTITUDE

How can our consciousness help with fortitude? That is a very good question. What does fortitude mean? It means strength and courage and determination in the face of challenges or difficult circumstances. It means you stand upright when all about you might be falling down. It means that you look directly straight ahead to see what are the possibilities and the positives, instead of falling into a hole. It does not mean you are Superman or Superwoman, a hero of our times, but you do need to be a hero to yourself, and you need to rise to the occasion and do whatever is necessary to keep you out of that hole.

Many people lack fortitude, for it is not taught at home and it is not taught in schools, not as a subject by itself. Certainly, parents and teachers and society will expect you to have fortitude as if it is something you are born with, and that you just need to press a switch and it comes to the fore. Unfortunately, this is not the case, for to have fortitude you will need to overcome your fears and limitations, and sometimes these barriers seem impossible to breach.

So, we need to school people in fortitude, for often it does not come naturally, especially if you have had a childhood full of traumas or disaster. We need to help people build up their confidence and their strengths, so when the time comes for them to be tested, they will find that inner resilience and determined stance.

We train people in the armed forces, and other defence forces like the police, to become strong and brave. We teach them how to tackle the enemy. But we don't always teach people how to have emotional strength and mental strength. And this is where we are falling down as a human race.

For fortitude is not only physical strength where you are able to stand your ground, where you are able to use your body to get yourself out of tough situations. Even the toughest soldier will tell you that they can be mentally broken by the circumstances that they face. And so, you have many cases of PTSD (post-traumatic stress disorder), where people's fortitude has cracked and they have not had the strength to go on and live a happy life.

So, we will need to teach about emotional resilience and mental resilience so that when the travails of life touch us we can muster our inner strength and utilise our consciousness to keep us strong.

Our consciousness is a playground for playing out our thoughts. And so, if we lay all our negative thoughts out before us, then this is what we are creating as our life. So, let us clear away the tarpaulin that is filled with dreads and fear, and let us begin to put in its place some positive and strengthening pillars. Let us rebuild our house with firmer foundations and solid walls.

Let us account for all the successes that we have managed in the past. You may shake your head but there will have been some. For instance, if you are reading these words, then you have had the success in teaching yourself to read. No small feat, let me tell you.

If you have been walking today or driven a car, then you have had the success of learning to walk and learning to drive. If you have ever had a job, then you have had the success of being offered that job and the opportunity of trying it out. If you have grown from a baby into an adult, then you have had the success of nurturing your body into adulthood. If you have ever kissed a person and made them smile, then you have had the success of a relationship. If you have ever created anything with your hands or from your womb, then you have had the success of bringing something new into this world. There are countless thousands of examples that I could give you.

So, start with these positives and all the successes that you have gained. Now take it one step further and think upon all those times when you have made it through a challenge. If you made it through school, then that's a challenge in itself, and you would have displayed fortitude to get you through lessons and exams. There will be many times when you have displayed your strengths. There will be numerous times when you have driven yourself on. So, don't tell me you are lacking in fortitude.

Now, when it comes to the larger problems of life, you might face them and blanch and begin to walk away. It is just a matter of scaling up your current fortitude. You'll need to be a bit stronger, a bit more courageous, a bit more determined, than ever you've been before. Can you not give it a go?

No one is judging you for turning away. But you will be judging yourself and wondering why you lack this fortitude. Sometimes the price is just too high to pay, and it will be sensible to do the reasonable thing. But are there times when you will wonder, if you had just made that little more effort, if you would have got through and survived and chalked up another success.

You will know how far you can push yourself, but your soul will know this too. And your endpoint may be a lot closer than your soul's, who wishes you to try and make out a little further. No one has ever improved themselves by staying where they are.

So, if you wish to become stronger and more successful, then you will need to take a step further than you've stepped before. If, as children, we hadn't taken those steps, we would still be sitting on our backsides and never known the wonder of walking. So, challenge yourself a little further every day and this will build up your fortitudinal muscles so that when a testing time comes you are ready and able to stand through the gale. Challenge yourself in the little things and the big things will take care of themselves.

And so, we must turn to trust, now, for when you are lacking in fortitude it means that you don't trust yourself. You think you will buckle under pressure. You believe it's all too much and you will fail. So, how about trusting that you will make the grade? How about trusting that your soul is helping you along? How about trusting that gods and angels are by your side? How about trusting that even if you fail you can get right back up again and try once more? Usually, the world does not end when you don't succeed. The only failure comes when you don't try for success once again.

So, don't be shy about putting your best foot forward. Be determined, have some faith, and feel your strengths. Fortitude is a trait you will need as a god. Practise it in your daily life. You never know when it will come in useful.

Chapter 32 – YOUR SPIRIT-SOUL TEAM

It is surprising what happens in the higher worlds, is it not? So, let us come down to Earth today and see what it means for us. When all is abuzz in the heavens, how does it play out down here?

In Heaven, your consciousness has been going about its business. Your spirit self has been leading another life apart from yours that you experience in your human body. Your spirit self is alive and well, and it is up to all sorts of activities and has all sorts of plans and dreams.

So, when something comes to fruition for your spirit self in the dimensions above, what does that mean for you down here on Earth? Will you be affected? Will your spirit's dreams become your dreams and drag you along that path? Well, yes, you and your spirit are joined at the hip, or rather I should say, through your consciousness. So, what either of you does in your individual planes, will certainly affect the other, whether they are the higher one or the lower one. So, if your spirit is having a successful time of it and has reached a crescendo on its path, then you will be the beneficiary of this and it will feel as if golden sparks are raining down from Heaven.

But the outfall from your spirit's victory will not just be these blessed energies. For, what is motivating for your spirit is also motivating to you, and if your spirit is following a certain line of action, then it can be sure that you are to follow suit. Yet, will you or won't you, is the question. For even though your spirit may be showing you the way and trying to lead you there, your part of consciousness may be resisting and digging in its heels. For you may have decided that your spirit's goals are not your goals. You may have made the choice to do your own thing.

Now, what happens when two parts of the same consciousness are pulling in opposite directions? There will come a split, a tear, and this is always painful, and will continue to be so until the rend is mended once again. You may ask, "Why do I always have to follow my spirit's bidding. Why can't they follow mine?" Well, this is the difference between divine will and human will. And you can certainly go your own way, but if your spirit is not on board you'll pay the price.

So, it behoves you to get together with your spirit, and also with your soul, and ensure that your destinations are aligned. If you are making for different goals, or even the same goals but at different times, then this will be the source of misery and conflict and tension. You'll need to get all your ducks flying in the same direction.

It is not that your spirit is always right, for sometimes the spirit neglects its human counterpart. Sometimes it forgets to use compassion. Sometimes it forgets to share its knowledge and its motivations. So, just like any team on Earth, you will need to get together with all members and establish that you are all on the same page, and that you all know the process and the techniques for getting to your destiny. If you do not keep each other in the loop, then one or another is bound to get off track. So, daily meetings between spirit and human would seem the reasonable way to go; understanding each other's expectations, acknowledging what each other can bring to the table, and where one or another of you might need extra support.

Spirit and human are two halves of one mind. If one is missing from the party, then you will stand alone. And you must learn to live with one another side by side, like Siamese twins. You cannot dump your spirit or ignore them, for they are your shadow, if truth be told. If you never acknowledge your spirit or dismiss them, then your spirit will go off into the ethers and wait for you to contact them at a future time. But then, who will guide you and get you to your stations? Who will protect you and help you manifest your dreams?

So, call upon your spirit and invite them into your life. Ensure that you keep up the contact and that communications flow between you regularly and often. When your spirit is part of your life, you will wonder what you ever did without them. They have remarkable skills and are well-versed in how to use the tools of your consciousness.

Your soul is the next level up from your spirit. As you make your way up the stairway to Heaven, your spirit gets closer and closer to the level of your soul. Then, one day, it will be time for spirit and soul to merge together, and your whole consciousness takes on a higher tone. For a while, spirit and soul will become accustomed to this merger, and all parts of consciousness assimilate these energies until it can work as one.

So, now, your spirit is at the level of where your soul was, and all of your consciousness has been heaved up to a higher level. In the background, a new soul will be waiting for you in the distance, at a higher level once again. So, always you are making towards a higher and higher soul.

What happens to the human, then, when spirit and soul have merged? Well, the human consciousness must also do its part, and it must raise itself up so that it does not drag its spirit-soul down. So, your whole sphere of consciousness, that of human, spirit, and soul, moves up the stairway, step by step, and at certain points it is time to merge with your soul. Now, things will take on greater clarity for the human upon the Earth, for the soul comes in like a new broom and there are new rules and new goals, new parameters, and borders, and the human will need to discover what these are.

So, when your spirit merges with your soul, it is like a change of management for your company. A new CEO takes the helm. And you, as the human, will certainly feel this change. Gradually, over the months and years, the soul integrates with your spirit and becomes your spirit friend once again. At this point, your new soul will make themselves known. And the process will begin all over again.

So, align yourself with your spirit and let them take control. The spirit is your director, and you are its valued employee. Join your team and play your part. Follow the company's strategies and you'll go far. Successes come when the team all works together, and you, as a human, will feel your destiny fulfilled.

Chapter 33 – PEAR-SHAPED SOCIETY

Let us speak about things going pear-shaped today. By that I mean that things in our life have collapsed around us, that our expectations have not been fulfilled, that plans have gone awry, and that events have taken other directions from the ones that would be fortuitous for us. Going pear-shaped is not usually meant to mean a great disaster or calamity, but that structures have fallen down and that which should have been sustained has collapsed into a heap.

We have many such events in our lives, and we wonder why this or that did not go to plan. And it is a setback for us, an upset. But I'm here to tell you that things that fall down usually have not been built properly in the first place. Perhaps they did not have firm enough foundations. Perhaps the structure was dangerous. Perhaps the outcomes would not have been beneficial. There are many reasons why the universe might take something down.

You yourself are the architect of these structures, so look to your creations and examine how they are built. Have you invested enough depth into your foundations? Have you done enough research? Are your plans rightly detailed, for, once you have strong and powerful foundations for anything in your life, then you can go on to build and create the superstructure, and from there you can fill in the details.

There are some who do not pay enough mind and apply their full consciousness to the beginning of a project or a plan. They are caught up in outcomes and put too much effort into delivery instead of the conception. So, if you are to bring anything into this world, by way of a little human or an idea or project, then you will need to attend to your birthing plans and get things correct right from conception. If an embryo for a human does not get the details right within the first few days and weeks, the result will be the birth of a deformed child, and no one wants that possible outcome. So, put as much thought into your initiation as to your finalisation, for good strong legs will carry you far. Spindly legs will see you wavering in the future.

I have been noticing those who ride only on the crests of waves. You could say they ride by the seat of their pants. And these folks may enjoy this ride for a time, but there is no depth to them, no anchor, and if the waves cease to exist they will sink without a trace. There needs to be depth to everything you do, for then, when the gales of adversity blow, you are pinned down well and cannot be blown away. And if things do go pear-shaped you are able to rebuild again from your firm foundations. If that underlying structure is not there, then all can be wiped away and you will have nothing left to speak of.

We welcome those who would do a good job of things, taking the time to plan well and to erect structures that will stand the test of time. We are not so interested in fads and something that will dazzle for but a dozen days. We are gods who reckon in billions of years. What will be left standing of humans in this timeframe?

You are a throwaway society and you are drowning in waste. So, let us invest some effort and consciousness in building a more robust and resilient world, not one which you tear down every ten years or even less. Let you build things which will last the distance, as your *New Horizons* spacecraft is doing. Why do you build this to last for decades, yet you build your phones and computers to last for only a year? Why are you so desperate to keep throwing things away?

It is not that we don't wish for you to embrace change, but change in your society has reached manic proportions, and people are suffering insanity because the treadmill is moving so fast that they cannot stay on it with ease. We applaud changes in technology and the status quo, and yet change must be manageable or humans will go mad.

And so, your society is going pear-shaped and most structures are falling down. There is little support for the man on the street, and when people are frantic, society will break down. So, while there is much investment in technologies and economies, there is little investment in what people really need. They need love, attention, education, housing, and food. They need support in all quarters. They need acknowledgement and rewards. They need training; as managers and as employees, and as youngsters and parents, and as teachers and youth.

It seems the world of humans has forgotten about what really matters. The foundational work is no longer done. It is all about outcomes and making money. There is little investment in making society work.

So, let us ask the consciousness of our souls to inspire us with brilliant ideas that we can bring through into the human realms, and modify the structures and underpin them to make them strong. A world that is built on such fragile foundations cannot survive when the waves come rolling in. Shore up your structures before these tidal waves reach your shores.

Chapter 34 – TRAVEL TO THE GODS' WORLD

Let us go exploring today. Let us take our consciousness within our spirit sphere and let us go travelling around this universe. There is much to see, and it would take all your days and more to get around it all. So, do not think that you would ever run out of enjoyment or adventures. It keeps rolling on and rolling on.

But today I have a particular sector of the universe in mind, not so far away and within your own galaxy, it would seem. Now, I say 'it would seem' for, to you humans, what I am about to describe would appear to take place in your galaxy. But, in truth, we are describing events and situations that exist in the higher planes, and these don't really exist in your galaxy at all. They are outside your galaxy at a higher level.

So, let us jump into our sphere of consciousness and let ourselves be taken there, for you know that we will be instantly transported to wherever we set our dial within our consciousness. So, let us look around us now, and what do we see? Alien worlds that bear no resemblance to ours? No, there will be many aspects of this world that look very much like that of Earth, and you will find that familiarity comforting. But around the corner you may find things that give you a jolt, for these will be things that have come from the imaginings of higher gods. And, some you will be able to work out their function, and some will leave you mystified.

But then doesn't a child have these same feelings on their first visit to Disneyland or other theme parks? So, this may be how you will react when you visit any of our higher worlds. It may seem like you are within a theme park. And that is good, for these places always tend to be enjoyable. So, don't be afraid but, come, step forward. Let us see what this world has to offer.

And it will not be just in the structures and architecture that you will find novel ideas and futuristic implementation, for society here is altogether changed. Love is the prime mover here. And this is why I have brought you to this particular world, for I wish you to experience how society can work through love.

You find it impossible to imagine at present down upon your planet because your hearts are not filled with love. It is beyond your reckoning that these philosophies would work. And yet here we are proving it, making life work in the manner of true gods. We esteem one another, and we respect all beings in our world. We do not always have the same opinions. We do not always embark down the same road. But we appreciate our differences and how all skills connect. We put everyone to work with the skills they love best, so our work force is happy and always gives their best.

Like you, we have managers and those who toil the fields, but this is not a source of conflict, for some like to direct and others like to be directed. Managers are not superior to workers, but all have equality in this higher world. One life is not more valuable than another.

We live for a long time, for we have learned the healing arts. And it is not that afflictions do not visit us, but we know how to resolve them and bring ourselves back into balance once again. It sounds very Utopian, you might say, and to be honest it is. But what is the problem with that? We have worked hard to settle our issues and foster good vibes. For we have wanted peace more than hatred, love more than ego, and a world that works as a whole rather than individual success. Can you see where you may be going wrong upon Earth?

So, this is the world of some of our gods. Other gods live in different places that bear no resemblance to Earth. And you may get to visit such places on your travels too. You may feel a little weird and uncomfortable, but you will survive, for your consciousness cannot die. We like to bring humans over to our godly world, which is very like Earth, for it is not too much of a stretch for you to take in. It is an elevation, to be sure, from your home world, but most of you can see the possibilities that exist in this new world.

And so, some of our ideas are beginning to find footings in your world down there. We applaud this and offer you as many tours as you would like. And if there are things you would like training in, be sure to ask and we will provide. We are not flooded with as many visitors as we would like, so at present we are having a hard time making inroads into your society with our ideas. But if you could spread the word to friends and family, we will be able to set up your world as a better mirror of ours.

So, come, take your sphere of consciousness for a spin. Travel our high roads and our byways. Poke your head in wherever you can. You will always receive a welcome and we'll be glad to show you around. And just as when you've had a trip to some theme park you return home agog and tingling and fully alive, then so shall you feel like this after a trip to our gods' world and it will be hard to contain all the ideas flying around your mind.

We do not copyright ideas in our world, so you are free to share them and use them and bring them into form. Delight your world with your creations for we wish our energies to be spread abroad. You are not limited in your trips to our world. Take daily excursions if you feel the need. We are brimming with energies, overflowing with love-ly ideas. We offer them freely to your nation. Can you offer them freely to your world?

You are hoping to discover new planets by flying in spacecraft and landing on their ground. You will not discover much that is notable to you. So, rather jump into the spacecraft of your minds and fly off to distant places. Here are the true worlds, the worlds of your spirit and soul. Here is where ideas abound, where love is bountiful, and success floats on the breeze. Come and join our teams and we will train you up. Then you can return to your Earth world and begin to make changes that will see your world transformed.

Chapter 35 – BELIEVE AND YOU WILL SEE

We are running today, so let us see where we are running to, for I have in mind a wonderful subject to explain. I would like to speak about tachyons today. What are these things? They are subatomic particles that fly through the air invisibly, and which no one can get to grips with, for you cannot catch one and hold it in your hand, nor have scientists been able to examine one in detail, yet they know that these particles exist.[1]

They are a little like ghosts, are they not, like our spirit selves? We know they exist but they are invisible to humans. So, why do scientists believe that subatomic particles can exist like this, in this state, and yet not believe that there are whole beings, and even whole worlds, that exist in this state too? There is indeed an invisible universe out there, unseen by human eyes and yet quite visible to the rest of us spirit beings. When your world would acknowledge this, then our world will begin to reveal itself to you. So, you must believe before you'll be able to see.

And really, the whole crux of this book is laid upon that tenet, that when you believe these things I am telling you, a whole new world and dimension will open up to you. While you have a closed mind, the curtains will remain quite shut. As you open your mind, your

---

[1] A **tachyon** is a hypothetical particle that always moves faster than light. Tachyons have never been found in experiments as real particles traveling through the universe, but theoretically it is predicted that tachyon-like objects exist as faster-than-light 'quasiparticles'. Most physicists believe that faster-than-light particles cannot exist because they are not consistent with the known laws of physics. Despite theoretical arguments against the existence of faster-than-light particles, experiments have been conducted to search for them, but no compelling evidence of their existence has been found. In modern physics the term "tachyon" often refers to imaginary mass fields rather than to faster-than-light particles.

consciousness, so windows will start appearing, giving you glimpses of the other side.

So, how do you open your consciousness? For there is not a door, as such, with a key. But there is a symbolic door, and the key is your belief. You must have belief enough to know that other worlds exist. And even though you are not sure of the details, have enough belief to go exploring and find out for yourself. Let not your colleagues put you off from this, sneering in the face of their evidence, for your evidence will tell you otherwise and you will not be able to deny the experiences that you have.

It is difficult for anyone to believe until they have had an experience of other dimensions. While everyone will have these through their dreams, dreams have been accorded as a natural human state and their significance has been downplayed as motions of the brain reordering your thoughts while you sleep. As you will know by now, your dreams are a record of your travels in consciousness as your human self sleeps. The spirit part of your consciousness takes off in its other worlds.

And so, at first it comes down to whether you believe in consciousness itself. For if you believe that you only have a brain, then you will not be game to explore your whole consciousness and thus enter into other worlds. If you believe that you are more than your brain, then you have the basis for believing in consciousness and thus you have the basis for exploring from thereon.

So, what would we do with this world that is divided into believers and those who will not believe in our worlds? We cannot force you to change your opinions, and, bar us gods coming down in our spaceships and landing on your Earth, we will not be easily able to persuade you to change your human minds.

Think about what it was that made you pick up this book. What was your curiosity that led you to read these words? Why do you have this hunger to know more? And yet the people around you are like those who once believed in a flat Earth. What are we teaching our children so that when they are adults they will have this belief or not?

For the most part, belief in our worlds is like some underground movement. People are not keen to admit they have these beliefs. And if you are a scientist or other professional, you would keep this kind of thinking under your hat, for it may impinge upon your career and certainly upon your reputation. So, people may be free to think what they like, but even now they are not free to speak about what they think. It is a terrible shame, in this day and age, that humans have not moved on to be able to share with more freedom.

What is the world afraid of if they discover there are worlds beside their own? What is the threat? What are they protecting? Perhaps it is merely the fear of the unknown.

We gods would have thought that humans would clamour to know more brilliant minds. Everyone awaits another Einstein or Gandhi or Christ, yet when these could be on offer humans are closed to this gift. It is not as if we gods are some alien race who intend to invade the Earth and take it over. We come to teach you, to raise you up. Our intentions are benign and beneficial. Yet humans are suspicious and protective of their own. They do not particularly like their world in many cases, but they sure as hell don't want anyone to wrest it away from them, gods or not.

You are like children who are dying and who are refusing to take medicine. We cannot help you if you will not let us in. Many of you are trying to put the world to rights. It is an uphill battle, for many are doing wrong. Who will win in the end is not a foregone conclusion. Yet if you would allow us gods to enter the fray, we can turn things around and introduce you to our ideas. Whether you take them on board is up to you, but we have new ways to offer you and we found these have worked for us.

So, don't be resistant, children of Earth, denying our existence, the existence of our worlds. You would be foolish to do so, for then you will battle alone. We are not your enemy; the enemy is yourselves. We live in a world of love. Can you say the same about your world? We live in a world of peace. Can you say the same about your planet? The universe we live in is respectful and kind. What kind of universe have you created around yourselves?

So, open up to this invisible universe that lies beyond your walls. Break down your barriers and bring yourselves here. We are your friends and we have many tools to help you. Do not be afraid to go out and spread the word, for once it becomes a common theme then it will seem like common sense. There are many of you who are working with us now and we appreciate your efforts. But we are a long way from being mainstream, are we not? At the moment we are just rivulets along the sides.

It takes a few hundred years for a religion to take hold, but in this day and age information travels fast. And we are no religion, although you might term us as gods. We are really just higher beings than yourselves, and what we teach is just a way of life. We do not wish to be worshipped or adored. We elicit no payments. We require no churches or palaces. All we require is just your open minds. All we require is a chance to open your hearts.

We are here in the higher dimensions. We will always be here; we are not going anywhere. We will continue to live out our lives in our paradise. How will you continue to live down there?

Chapter 36 – FINDING MOTIVATION

Let us speak about attitude and motivation today, and how consciousness can help us with this. We spoke previously of fortitude and needing to brave up to the situations we face in our lives. But what if there is no situation and we need to create one, where we need to make something happen and bring it all alive? It does take fortitude to be able to do this, but it is a special kind of strength where you can motivate yourself and get yourself going.

First, we must explore our consciousness to understand why we can't start ourselves up. Where is the life force and the spark? What would enable us to be set alight? Often, we have fears and projections barring our way ahead. We are assuming this might happen or that. We feel we could not cope. Often, we don't know how to go about doing something. So, if we lack the skills and the know-how, then this is easily remedied, and you go and search out the training and information.

If it is fear that holds you back, then this is a little more difficult to remedy. But we know now how we can go into our consciousness and look around. And we can find those parts of our fearful self and we can adjust their reasoning or let them go. Fear is just an emotion. It is not an object that you must chisel away. Fear is merely a thought that you have. And if you take away that thinking you will have that fear no more. So, tear out that page in your consciousness and replace it with a new one filled with positive thoughts. Then fear will no longer be your barrier and you'll have more energy to put towards other things.

Your motivation might be lacking due to experiences in your past. You may have failed or made no headway, so you are projecting this will happen once again. If you are trying to do everything exactly as you did before, then this may well be the outcome, so you'll need to adjust your tack. Make sure your idea or project is as well-formed as it can be. Check with your soul that this is right timing and check with your consciousness you have no negating thinking.

Then, why shouldn't you find yourself succeeding? Fear of failure trips up many, and so they are doomed. But trying to succeed is never a failure. It is but one more stepping-stone on the stairway to success.

The ultimate motivator is when you picture the outcome of your journey; the winning post, the final step, the delivered idea, all smiles and all rewards. You must post this image into your consciousness and never let it fade. It is your key to motivate you and will keep you going through long dark nights and woes.

Do you have the idea that things should always go smoothly and be successful every time? This is not the way the universe works, for it is teaching you how to think creatively and how to overcome adversity and make yourself strong. Certainly, there will be times when things will flow, but there are so many energies interacting in this universe, that others' energies will interrupt your flow and send you on diversions. You will need to be prepared for this and able to manoeuvre down any channel that you are taken. So, drop the illusion that everything should work like a charm or dream.

You must make use of what is presented to you every day. Be resourceful. Be clever. Be adaptive. Be accepting. Do not rail and rage against the universe when things go wrong, but negotiate with your soul and other gods to get things back on track. This is the nature for all of us in this universe, not to sit in our consciousnesses and hope we'll have a straight run. For there is no straight road between you and your source. It zigzags around many obstacles, goes uphill and down dale, careens around corners, slides underwater, and shoots into the stars. Your path will take you everywhere and to corners yet unknown. So, be prepared to face what you are facing. Get on through and move yourself on.

If you are waiting for the perfect time, the perfect place, and perfect resources, then you might be sitting there for quite a long time. So, make a start down your road, for you must meet your destiny; your destiny does not visit you.

What is your resistance, you'll need to ask yourself? If you were to motivate yourself, what would that cause to happen? And if that were to happen, how would you feel? Removing the blocks to your destiny is one of your commonest tasks. There's not a person who doesn't have these, so get out your toolbox and move on past. We could all have excuses of why we cannot move on, but your soul knows the truth here and will want to lead you on.

Motivating yourself is a crucial trait for being a god. Your mentors in the higher dimensions can help you to a degree, but it is you that must find the wherewithal, the energy, and the nous. The gods cannot do your journey for you; you must walk this part alone. Yet your soul is always right beside you. As a team you can make it Home.

Finding your core resistance will be like finding the plug to the bath. Once you pull it out, all the dirty water and emotions will drain away and you will be left clean and shining and eager to do your work.

Get yourself motivated and you'll fly along your path.

Chapter 37 – EDUCATING CHILDREN

Thank you, Sophia, for pitching up every day. I am most grateful to you, and the Aquarian Universe-ity[1] will be most grateful to you as well.

Let us speak about simpler things today than universities, for universities are complex worlds with many needs, and much needs to be on offer if we are to produce complete students. So, today let us speak about primary school children, those toddlers to pre-teens who require our education but in a simple format which nevertheless is enriching and character-building.

Gone are the days when masters stand over their pupils with canes which they were eager to utilise. And we gods, we Masters, do not espouse this method, for there are gentler ways. The consciousnesses of children are sensitive and delicate things, so we must pay mind to this, for to damage these consciousnesses early on is to produce a damaged adult whom we may not be able to bring back into form.

So, much thought and consideration need to be applied to how we educate our young fledglings. Do we do this with the utmost care right now, or do we just try to get them through the treadmill of learning the very basics before they are thrust into a higher school? Bear in mind what I spoke about in an earlier chapter about building foundations so that you will have stronger walls. Why do we have so many adults these days with mental and emotional issues? It is because foundations have not been laid quite right when these people were little children.

So, much care needs to go into every little individual, not only teaching them to read and write, but in monitoring their emotional state and their angst, their vulnerabilities, and their issues. Your teachers

---

[1] The Aquarian Universe-ity (AQU): a project that the gods are working on at this present time to educate humans in the ways of gods. This book is destined to become some of the source material for AQU students.

of today would say this is not their issue. But we gods would take a different tack, for in educating a child we need to involve all their senses and all their sensibilities too. For how can a child learn the rudimentary skills if it is bathed in pain within its consciousness? No one can apply themselves when they are wreathed in pain or confusion.

So, let us take the whole world of these children and begin to understand what matters to them and makes them tick. We do not come with one general manual and make it work for all. Each child has an individual consciousness, and this must be treated like a jewel. Every facet must be exact, contemplated, and worked upon according to its lines. Where your human education system has gone wrong is that you have applied the same Band-aid as the solution to everyone, and not checked what is going on beneath the wound.

So, you will be able to see that considerable changes will need to be made to your systems. Your schools, your universities, your teaching colleges, and parental attitudes, will all need to be vastly transformed and most things turned on their heads. A big shakeup is needed, and who will be the ones to lead the way?

Your politicians will tell you it is all too expensive, yet what is the cost of bringing damaged adults into this world? If you totted up the cost of the medical facilities needed for emotional and mental issues, and the cost of your prison systems, and the cost of abuse and fraud and inefficiency and laziness, if you garnered all these costs together you would amply be able to afford to implement this new kind of education.

But where shall we get our teachers? For they would need to be Masters in themselves, and most of your teachers at this present time are damaged adults and a product of your education system thus far. So, we will need a new kind of teacher, a true mentor and support, a person who understands the psyche of little children, who understands how consciousness works. If you are one of these teachers who is reading these words now, I urge you to apply for one of these new posts, so that we may begin to spread this system far and wide. And if you are not quite there yet, at the level of the gods, then we invite you to attend our teacher training school, for we will patently need many with these skills.

And how very fulfilling it will be for these teachers to impart their wisdom and their love. Gone will be the shenanigans of the past in your classrooms, for each child will feel attended, listened to, and loved. They will not be punished for things they do not know, but they will be encouraged to explore the unknown with gusto. We will bring back a love of learning to these children, and so they will grow into adults who search for more, and the teachers will feel gratified and rewarded from their skills.

Adults who have been given a firm foundation will become winners in your world. They will need no mollycoddling or attention. They will contribute much and add value to your world. Gone will be the days of burgeoning prisons and mental institutions. Suicide and murder will be unknown. Humanity will at last find some balance, and you will be able to go on and create societies of love. Taking away the pain in childhood will result in adults not projecting their pain. And when mankind is pain-free, then your consciousnesses will be free to work on other, more fulfilling, projects and ideas.

So, who will start this ball rolling, making changes for our kids? How can you steamroll over governments and education systems set in stone? It is like the old joke about the elephant. How do you eat an elephant? A little bit at a time. This is how it will be with our foray into schools. We cannot overturn the system overnight, but little by little, every day and every year, we will bring about our target, for we have fortitude and we are strong.

So, let your consciousnesses now be flooded with this idea, for this is one way we can change the ballpark, for, as you know by now, everything on Earth first starts in the minds of gods. You are now channelling this message—broadcast it far and wide. Look at the mess we are producing in our children and be determined to set this right. Even if you never put pen to paper or lift a finger to support this in any way, if you approve of this idea within your consciousness then you are giving us your vote to proceed from here. We appreciate you have your destiny, and it may not be inclusive of ours, but if you can accommodate these ideas in your consciousness then you are electing us to move forward with this idea. Do not underestimate the strength of your support that can be offered in this way.

So, here we are, with ideas for changing your world. Back us with your positive thoughts and you'll see action emerging a little down the tracks, and you'll get a little frisson of excitement as you realise you helped create this change.

There are many areas of society that will need transforming, but educating our children is priority number one.

Chapter 38 – UNIVERSE ODYSSEY

We are going to embark on a bit of an odyssey today, so hold onto your hats. The journey begins now. Get yourself into your sphere of consciousness. Get behind the controls and see the dials and let yourself take off for a higher plane. This is easy for you to do, so let's not hear any excuses. Just let yourself go, release yourself, free yourself, surrender. Some of you hold onto your earthly human consciousness as if it was life or death. You'll still live to tell the tale, even if your spirit is traversing the universe. So, allow yourself this little trip abroad.

Space is a peculiar thing, for you would think there is nothing out there except for the odd planet or star, yet you will find yourself buffeted by many a solar wind or planetary ray. Magnetic forces will throw you this way and that, and gravity will pull you in or push you away. So, although it seems like there is nothing in space, except empty air for you to travel through, you will be at the mercy of the energy grids of the universe.

And if you tried to navigate these with your human eyes and senses then you will be lost. So, it is incumbent upon you to look through your spirit eyes and utilise your tools of consciousness. And this is somewhat how your latest cars are programmed; they use electronic eyes. And you even have creatures in your world who use other forms of sensing to find their way around. Think of bats and birds, whales and turtles.

So, using your human eyes to navigate is very limiting, but when you utilise your entire consciousness there is so much to be seen. So, turn on your consciousness' computer. Let it perform all these marvellous tricks of getting you around to where you need to go. You do not need to worry about the hows and the wherefores; your scientists will one day figure it out. But know that your consciousness has a wonderful GPS and it will get you arriving at your station or desired location.

You can hop from one planet to the next or even from one star to another. Neither are you contained within this galaxy. But bear in mind your boundaries will be where your wavelengths stop. So, if you wish to explore further, raise your frequencies, and doors will open. We need no fingerprint identification from you, or iris scans. The level of your vibrations is telling enough for us.

Now, if you are into science fiction, you may get to visit worlds that you've seen portrayed on Earth. You are not making these things up, for the ideas manifested upon your planet have come from spirits that have visited these places high above. And those with little imagination, don't think that you will need to create these magical worlds, for they are existing already. All you need to do is get yourself there. Your soul knows the way, so give up all control. Let your soul manage the joystick or the wheel. You can be a passenger on this ride.

And when you are done and back in your human world, you may be thinking, "Wow, that was some vivid dream!" But it is not some dream but the reality of your spirit, the part of you that lives in the higher and hidden worlds. It is wonderful when you and your spirit get together, for there is much you can teach one another, and it benefits both. So, do take the time to get to know your spirit and your soul. They are your kith and kin, closer to you than any family on Earth.

And when it is time for you to depart your planet, then it is to your spirit and your soul that you will go. And for a while you will get used to living with your other half and being monitored by your parent soul, until eventually you will merge back into the consciousness of your spirit and become unified and one. Then, one day in the future, you will make plans to incarnate once again.

But let us continue our odyssey, for there are many places to see and much to learn. Without a human body you can go anywhere; into the centre of the sun, or down into the depths of methane seas. You can fly through rocky mountains and squeeze through holes. You can ride on a star beam and go circling around moons. You can mine for gold or diamonds, or crazy gemstones that you don't get on Earth. You can hear different music and taste different food. You'll meet aliens aplenty and be astonished at what you find.

You may applaud those with imagination upon your Earth, but let me tell you, this is but the tip of the iceberg for what you'll find out there. Billions of years have served to create masterpieces, and if you think your Great Pyramid is some work of art, then you will be dumbfounded at what you find elsewhere.

What you have managed to produce on your planet in just a few hundred thousand years is nothing short of miraculous, so you will appreciate what has been created since the universe first began. You are just a junior civilisation compared to others that have been up and running for quite a while. So, come, visit these civilisations, for they will welcome you and share their worlds. Be polite and carry the gift of your love and doors will open for you everywhere, for all beings are anxious to help.

You will not get tired on your trips around the universe, although you should take time to assimilate all you see. It is not as arduous as travelling around your planet, for it is easy to get around when you use your spirit sphere. If you don't like the thought of travelling all alone, then invite another spirit or join with a spirit crowd. You can travel in your vehicle or another's. Consciousnesses can join together and travel as a group. You do not need any kind of physical vehicle. Everything you need is within your mind.

So, get used to going out on forays so that when you leave this human world you won't have to take the time to learn how to drive. When you pass from this human world and leave your human body behind, you will have a new kind of body in the spirit world. It too is physical but not quite the same as the body you had on Earth. You will be a physical body of pulsing lights, light that will have the hues of all the colours of the rainbow and more. And yet you will be able to manifest yourself into this form or that, and you can even make yourself look like your human form if that is your wont. Your consciousness will be the same as that with which you left the Earth. There will be some confusion at first, as you make the transition over, but soon you will adjust and you'll come to love your new form.

We have societies and structures in our civilisation on the other side. All is not freeform, energies just moving in a tangled web. No, we have great structure, and you will come to know our rules. And the first abiding rule is that you be love. Everything else is secondary to that.

So, you will not get very far if your heart is set in stone, for your heart dictates your vibrations, and vibrations need to move to play their music. So, let your heart soften and move up on the scales. Let you fly on the higher wavelengths and discover all that's hidden from your human eyes.

Chapter 39 – GHOSTS IN THE CRYPT

We are going to speak about a side issue today, something a little off the beaten track, something that people do not often think about when they think about their consciousness. And it is a little like raising Lazarus from the dead.

There are multiple parts to yourself, as you will well know by now. You have the part of yourself that you are used to seeing and working with; the human part of your consciousness. And then there are the subconscious parts of you that are doing many things for you in the background. And then there is the part of you that is in spirit, and a higher yet part of you that is your soul.

But there are still yet other parts of yourself, and these parts could be seen as hiding away in crypts. These are the old parts of you. And you might ask, "Are these my past lives?", and I would say yes. But parts of these parts of you are still alive and they are still working in your consciousness, enlivening you, or trapping you, tripping you up, or making you go in a certain direction that you would not normally have followed.

So, you might like to think of yourself going down, down, down, into the crypt of a church, and in all the dark niches there are these old parts of you who are still alive in your consciousness today. The skeletons might be mouldering there but the consciousnesses of these old yous are still in effect.

So, you might like to go and visit these old skeletons in your cupboard. Take time to understand what they are representing in you today, for they can pull you back from the path you should be taking, for they do not understand the you that you are today. They are still stuck in their old own experiences; their fears have not been cleared.

So, it is as though you must put each of these skeletons into their graves and seal their coffins once and for all. For their ghosts are still haunting you. They are still writhing through your consciousness. And you might be asking, "How do I put them to bed?"

We have spoken in past chapters how to let go of the parts of our consciousness that no longer serve us. And here we can do the same thing. You may want to understand this skeleton's angst and worries, for this will help you understand what you are going through today. So, speak with this old part of yourself. Enter into dialogue and conversation. Let them speak freely and offer up their fears. And you, with all your new tools of your consciousness, will be able to calm them and reassure them and offer them a way out.

The way out is not to shatter their bones but to take their anxieties into your confidence. And, as a good counsellor, you will sort out the negatives from the positives and let them see things from a new perspective. Help them to know where they stand within your new advanced consciousness that you carry today. And if there is no longer a place for them here, then offer them the chance to dissolve into Heaven's river. We are not so much killing them off as allowing them to merge back into the greater consciousness where they will meet with love and comfort.

Walk around your crypt to every skeleton there. Tend to each casket until nothing but love remains. If there is a feisty one who insists on staying, then you may need to work with them for several days or weeks. They cannot always see the benefits of going Home.

But soon you will get to clear your crypt. Then it will be time to climb the stairs again, back up to ground level, and then up more steps into the bell tower. Climb up onto the spire and sit atop the pinnacle and look down upon your world. You will have cleared your crypt and now it will be time for you to clear your church. Clear everything beneath you, even the spire itself, for we have no need of what has belonged to the lower world. It was necessary for you to go through these enactments, for this is what has shaped your consciousness, but we have new structures awaiting you in the higher dimensions now. So, let us climb up the stairway into the heavens. Let us enter the future. Let us see what it can bring.

If you feel any of those skeletons still clawing at your feet as you try to move to these higher realms, then go back down there again and speak with them and resolve their fears. For it is not always a clear path from crypt to Heaven. Sometimes skeletons arise from the dead, those whom we had long thought we had put into the ground. So, be sure that all your ghosts are laid to rest, for you do not want them to come haunting you as you are trying to get ahead.

Do not kick their hands off the rungs of the ladder. Do not push them over cliffs, or into the great abyss. Deal with each ghost with kindliness and love, for this is still a part of you. And isn't this the way you would wish to be treated too? These skeletons were once you in an age long past. They may have been troublesome, or just troubled, but they deserve to be treated with the greatest of respect.

So, this can sometimes be our journey as we make our way through Heaven's gates, that we are pulled back again by this skeleton or that. We cannot turn our back on them. We must face them and deal with them through love. It happens to all of us, even to the most senior of gods, that now and again one of these skeletons will be uncovered and you must make that journey back into that crypt.

It is very satisfying once you lay your ghosts to rest. There is a feeling of calmness, and all the anchors will fall away. Your journey will then be unimpeded. You can race back up that stairway and into newer climes (climbs).

So, be prepared for these times of entanglement with the long dead. They cannot always be predicted but they will shackle you, nonetheless. Free yourself of these devices and then you'll be able to fly. You will still have the consciousness of these past folks, but you will take with you on your journey only those traits that serve.

Think of all the hundreds or thousands of lives that you have lived. You are a multi-media mish-mash of every one of these lives. Bringing them all together in your consciousness, as you are now, takes some balancing and coordination. So, be patient while you work all this out. It can be like having a class of a hundred schoolchildren sitting in your head. Are they all going to be quiet and well-behaved, or are some of them going to give you the runaround? So, you will need to be on top of your game, the best parent, the best Master, to harness all these minds, taking the very best of them and bringing them to potential. But also noticing which ones trip you up, and dealing with these in a kind and gentle way.

You are the conductor of an orchestra. Each of the children within your mind is like a different instrument, all wishing to play their favourite song. You must bring them into concord and have everyone playing the same tune. So, let you pick up your conductor's baton, your magic wand. Let you bring your orchestra into harmony and let us gods hear your music, and may it fill our hearts. We will not allow any discordant notes, so, if you have a broken instrument, then fix it and return to your seat. We will enjoy hearing your symphonies in the years to come.

Chapter 40 – KEEPING ON TRACK

Let us take care today of where we are going, for there are deviations and detours, and if we are not looking smart we may miss our track. Let us set out on our journey as we do every day. There is always something new on the horizon and something that takes our attention on either side. And we are often pulled back by what is behind us.

So, if we are to make progress then we need to be one-pointed in our advance. It is not that we shouldn't care about all the little things that go on in our life, but our major thrust should be forwards. We should not be dallying on the sidelines at the expense of movement towards our goal. Let us always be mindful of our target and our mission, or we will find that we have procrastinated for far too long, and months or years have spun past and we are no further along our path to our destiny.

So, let us keep a check on where we are going, for it is too easy to dither here and there and get caught up in minutiae and things that do not serve our ultimate goal. We need to be clear about where we are heading, and then we will find that momentum will take us there. A train does not stop to prevaricate in the sidings. It has stations to arrive at and schedules to maintain. Ultimately it is heading for its terminal, and then another journey shall start from there.

So, we must ensure that our consciousness contains our itinerary and our schedule, and that it is very aware of our ultimate goal. For then the universe will keep us between these tracks. And when we are in danger of slipping away from these, the universe can alert us with signals and messages to that effect. But if we have no idea where we are heading, then our train will take the most roundabout routes and it may be a while before you see your chosen destination.

So, pay attention to your itinerary and all the stops you'll need to make along the way. Be cautious about getting side-tracked, for there are many elements on Earth that will pull us away from our golden road.

This is not to say that we cannot have fun or leisure or refresh ourselves in certain ways, for balance is certainly needed between our work and play. And it is when we are most relaxed that we will find love seeping into and out of our auras. Yet we have not come here just to bathe in a pool of love, much as that would be the ideal lifestyle. We do have missions to complete. We do have tasks that we must undertake. We cannot be frivolous with our time here on Earth, for we would regret that when we arrive Home in the higher world.

By all means, cultivate friendships and relationships and weave your magic into society and your world. But let us always have, at the forefront of our consciousness, the goal that we are making for, the reason why we're here. Too often we have folks arriving Home who have forgotten to do their mission.

It is not a requirement that you slave every day. We gods are not hard taskmasters who wish to run you into your grave. But you do have responsibilities and these we urge you to maintain. You will only feel you have let yourself down if you shirk your tasks and put them off for another day. As I have said before, your soul knows your plan for your journey. Ask them where you are and what's to do. There will be a list of 'whats' to be tackled, and where you are making for as your next station. Don't drop the ball, for it may be hard to find again. Keep on moving and checking you're on track.

And while you have your own train and your own track and your own terminal to arrive at, you are also part of a greater journey, a passenger on a larger train with a greater mission to fulfil. So, even though you must be assiduous in completing your own journey, you will find yourself flowing down another river where other tasks shall be expected of you. So, not only will you need to develop yourself, but you will need to develop humanity too. So, be prepared to share your time and love. There is much work that needs to be done on this godless Earth.

But do not go the other way and devote all your time to humanity's woes, and forget to work upon yourself and bringing yourself to your destiny. So, you are playing two games here, and often the one game plays inside the other. Just be aware there may be several different tracks to follow.

How can you make sure you keep on track? Working with your soul every day is a good idea. And bringing to the forefront of your consciousness the intentions for your destiny, will help to remind you of your journey every day. The details of your human life clutter up your consciousness in every way. So, it is as if you will need to create yourself a billboard in your mind and advertise your destiny which urges you to get on board. Whatever works for you to remind you of your mission, do it now!

It is too easy to slide down the embankments from your track and end up in the lower worlds and missing your date with destiny. Many of you will have had dreams where you have missed your train. And you wake up with a feeling of anxiety, and this is your soul worrying if you will make it to your terminal on time.

We do schedule in holidays and rest stops and overnight stays. But make sure you keep on travelling at other times instead. If you were making your way to a holiday destination you would have a schedule and itinerary in mind. And you would not want to waste time on platforms or at airports, missing connections and getting stuck in unlikely and lowly places. Treat your mission with the same kind of zeal.

If you are going around in circles and you don't know where you are, then stop and take the time to connect with your soul. If you are in darkness, they will have a light. If you are in confusion, they will know the exit from your maze. If you are uninspired, they can light the spark within you. If you are resisting, they can help you let go of your fears.

So, take some time now to put your map up on your billboard of your mind. Place the marker for 'You are here'. Place the marker for your golden goal. And buy your ticket and board your train. This is a wonderful excursion and it will transform your life. Forget about your baggage. Come as you are, along with your soul. All you require will be provided along the way. Get into the spirit of things and make that journey now.

Chapter 41 – WHAT IS REALITY?

Have we delved into consciousness enough? Not by a long shot! For consciousness is as large and varied as this universe and we will never get to grips with all that goes on there. So, consider this book merely an introduction to consciousness, for there will yet be many years work to unfold all its pages.

Consciousness has a devious nature. It is not all that it seems, nor does it project out there all that would seem to be your reality. You see what you are meant to see. You see what your filters allow you to see. You see what you have been programmed to see. And yet is this real? You would be astonished at the illusions that have been played upon you, not maliciously, but just through the nature of how this universe works.

So, although you think you are this person that you are, and that you have this life that you have, and that you think this way and not that way, much of this is not the truth. And it comes as a shock to many people when they find that all they have hung their hat upon is crumbling away and has not much basis at all. It is disconcerting, to be sure, when the rug is pulled from under you, when your structures are falling down, when all that you had thought was solid begins to melt into a miasma.

You find out that not only do you live upon Earth, but that a part of you lives in another dimension. You find out that you leave your body when you sleep and that your spirit goes travelling, who knows where. You find out that there are aliens who call themselves gods. And you find out that matter can be manifested at your feet.

This is patently not what you are taught at school. And so, your school years are mostly a lie. Your brain is filled with all that stuff and nonsense, and you grow into an adult and still cannot make head nor tail of your world. But you know that you exist and that things around you feel real. And so, who is telling the lies? Those around you, or the gods up here?

Of course, you will not doubt the evidence before your eyes. And so, lies become facts, and facts become your beliefs, and your beliefs go on to create your world around you. And so, we have a vicious cycle.

It is almost impossible for us gods to knock out those beliefs, for they have been ingrained into you from an early age. You have built your whole life upon these beliefs, and questioning these beliefs would mean dismantling your life. So, who could be bothered with that? It is much easier to go on believing, for it seems to do no harm and keeps you safe. Whereas, believing in another world will shake your foundations to pieces, and not many will choose to go through this angst.

And yet, if you had a broken bone that was set all wrongly, you would allow the doctors to break that bone again so that everything could be set back right. Your world is a collection of broken bones that have been set wrongly, so you know what must be done to put it right.

There will come a time when this resetting can be put off no longer. And it is already happening in some quarters where lives are being demolished so that people can start once again. You might hope that it will never happen to you, but if your beliefs and your life are not aligned with the new energies, foundations will crack and walls will tumble. And you will find yourself having to rebuild all over again.

However, we do not wish for people to rebuild in the old way, the old styles. We have new building codes where we come from. So, you will need to take on board our beliefs, for these beliefs are born of higher vibrations, and it is with these that we can rebuild strong and true.

So, we are going to have to take out every segment of your consciousness that does not conform. And this could be pretty much all that you have ever known and done. We are not just fiddling at the edges here. We are going into the deepest crevices of your mind. We are scraping things clean, removing old waste. We are dealing with back issues. And we are setting you up to shine.

You may go on with your old ways and world, thinking I am speaking nonsense and these things will not come to pass. This is your belief right now. Come visit me in the future, for no one will escape this cleansing and rewiring.

If you refuse and resist these renovations to your life, then you will be invited Home where your spirit can be dealt with more helpfully.

This is not a threat that you will be punished or killed, but the frequencies levelled at you will break you down all by themselves. We gods will not lay a finger upon you. We do not send devils or demons or put you in hell. Your consciousness must deal with the wavelengths of your world, and if you are not prepared and ready, then your world will start falling apart.

It is appalling that any one of you should suffer, for the gods feel compassion and great love within their hearts. But, like the doctor that must reset your broken bone, we know it must be done in order for you to heal.

The easiest way to prepare for these times is to begin to believe these things I have written here. When you make that shift of perception in your consciousness, doors will open and you'll see with greater clarity what really exists in your world. I cannot force you to believe these things; the choice is up to you, but do give yourself an open mind, that perhaps there is more to this universe than you've been told. Allow yourself to be open to new experiences and ideas. And keep in mind that what society has taught you may have glossed over many secrets hidden from human eyes.

We may sound like conspiracy theorists. We may sound like woo-woo agents of supernatural gods. We may sound like we have smoked too much hashish or have drunken too liberally. We may sound like a fantasy come down from a made-up world. These are, of course, your defences of your human world today, for denying our existence keeps you safe from the fear of change.

Throughout history there have been those who have come to change the world. Many have been given short shrift. For the world does not like changes when people have investments here. So, examine your beliefs and your openness to change, for times they are a-coming where nothing shall stay the same.

Chapter 42 – YOUR SPIRIT COUNTERPART

Let us speak about your divine counterpart today, your spirit self that is on the other side of the divide, the line that separates Earth from Heaven. It is no physical line as such, not a wall that you have to climb over, or a physical door or portal that you have to enter through. But it is a line that separates one set of vibrations from another. Below this line, in the lower vibrations, you have Earth and humans. Above the line, in the higher vibrations, you have spirits and souls and gods.

We have spoken about your spirit self before, that other part of your consciousness that lives in a parallel world but does not necessarily lead a parallel life to yours. All parts of your consciousness can lead individual lives, and your spirit is no different. Think about the consciousness of the cells of your body. They are certainly part of your consciousness, but do your cells not lead a very different life from you? So, get to understand that your consciousness is here, there, and everywhere, and having experiences that are quite in contrast to the human experience you are having right now.

Your spirit is in their spirit sphere, travelling through the higher dimensions, perhaps at work, maybe at home, even perhaps visiting another galaxy. You may be aware of what your spirit is up to, or you may not. Most of what your spirit does is kept secret from you, for it would overwhelm your human mind if you were to know too much. And yet if you ask your spirit self, they will gladly share some of their experiences with you.

Your spirit self is preparing you for a better life down below, but also for the time when you will return Home and you will merge back into your spirit and be as one. Your lives upon Earth are good lessons for your spirit consciousness to learn. They are not wasted.

All that you do down here on this planet is analysed and utilised by your spirit and your soul. And similarly, if your spirit discovers something useful to its human counterpart below, then it will try to share this discovery with you, if you are open to receive.

So, you are like twins, one on other side of the divide. And you come together often, hopefully, and you collaborate and you share. You are both helping one another up that stairway to raised vibrations. You do not work at cross purposes with one another for that would be sabotaging yourself. So, try to imagine this consciousness spread across two dimensions, two halves of the one mind.

And spare a thought for your doppelganger, for what happens to them will drizzle down the wavelengths and affect you. Similarly, events that have a crashing effect on you will also be felt by your spirit in the dimension above. It is like your cells in your big toe go about their business without you paying them much mind, but if you stub your toe then you will become very much aware of those cells down there. Your whole consciousness reverberates with their pain.

So, sometimes you might not know where your feelings are coming from, for they would seem to have no basis here on Earth. Begin to wonder, then, if your spirit is not going through some challenge and you are feeling the waves of the outcome from up there.

Your spirit has a clearer mind and clearer sight. They are not confused by the befuddlements of Earth. They do not live in a dimension where time is all. And so, your spirit can make sense of things and see the big picture which might be denied to you on Earth. So, converse with your spirit and get them to share their views. It is not that they will give you the winning numbers for the lottery, but they are adept at showing you the best way to go.

You might ask, "How do I converse with my spirit?" Well, they are within your same mind. So, imagine them standing in front of you and strike up a dialogue as if you were with a friend. You may think you are making up your spirit's part of the conversation. It is natural to think you might be going insane. But, I can assure you, your spirit has a voice of their own and they are quite capable of speaking with you in an adult and articulate fashion. Try it and practise, and you'll soon get the hang of what I mean.

Your spirit will not bother with the mundane details of your life. They have bigger fish to fry. So, they will be more interested in getting you on track and to your station. They will see your issues and try to get you to let go. They will see where you may be stalled along your path and what is the barrier that prevents your progress. And they will always be concerned with getting you to raise your vibrations, for this is the nub for both of you on any day. Always, you are making for a higher station, a higher level. There is not a day where you will want to go backwards or stay the same.

So, you will always feel your spirit gently pushing and, at times, they might be kicking you if you are refusing to budge. So, it is not generally us gods that are doing this work with you. We come on occasions and give our advice and love. But it is your spirit who is with you on a daily basis. In every moment they are walking a parallel world beside you.

So, think what you could do for your spirit, your best friend. How could you make their life more palatable, more enjoyable, easier, and more loved? When you begin to think this way about your other half, they will act similarly, and you will feel their love, and treasures will rain down on you from the oddest of places. For your spirit loves to cherish you if you are cherishing them.

But if you pay your spirit no mind and forget about them from day to day, your spirit will go about their business too and they will make no connection with you, which you will feel. You will feel this disconnection and probably a sense of loneliness too. There might be a feeling of abandonment, and all this will reflect in the external world around you.

So, if you wish for the world to love and cherish you, then you will need to get your spirit onside first. And when this relationship is up and running and travelling well, then you will find all other relationships on Earth will begin to be smoother, more harmonious, and natural. When there is a divide between you and your spirit, that division plays out too in your reality down on Earth.

So, you know what to do. Get hold of your spirit, connect, and make peace. There is nothing more beautiful to us gods than to see a spirit travelling with its human counterpart with smiles and love all round. You will not get far in your travels into the higher dimensions if you do not have your spirit on board too.

Chapter 43 – SOUL GRADUATION

Let us speak about graduation today. How does a human graduate to the next level, and how does its spirit do likewise? These are questions you will be asking one day, if you haven't done so already. For as I have said, you are making your way up the stairway to Heaven, but every now and again there are gates that you go through that define where one level stops and the next level begins.

These are graduation gates, and it is like moving from one class at school at the end of the year into a new class for the coming year ahead. It is not that the duration of this level will be for one year, for your progress depends upon yourself. You could be here several months, or several years, or even several decades. If you do the work, you will progress. If you shirk your work, then you will remain in the confines of your level until you raise your vibrations sufficiently to break through the barrier and through the next gate.

My advice is to keep working at it every day, and even though it may seem you are making imperceptible progress, you will be moving forwards and upwards and you will reach your goal given time. Some people like to make a drama of it, and they do all their work within one small period, but this transformation is a little exhausting and complicated. It is not recommended that you do it in this way. Slow and steady wins the race, is one of your sayings upon Earth.

So, where do you go to when you graduate? It is not that you will move somewhere with your physical body, although you may choose to do this, of course. You are graduating to a higher level with your consciousness. And at this higher level, new doors will open for you and new vistas will be exposed. New people will come into your circle, and you will discover things about the universe that you had not known before.

When you go through one of these major graduations, what is happening is that you have lifted your vibrations to the level of your soul. The consciousness of your soul now merges with the consciousness of your spirit and of your human too. And so, your human self will feel elevated, and all will change in the world around you upon Earth. Your soul is now sitting next to you within your body, and this is a time now where soul and human will blend.

The soul does not come in and take over the human completely. This is an integration, an assimilation, and gradually the two consciousnesses will begin to merge as one. This happens already on Earth between two marriage partners. They have lived independent lives and now they come to live with one another in one house. Compromises will have to be made, perspectives changed, and there will be new ways of going about your lives. This is the same for human and soul when you graduate and merge. It will take time to get used to living with one another. And because the soul is wiser and more experienced, it will take the human under its wing and it will teach the human how to surrender to greater love and harmony. It is not a taking over but a transformation, until both consciousnesses are aligned and working together cooperatively and in joy.

Your spirit too on the other side will be going through similar challenges of merging with your soul. There may be different problems there to accommodate one another but the outcome needs to be the same. So, it is like pouring cordial into water when your soul merges with your consciousness, and what you will get in the end is cordiality.

At first, when your soul comes into your human consciousness, you will be very aware of the differences between you and them. But over the weeks and months you will find ways of working together peaceably. And one day you will come to realise you no longer know where you end and they begin, for, now, you are unified and harmonious.

Way in the background, another soul is slotting into place to take up the position vacated by your recent soul. There is a line of souls stretching back to your source, and as each soul merges with your consciousness, the next one lines up for its tour of duty, each soul being at a higher level than the last. You will not get to connect with this new soul that has come down the line until you have properly integrated with your most recent soul. So, focus on this part and then you'll keep on track.

All the while, remember that you have a spirit in the heavenly realms. And you will need to keep connection with this spirit for it is still your guide and knows the plans for you.

After your graduation, there may be a period of mourning, for you may feel like you have lost something or someone. For the human part of your consciousness is now fading away to be replaced by a higher level of consciousness from your soul. Try not to resist but let go with grace. You had this time as you. Now you are entering a new field of experience as you. It is a little like leaving your childhood behind and entering the field of an adult. Or leaving behind your time as a single person and entering into a new commitment as a marriage partner. You must look at the things to be gained rather than the things you may have lost.

Moving into a new and higher level brings with it more responsibilities and tasks. You cannot just float on a bubble of ease from level to level up the stairway to Heaven. With any promotion, you will face new work and new challenges, but also new rewards.

So, be prepared to face your new world with strength and alacrity and a positive note. Certainly, it may feel unsettling at first, for your new soul will have you facing in new directions and taking new roads. All can never be the same again. But let us face the coming days with equanimity, for feeling hassled by them will not stand us in good stead. Bring to your new world an open heart and an open mind. You do not know where the new road leads, so allow your soul to show you. Don't make assumptions or feel glum. I can assure you that all roads at higher levels lead to better things.

So, do not put on your armour and defend your old school of thought. Liberate them from your old ways and come with a clean slate to explore your new domain. Have no expectations and no negations. Allow all to unfold as if you were in some magical land, for your soul has plenty of tricks up their sleeve. Your soul has been saving them for times such as these.

Take a deep breath and calm yourself down. Going through a graduation is a wondrous thing. You are the butterfly emerging from the caterpillar. So, come stretch your wings and fly.

Chapter 44 – RAISING YOURSELF UP

Let us take a turn around the block today, and by that I mean, let us see what new things are out there for us to discover. If you stay in the same place, looking at the same views, all you will get is the same kind of life. So, pick yourself up and walk about, or you will never know what is on your doorstep and further afield.

Always walk with your spirit self for they will have a different perspective than you. And so, you will find yourself discovering a lot more than if you were on your own, just travelling with your human consciousness. When you have the divine element with you, then you will find your life becomes more divine too. So, give it a go, take a turn with your companion and discover the wonders that are out there beyond your eyes.

Many people sit waiting for the divine world to come to them. As I have said before, it is you that must step up into the heavenly realms. You must bring your vibrations higher, then all will be revealed to you once you make that effort and you are riding high. Miracles abound and await you, but they do not come searching for you; you must go to them.

So, if your life is a little tired and needs a makeover, then you know what to do, for sitting there waiting for miraculous change will never happen. You must be the force field that triggers the change to come. Now, if you do not have the motivation or the enthusiasm or the pep, your world is going to stay pretty much the same, or even spiral downwards, for your vibrations won't be high. So, kick yourself into gear and find a shred of life-spark. Hustle to get that fire going, for nothing can be created without fire at its source. Bring yourself to the boil, even if it takes all day or all week, for living with flatness or hopelessness is not living at all and will just make you sick.

Spiral yourself upwards; you could imagine climbing a spiral staircase in a tower. But whatever way you do it, get yourself into higher climes (climbs). Once you are out of the doldrums, the air will be clearer, and you will be able to see further, and all that miasma will fall away from you. And now you will begin to feel the sun's rays on you and the sparkle will begin to take effect.

Too often we let life's vicissitudes keep us down and keep us suppressed. It is the trait of a god to know how to handle this and to inject life force again and break through the barriers and into clear air. It needs nothing more than the force of your consciousness, for your mind is the tool that works for every occasion. This secret is not the possession of the gods. It is a well-known fact upon the Earth, and here I am broadcasting it to you again.

Your thoughts dictate your reality so, using your thinking, get yourself out of there and higher up those stairs. Anyone knows how to climb up steps within their mind. So, let there be no excuses. You can raise yourself up in 101 ways to suit. No one is holding your consciousness down. You are not a prisoner except through your own thinking. So, begin to act as your spirit self in ways that set you free. In your mind, do all the things that you have ever dreamed of. Let your spirit play the part and play it well. Pretend that you are a king or queen of your domain. Pretend that you are with this person or that, or doing the work you have always favoured.

In the world of consciousness there are no limitations or barriers or holds. You are free to travel and wonder and explore. And as your consciousness takes on this new world, so these aspects will begin to filter down into your physical world upon Earth. Your new reality starts with the thoughts within your head. So, get changing your thinking and your world will change likewise too.

I see so many stuck in the pipeline of their dreams. Their dreams are waiting at one end, but the thinking is going round and round in circles along the pipe. You cannot think the same thoughts and find yourself making progress. Only new thoughts will edge you closer to your dreams. If we could educate all people in this one fact, lives would be so different and your planet a happier place.

What does it take to sit there for a minute and think a happy thought? This one action will raise you a degree above where you were before. Keep shoring up these happy thoughts and you will find yourself rising to new levels. New levels will offer you new fields of existence. And here you may find life is much more to your liking than those fields much further below. So, give yourself a present and stir your blood and stir your thoughts. Are you really so happy in your current situation that it is not worth moving to a step or two above?

We hear the wails and woes of you humans from where we live. It is a terrible din, a cacophony, and it pulls on our heartstrings for we know that you could change. Why do so many choose to live in pigswill when, with a few choice thoughts, they could elevate their lot? I don't understand why so many don't make an effort. It is hard to imagine they enjoy their bedevilled lives.

Your consciousness is a gateway to your dreams. It happens in no other way. You can take all sorts of actions upon your Earth, but the universe works only with what is carried in your mind. You cannot think to cheat the universe by thinking one thing and doing another. Your thinking is what sets the tones for your vibrations and, as you will know by now, it is your vibrations that set you free.

So, let us have more action on raising the timbre of your wavelengths. No matter how dire your circumstances, your thoughts can let you fly. Begin to cultivate ways to raise yourself often, for this is the magic that will create a magical life.

Chapter 45 – SEEING THE SIGNS

Let us speak about something significant today, something that signifies. We are speaking about signs. Signs are all around us, not only on Earth but in Heaven too. We are directed this way and that, forever being guided by well-meaning persons or gods.

Do we always see these signs? No, we do not. Sometimes we are blinkered, and our filtering systems in our consciousness make us see only what we want to see, and we ignore any other signs that fall outside this remit. This is why we must open up our minds, our consciousnesses, so that we may see all the signs that are offered for our guidance, for missing one may mean we could lose our way. And this is what happens on a daily basis, yet if we had followed the signs we would have kept on track.

Signs are not always in our face, written in words that we can understand. Signs can be displayed as symbols, and then we will need to interpret these symbols correctly if we are to know in which direction to head. So, signs can be a bit of a minefield if we do not have the right intelligence to interpret them in the way that they are meant. We can read all kinds of things into signs and symbols. We can often make them say just what we want them to say.

And this is why you will need to employ an interpreter, a translator, in order to know what your sign or symbol is telling you. And you have one of these interpreters right beside you at all times, for your spirit or your soul will be able to unravel these clues and set you right. Do not rely on your human consciousness to guess at the meaning of things. You may be right, but you may be terribly wrong. So, employ one who knows, one who is used to using this language to communicate in higher realms. For we are not a wordy society up here; we speak more with the language of symbols which can convey many meanings at once.

Think of the symbol for McDonald's; the golden arches. If you were to see this symbol anywhere around your world, you would know immediately what it meant and what it offered. It would not translate merely as the word *McDonald's*. You would be having visions of food and drinks, and you would know exactly the kind of place you would be walking into. The golden arches symbol represents an entire environment that you can conjure up in your mind.

And so, symbols and signs are very powerful. And these are being transmitted to you from Heaven to Earth at all times. When you really look around you, you will see them. Your environment is speaking to you. Do you hear? And it is not just something special or unusual that you can see. There, of course, will be the moments that stand out for you but, in truth, there are messages on every breath of wind, in every blade of grass, in every corner of your world.

If you were experienced, you could look around you and read your world like some wise book. Don't take my word for it. Go out there after reading this and see the signs and hear the messages and feel the touch of the messengers of the gods. You will laugh when you get to understand these things, that you had not seen or heard them before, that you were blind and deaf to all that was really going on in your world, that you had been aware of only the top layer and nothing deeper underneath.

Most humans are too wrapped up in their own little spheres to notice what is going on around them. And yet other worlds are intersecting with their own in every moment, and they bypass these things and are none the wiser.

Certainly, if you were to take account of all the interactions that are intersecting with your world, you would become quite overwhelmed and quite astonished. Your human consciousness protects you against these things, filtering out this and that until you are left with the essentials. And yet there are essentials that are being left out of this loop. Your human mind is cutting the line too thin. You must broaden your trajectory and take on board more news. As a god you will be able to process it all, and as a god-in-training, humans must learn to broaden their minds.

So, don't just see the obvious and the commonplace and the familiar things you know. Begin to look around corners and upwards and downwards and in directions you rarely scan. And look over your shoulder once in a while, for you never know who might be following you.

Consciousness is all about awareness, so train yourself to be aware. Train yourself to be more conscious. Most humans live life on autopilot. It's a useful trick to have, but pretty useless if you are a god.

The signs will not only be in your physical world. They will pop up in your consciousness too. Don't dismiss them as if they were not there. Ponder on their meaning, their meaning as pertains to you, for a sign can mean different things to different people. So, don't ask for others to translate, for this may bear no resemblance to the message that's come for you.

Signs are the way that your spirit or soul guides you on your path. Notice what is happening and correct your trajectory as suggested. Your life will be very rich when you learn this language and keep it in play. And you may set up a system with your divine counterpart to be shown certain symbols which will have meanings that you've agreed. Playing this game with your spirit or your soul is very fulfilling for the human, and the spirit or soul will feel grateful that they've been able to make themselves heard. So, set up this system of communication between you and your spirit and soul. You will soon get to know the symbols they like to use, for these will be symbols that mean a lot to you.

Wake up your consciousness and begin to learn its language, then you'll find that the colours and tones of the universe become much more meaningful to you. I'm giving you a sign now; act upon it without delay.

Chapter 46 – A TRIP TO THE NEW WORLD

I am going to embark on a bit of an odyssey today, so come with me on this journey for it will be instructive and informative. We are going to go around the houses a bit, so bear with me if it may seem like I am not getting to the point.

We welcome all the new gods and new spirits into our new world. Many of you are joining us now, and it is very gratifying to us more senior gods to see our next generations spread before us. We are delighted at the progress you have all made.

So, what do you do now, now that you are here? Will things be so very different for you than they are right now? We are hoping that they will be indeed, for if you carry on as you are, then the world will carry on as it is currently, and you would agree this is not the outcome that we would want. So, things will have to change, up here and down there, if we are to transform our worlds and make them a better place.

I am speaking here of the heavenly world and the earthly world, two different dimensions that your consciousness must needs straddle. You will be jumping from one world into the other and back again with regularity like some commuter. It is becoming one and the same world, merely living at different vibrational levels. So, move yourself up on the vibrational scale and you will find you do not have to live at those lower disastrous levels. You will be pretty much cocooned in your own little world, far away from the worlds of those with the lowest frequencies. This happens on your planet already and has always happened to some degree, but now you will begin to find there is definitely a schism between them and us.

The new world will break away further and further from the old world. They will be poles apart, you could say. And those who have done their work and have raised themselves up to the higher levels of love and grace, they will enjoy a life of peace and plenty. Those humans who have not bothered with the niceties of their world, they will find there is nothing nice about their living conditions, and all shall seem dark.

It is nothing to do with the gods plucking a favoured few and bringing them into Nirvana, and nothing to do with the gods casting the sinners into hell. Every human has chosen their vibrational level they wish to sit at. You have judged yourselves. The gods are not involved. So, please do all you can to raise yourself further and bring up your family and your friends too. The new world has a very different playing field from that which you're used to down below. We abide by certain rules and ethics, and if you cannot match these you will fall again down below.

So, let us carry on with our journey through the new world and notice the state of the air. It is clean and fresh and purified; no pollution from man or poisoned minds. Our climate is very stable, be it weather or emotions or politics. We do not seek to upset the peace, and if something is working we let it alone. Yet innovation is high on our agenda and we are always looking to improve. But changes are brought in justly. We do not ride roughshod over anyone, but all are catered for and considered.

A happy person makes for a happy planet, so we endeavour to work with the well-being of all. And it is amazing how productive people can be when their heart is in the moment and they are devoted to their life. When people are in love, they share and give and help. And this in turn engenders more love, and so, love cycles through the planet and helps everything to work.

Your old world placed power as its combustion engine, and believed it was power that made your planet tick. In the new world we have relegated power to a lesser place, for we believe love is the powerhouse, and love is what makes things turn. And so, you will come across evidence of this as you begin to explore your new world. And you will be amazed at the hefty power of love. It truly can move mountains, soothe troubled seas, and bring smiles to every heart.

In the new world you will be required to do your bit. You cannot sit on the sidelines and watch it all go past. You are here on this planet to add value in your own way, and now you will be tapped on the shoulder and asked to contribute in the best way that you can. No one will be allowed to dodge their input, for that would be patently unfair, and all who have made it into this new world have come here to know fairness and justice for all.

We cannot claim to be Utopia, certainly not from the start, but we are laying the foundations to one day get us there. So, bear with us as we transition, for the old must be shaken loose and the new put in place and bedded down. This will not be an overnight process. We are speaking of years and even decades, and you will be asked to do your bit to help this process along.

There are many now who have jumped over the wall and climbed up the staircase to reach our doors. You are not so few in number. We have a majority and thus we know this can work. Chaperone the young ones and teach them these new rules. They are our future. We must let them see this hope.

Where is this new world? All around you and inside your mind. It dictates what you will see now, what you will hear, and how you live. The energies may be hidden but they are potent and will turn you around. So, come, allow yourself to be guided through these halls. There is much to see and touch and taste. Immerse yourself in this new world. Bathe in its energies, breathe it in, and swallow it down.

You are no longer a member of the old human race. You are walking with gods now, and following in their footsteps. Some of you are transforming into a god yourselves, and some of you have just started on this path. All are welcome, and you will be guided to what you need.

Don't let this be just an excursion. Pack your bags and move here permanently. You are not refugees, but the first phalanx of the new human-godly race.

Chapter 47 – SPACECRAFT AND UFOS

We are going to speak about spacecraft and UFOs, for it is a subject that enchants many of you upon Earth. So, I would like to give an explanation of this phenomena.

You are wondering if aliens are coming down in their spaceships and looking at you and evaluating you and then speeding off home to report their findings to their particular race of beings. Well, you would not be far wrong. But the aliens that you think you might be seeing, are not beings from other planets or distant parts of the galaxy, or indeed even further afield. As I have stated before, it is not yet time for you to meet your neighbours. And yet what you are seeing is us gods.

It is not that we need spaceships to travel around. But we have invented them in our quarter of the universe, for at times they do come in useful for carrying physical bodies and objects around.

Now, when you see these spacecraft, or UFOs as you have termed them, you are seeing through the veil into the dimension of the gods. And we have allowed this for you to see us, for it is one of the ways that you can begin to understand that you humans are not here alone. We are not coming as huge battleships to hover over your cities, as portrayed in some of your movies, but we can give you a glimpse here and there to excite you and get you thinking. What you think is up to you, but the general idea is that you know someone is out there.

Some people will say they have had experiences of boarding these ships, and they have memories of their time there. Well, as you know now, your consciousness can go anywhere, and why shouldn't your spirit self be allowed to get on board one of these craft and experience the other dimension in a more conscious manner?

Arguably, not all these experiences are hosted by our gods, for your own consciousness can conjure up many scenarios to teach you what you need to learn. So, you will need to be discerning around what you believe about us gods, and what it might be that a consciousness is undergoing as a challenge or a trial. You will know by now that the ethics of us gods is to do no harm and only to propagate love. We will leave it up to you to make your judgements.

But certainly, there are many things in the air above you that are hidden from your eyes until it is time for you to see them, and, even then, some will miss out for they cannot believe their eyes. We have all kinds of craft that skim your skies. We have been very inventive and innovative up here. And because we do not use the same methods for propulsion that you employ, we are quiet and invisible and cannot be detected by your machines.

It is not in guile that we come, nor to pester you, but we are monitoring our domain, just as you use cameras and drones and satellites to do the same. Not only that, but we enjoy flying around your world, for it is beautiful and its consciousness speaks with us, and we visit it in the places where we have been requested to go.

So, know that if a UFO has been sighted, it is not just some fantasy on the part of some kooky people. It is the truth. And we laugh at all the conspiratorial agencies that dive into action to cover up this truth. What are they so afraid of? That Martians are coming to invade their little world? It is in the psyche of most humans to fear the unknown and especially those from other worlds. This is why we don't show ourselves to you in any forceable manner or display. But those who are ready to see will see us, and they will just need to bide their time until we can pull the curtain wide open and be on show for all to see.

Really, what would you do if a spacecraft truly landed and you saw it on your news? It would certainly wake up the consciousness of this world. But it would also generate fear and panic, and we are not about upsetting the population of this planet.

So, accept that our little UFO visits are targeted events to let you see that we are waving at you from above. You can see us now, and you know that we can see you. We have made contact, and if you tune in your consciousness to our frequency, you will be able to converse with us mind to mind.

You wonder what we are like. Are we little grey men with black slanting eyes? If that's what you expect then maybe it will be so. But you know now from my previous chapters, that gods can take on any form. So, how about we come looking like humans, then we won't be so frightening? We'll be normal and just like yourselves. Remember that we created humans in the image of ourselves, so why would we look any different? We like this form; it has served us well.

So, if you were to see a man or a woman stepping out of an alien spacecraft, what would be going through your mind? Would you be disappointed, or scratching your head that other humans could live out there? Well, we are not humans, but we are human-looking gods. And as you begin to speak with us, you will start to realise the power of our presence. It is an exciting thought, is it not, and many of your movies cover this kind of scene; the arrival of aliens and first contact. For many, this is their dream.

And as the higher dimensions begin to envelop your Earth, and the planet herself is raising her frequencies to accommodate the wavelengths of the gods, so will you find the frequency of our visits will increase. The veil is thinning in many areas of your Earth right now. Do not be surprised when you start seeing things that occur in the higher dimensions where you had never seen them before. Physicality is changing. The environment is transforming. And as your consciousness raises itself up, new forms will appear and will need to be understood. This is why I say you must broaden your minds for, if you look with old eyes, you will not see the new.

Will you get to take a ride in a spacecraft or UFO? It is unlikely unless you have the physical body of a god, for your human cells could not cope with the higher frequencies of our world. That said, your consciousness, your spirit self, is always welcome to come on board.

So, you can see, or I hope you can, that exciting times lie ahead. We are on the cusp of entering an entirely new world. The lid is being lifted, and some of you are getting a peek. When you believe, then we can show you more. Until then, we will need to keep a lid on it. But be ready, for any day now we could be appearing in the skies near you.

Chapter 48 – DISBELIEF

Let us carry on with our tales, for I have much to divulge before we near the end of this book.

Disbelief is a commodity not in short supply in your world. Everyone, to a degree, has a modicum of disbelief about us gods and our worlds. Even though people may declare that they believe, if we were to really quiz them about it, they would crumble under our questioning and they would say that there is no evidence for our existence, and therefore what they have is just blind faith.

It depends on what you mean by evidence. If you wish to be shown the physical body of a god in a courtroom in front of a jury, then we could give you some such thing, but then how would you prove that it was really that of a god? For we can look the same as you and we have the same DNA. We have blood, we have tears, we have bones, and we have tendons. What marks us out as different is our consciousness, so how would you test for that?

There are many gods amongst you now, and yet most of you have not realised or noticed. Some of you are gods yourselves and you are still having trouble believing it could be so. Your evidence is your experiences, and many of you have had plenty of these. For your spirit has met us gods many times in many places across the universe, and if you deny these experiences, you deny your very existence.

Your scientists will tell you you have conjured up these things in your imagination. As I have said before, your imagination is your consciousness. And your consciousness is not contained within your human body. It swirls into it and swirls out of it at will. But, of course, you will have to choose whether to believe this or not. Your society makes it difficult for you to believe these things that you go through, these experiences that you have. And unless you find others like yourself who can corroborate your tales, you would be inclined to think that your mental state is not all that it should be.

But perhaps it is the disbelievers who are in error here, perhaps because of their inclination to stick within the known rules of physics at this time because they are afraid to go beyond. The believers have ventured beyond. They have moved beyond the known world and into the unknown and gone exploring there. And it is always difficult for the pioneers to make themselves believed, for they return with tall tales of things that are not present in their current world. And until these things are seen with human eyes or experienced first-hand by a multitude of people, then these things are relegated to fantasy and the pioneers are derided and not believed.

All of you who believe in us gods and the higher dimensions, you are all pioneers for this earthly world and this human race. You are suffering somewhat from the lack of support on your ground. So, stay strong and keep the faith, for in the years to come all shall be unfolded and revealed, and then you shall feel vindicated about the stance you took right now.

So, give yourself some confidence and build a stronger faith. Think back to all the times where you knew, without a shadow of doubt, that you were interacting with gods or angels, and flying through sacred halls. All of you will have had crystal clear moments where you have felt the love and the wisdom of the divine. Do not crumble on us now and give your faith away. For what will fortify you in the future, for the earthly world holds little promise or support?

It is time to elect which side you stand on. And it is not that we gods are fighting humans, but we should like to know which side of the divide you support. There is no punishment from us gods if you decide to renege on your divine deals. But your spirit would be in anguish, and you would feel their sorrow as they had to take their leave. You cannot have a foot in both camps any longer and only half believe. We either exist for you or we don't. Do not use us as entertainment and then switch us off when it suits you to be human. And once you have made it into godhood, there is no going back to being purely mortal. You will have made the transformation and your body is now divine. So, think long and hard about your choices for the future.

We understand that you will be called upon to explain yourself and your beliefs. Can you do this and state your convictions, or will you be a Judas and betray those you love and who love you? At times you will be tested to see how strong is your faith and love. Although you might feel a little shaken, come back to us and regain your higher place.

We feel sorry for those who do not care to look beyond, for they are missing the best parts of our universe, exciting experiences, and options for love. It must be miserable thinking that there is nothing more than Earth, that this little life is all there is, and beyond the grave is darkness and non-existence. How surprised these folks will be, when they arrive on the other side, to find fully formed worlds of brightness, cheer, and love.

The worst thing you can do is to separate from your spirit or your soul, so keep this relationship going and you will survive the onslaught of disbelief. You believe in these things because they make your heart swell with good grace. You would not believe in them if they made you feel murderous and bad. You are following the road that makes you feel blessed. Do not snub it or be ungrateful. This road supports your being and will lead you to become like a god. If you do not believe this, what will you become instead?

Your consciousness knows what is good for you. Your consciousness tries to steer you to your brightest star. If this includes believing in a higher world and higher love, then shouldn't you follow it even if you don't believe? We all have crises of faith at some time or another along our path back to our source. Try to float through it and not be taken back down below, for it will take quite a while to get back here once again, and you will lose all status and privileges and, most of all, that feeling of great love.

So, come, beautiful people, steel your hearts and make your way across the borders to this great land of love. Experience our oneness and the brilliance of our minds. We understand your shortcomings but please don't sell yourself short. You are gods and gods in the making. Allow yourselves to believe that and get yourselves Home to our hearts.

Chapter 49 – DESIRES

Let us speak about desirability today, for desires come from within our consciousness, so we will need to know how to deal with them, especially when they are excessive or not for our greater good.

Everyone has desires, be they human or god or even animal. We have been put upon this Earth and in this universe with the capability of desiring things, for this is what motivates us and leads us on. So, desire is not ugly or forbidden. Desire is a good thing when we are following it like a carrot to complete our destiny. But you know the saying, "Too much of a good thing…." And so, we need to keep our desires in balance or in check, but not suppress them altogether. So, it is a fine line that we have to dance here.

Desire can be for anything or anyone. It may be for wine or food, a beautiful home, a prestigious job, or sex. And the desire to merge with another being is inbuilt in every one of us, for this ensures we get to meet the right people whom we need to have dealings with in this lifetime. As far as people are concerned, we are all like Geiger counters, tracking down those people who make us click.

You might also have the desire for peace, or more money, or to travel the world. There is no limit to what our desires encompass, and the universe has no rules that say we should not desire this or that. So, be aware of your desires, good and bad, and follow up on those that would be right for you and let go the urgings that would see you take the wrong road.

And let you yourself be someone who is desired through the traits that you display to humanity and to us gods. Let all desire to be near you, to hear your wisdom and feel your precious love. Let all who have been in your presence, bask in your glory and take it home with them. When you work on your own desirability, you are transforming yourself into a finer human and ultimately into a god. But desirability does not mean becoming some sex symbol or human icon. You will need to be known for what is in your consciousness rather than what you wear.

So, if you desire good things, then be a good thing yourself. If you would like a man or a woman of this or that ilk, then be of that ilk yourself, for I have said it before, like attracts like, and it shall always be so in this universe.

When your heart is full, others' hearts will be full towards you. When you are down and cranky, this is what you can expect to receive all around you. So, be a role model for the world you would like to see. If you want a pleasant world, then be more pleasant, and niceties will play out all around you. Get your own world in order before you go about judging others. Are you the best you can be at all times? I'm sure you're not, so forgive others who are not always at their best also.

Be patient with people and accommodate their whims. They have desires also, which may not always match yours, and so you can feel opposed. Do not butt heads through the opposing desires of others, but come to some agreement and foster harmony. And understand that you cannot win all your desires, all the time, not when you live amongst billions of people on the same planet. Pick the right time to forge ahead with your desires, and know when to step back and with grace let others win.

The desire to fight is inherent in human minds. It comes from the days when you struggled to survive. It is a basic emotion within your consciousness, and it is often triggered when you feel threatened and when your desires are in danger of not being met. Be aware of this prehistoric trait within you that will need to be gelded as you train to become a god. For higher beings cannot be fighting; it is against our tenets and not necessary in our realm.

So, ponder on all that you desire in your life. Could you live without it, or does it move you on? Where are the triggers that set you raging when desires are not met? Let these factions slide away and focus only on what brings you peace.

Desire, truly, is what makes your human world turn. All is focused on the desire for something, and when one desire is alleviated, the next one is already on the burner. Humans have become puppets of those who control the satisfying of desire. Thus, many people are led by their noses, or their genitals, into worlds that do not suit them and bring them down.

So, if you are to live like a god in the higher dimensions of consciousness, desire is something you will have to take a long hard look at and shake it out until it works to bring you Home.

I desire that your desires will always complement your destiny.

Chapter 50 – FALLING FROM GRACE

We have spoken about consciousness at length. Are we friends with it, or is it our enemy? For there will be some parts of our consciousness that we are delighted to fly with, and other parts of our consciousness pull us down again and again.

And so, we must build a bridge to the higher parts and leave the lower parts behind. And this is what all humans must learn to do, to say goodbye to their old ways, their old habitats, their old reactions and beliefs, and make their way across the bridge to the higher world of their consciousness where love prevails and justice and reason and peace.

It is not as though, when you are in the higher world and you have crossed that bridge, that you will remain there forever, basking in delight and the light. For you must maintain your position here, else you are sucked back over that bridge again into the lower realms. So, your daily task is to raise yourself up, to fill your heart with all that is delightful and harmonious, with memories of loveliness and goals of future happiness. When you focus on love, then your world can only be love. But when your thoughts are shrieking with anger and anguish, then this is what your world will reflect back to you, and you will know that you have fallen back over that bridge again and you will need to reverse pedal to get you back to that bridge and cross it.

Be mindful every day where you are. Are you in your lower mind or your higher mind, or zigzagging between the two? Make your mind up to live in the higher world, for why would you choose the pigswill of the nether regions of Earth and of your mind?

Sometimes it is a constant battle to raise yourself up out of the mire. We are cognisant of this fact, for we too have had our battles and know them well, but we cannot keep pulling you out of the muck and the mess that you find yourself in at times. You must learn to get yourself out, and do it fast, and then bathe and cleanse yourself and return to us in Heaven. We will not laugh or jeer at you, that you have fallen on hard times. We welcome you back and delight in your freshness. We bring you back into our circle and get you doing the things that you are destined for.

Do not feel guilty about your tumble, for challenges can be severe and you are not always aware of the right way to deal with them until you have made several attempts and finally become successful. This is the way we learn best, by experimentation and trials. Some of these are not trivial and really put us to the test. But when we survive them and are victorious, then our persona is better tuned to eventually become like a god.

So, always focus on returning to higher climes where the air is much brighter and your heart will feel lighter and more refined. We all have blips on our journeys; the path is never straight and true. Learn to accommodate them and move on quickly, for you do not want to get anchored in the lower worlds, for the deeper you sink, the more effort it will take to get you back to that bridge once again. Do everything you can to settle your heart and make it smile. There is always a silver lining, and a golden one too.

Be prepared in case you fall from grace every now and again, and climb like the devil is behind you, to make tracks out of there and into the place of gods. Your control centre is within your consciousness, so take control and put things right again. Control those thoughts and your emotions. Rein in the negativity and put it all behind you. Create only a beautiful world for yourself to live in, for you are living within your mind.

All the controls are to hand; all you need to do is use them and begin to change the scenes you are projecting. We have learnt about the tools in the toolbox of our mind. Get them out now and utilise them and put them into play. This is what a god would do, and this is how we are training you humans too.

So, if you wake up one morning and you don't like your world, then get out your toolbox and begin to change your mind. All is a reflection; change its source and you will change the view. Everything can be thought about in a different way. Nothing is locked in or set in stone. So, chisel away all that no longer serves you. It doesn't need to be there and patently does you harm.

Open your heart to the love and blissfulness that truly surrounds you. Breathe it in through every pore. Become light-hearted and light-headed. You now know what remarkable things are hidden all around you in this universe. Come back onto an even keel. Find harmony and balance and peace within your mind. It is easy to do when you set it as a target. But if you ignore this work, then chaos will continue to rule. Don't let the lower world retain you in its clutches. Escape from this vibrational miasma as if your life depended on it, which it does. See that bridge and get to it as fast as you can. Make the crossing and know you have survived.

There is no punishment for falling from grace, for you punish yourself through the darkness that invades. Develop wings and fly up high, for once you have tasted the glory of Heaven, the graspings down below will be more than you can bear. We are but a thought away in these heavenly realms. Tune into our wavelengths and get yourself here.

Chapter 51 – MERCY

Let us turn our minds today to a different subject altogether, one that we have not covered before, and that is the subject of mercy.

Many of you will know the quote from Shakespeare's *Merchant of Venice*, "The quality of mercy is not strained. It droppeth as the gentle rain from Heaven." And this is true. Mercy is abundant in the heavens. We are compassionate gods and we forgive all things, for we know that the trail to these higher dimensions is a difficult one and we sometimes get waylaid and forsake ourselves and others.

So, by the time you get to become a god you are well aware for the need for mercy. For you yourself will need to have been forgiven umpteen times and now it is your turn to show this mercy and forgiveness towards others.

Mercy is not so apparent on the earthly plane. In fact, it is darn hard to find in some corners of your planet. There are some humans who do not know what the word 'mercy' means, and they certainly do not ever apply it to those around them. And even in your more refined quarters of your world, where you would like to think you are compassionate and loving and full of grace, mercy there can be in short shrift too. For in your justice system and your courts, in even the most civilised of societies, draconian sentences can be passed down and not a shred of mercy is forthcoming.

In schools, your teachers can be quick with the sword of the tongue, and they are often merciless towards their students, and these young ones are not forgiven for their missed deeds (misdeeds). Surely the quality of mercy needs to be evident in all your schools so that children become accustomed to it and take it with them into adulthood. If mercy is not shown to them, then they will not know how to use it or show it unto others. So, let us bring the subject of mercy and forgiveness and compassion into our schools, and it will create better citizens of our children. And isn't this why we educate them, after all?

The quality of mercy is certainly strained within many families. Parents do not forgive children; children do not forgive parents or siblings. And so, we foster an environment of non-forgiveness. Grudges are stored away, to be brought out again like open wounds in the future. Yet, if we taught people how to utilise forgiveness on the spot so that there was no anger or resentment stored away, think how the world would be much changed. And all families would work together, and all people would cooperate in harmony.

It is not such an odd idea. And it starts with our children and teaching them when they are young. Imagine the outcome of this. There would be no conflicts and no war. And so, you could say that mercy was a foundation stone for this universe. And if we are to build godly societies, then this brick must be used and go in there on the ground floor.

And what about mercy for yourself? Can you forgive the things that you have done, not only in this lifetime but in all your lifetimes past? You have been a child of nature, and you have played out your rawest emotions and desires. Your ethics may have been non-existent in some parts of your journey, and you will have fought to survive in the only ways that you knew how.

So, realise that you were coming from the very lowest parts of your consciousness and that it has been your mission to raise yourself up. Each lifetime you will have refined yourself a little more, and you will have dusted off the dirt and darkness and brought in more light and understanding until you are where you are today. If you are reading these words, you are not that savage of yesteryear. You have improved yourself and transformed. And yet in your psyche, there are memories of your wrongdoings and murderous ways. Let go of these scenes now for they serve you no longer and your consciousness has moved along.

Yes, you did these things and you are guilty. There is not a god amongst us who hasn't been there too. But how does wallowing in your guilt and self-pity serve you now? Intend to be the very best that you can be and administer love in every quarter. Love is mercy, so serve this to yourself. Forgive the experiences that you have gone through and the actions you have taken to keep you safe. Let mercy rain down upon you from your spirit and your soul. Bathe in the richness of this emerald love and no longer weep.

Raise yourself up out of the ashes of your past and be determined to be godly and merciful to all in your path. Until you have forgiven yourself, you will not be able to forgive others in an unconditional way. So, put priority on this task and flood yourself with love and mercy, and bid *adieu* to the old you and your old ways. Cast them out on a boat into the ocean. Send them off with grace and gratitude, and turn around and never look back again.

You are going forwards now up the mountain. And as you crack through into the higher dimensions, mercy will abound. And that forgiveness will make you cry, for there is nothing so sweet as being absolved of all our sins, of being cleansed of the tarnishing that our error-full ways have placed upon us. We are cleansed and cleared of all our past. It feels miraculous, and life ahead will look so blessed.

So, imagine that you have been given a full pardon by a judge, and all traces of your misadventures have been erased from the record books. You are given a clean slate to start anew. How does that feel? This is the quality of mercy.

So, what has been done for you, we ask you to do unto others. Clear their slates for them too. Forgive who they were back in the old days, or even yesterday. Let them work now with a clean path, and you will no longer be an obstacle for them. The joy this will bring you will be immense, for the act of forgiving is comparable to the act of being forgiven. There is a huge releasing and the opportunity to start afresh.

So, let us no more get mired in old grudges and ancient enmity. Feel these lower parts of you fall away, and drink in the new air that will surround you now and watch as new doors open and new vistas are revealed.

Mercy is your tramline, and it will take you to the gods.

Chapter 52 – YOUR TURBINE POWER

Today we are going to speak about turbines, those engines, those motors, that turn things, essentially to produce power, as in hydro-electric schemes.

We will need to have turbines within us, to generate power to get us through the day and through our life. This turbine engine cannot be allowed to just sit idle, for it is a precious piece of equipment and valuable and needs to earn its keep. Your body is on Earth for a reason. It too is a valuable piece of equipment, and it would be a crime to let it just sit there and rust away, for it could be churning out much useful power for yourself and also for those around you and for humanity at large.

There are small turbines and massive turbines, and you will be equipped with the size that you need to complete your mission. Some will have much generating power, and others will be much more small scale. But, nevertheless, they are there to be utilised, so understand how your turbine works and get it going.

Of course, the turbine for a human is in your consciousness. Here you will generate the inflow and the outflow and control it how you want. And what provides the inflow, the food that feeds your turbine? Well, these are your positive thoughts and motivations, your goals and your dreams, your determination to get ahead. This is grist to your mill. And if you don't keep the supply up, then your turbine blades will stop spinning and you will come to a grinding halt.

Every day, you will need to feed your turbine. It is like the engine of a steam locomotive; it cannot run on merely thin air. You must provide the fuel and fodder. And the more you can input, the greater the power your turbine can raise. So, don't stint on shovelling in that fuel. Bring your turbine up to top speed and let it begin generating enough power to serve a nation.

And what will you do with all that power that you have generated in this way? There are no end of creative uses and tasks you can bring to bear. You will find yourself able to fly in every direction, and not just north, south, east, and west, but up and down and diagonally too. You will have the capacity of a dozen humans. Nothing will be too much for you. You will cope and enjoy your ride.

But when your turbine is working at only half power or less, you will notice that you are only just surviving and it is a struggle to get through your day and work. So, if you wish to work at full thrust and not on idle, then spend time every day bringing yourself up to full power. Feed your consciousness with the right thoughts that it needs. Ponder on your dreams and see yourself there. Play out the paths to your destiny. Get creative with your thinking and invent the scenes you need. Visualise the outcomes that you want. Feel into the desires that you want met. All in all, enter that world and find yourself there, and this is the fuel that will feed your turbine.

Most humans are afraid to conjure up their world. They sit by and let it manifest around them from the dreams of others who are utilising their turbines. In this universe you are either power-full or you are power-less. It is up to you to get your turbines going and keep them at full steam. Those who have parked their turbines will feel the price, for they will have no power to change things and then they will complain that the world is so unfair.

All of you have been given a splendid turbine. Not everyone makes the most of it, and some never even crank the handle. Yet it is never too late to start it up and get it going once again. You know what oils your machine, so begin to do it now.

Most people are woefully under-powered, but it is not that their consciousness is under-resourced. They have all the machinery that they need, but they have let it just sit in the shed. So, it is time now to take the covers off if your turbine has been laying low. Give it a cleanse and an oiling. Top it up with right thinking and watch it go. And each time you think that this will never work, you are adding a pollutant into your mix, and it will choke your throttle and make you splutter to a halt. So, clean up your input fuel and things will go more smoothly.

If you have enjoyed these lazy salad days, then we are glad for your joy but now you must get pumping. The energies are forceful that are coming in from the universe and, if you do not have the power to withstand them, then you will be bowled over and powerless to gain any ground.

So, power is important, even whilst we are advocates for love. For love without power behind it can be somewhat ineffectual in getting things done. While it would be wonderful to bask in the pure love of our consciousness, and whilst this treat awaits us in the years to come, in these times we must ensure that we use our power to create, for this world is at a crossroads and our choices now will dictate our fate.

So, becoming powerful is a necessary trait on the path to godhood. We cannot have gods who are ineffectual, or gods that do not have the power to create. And we do not wish for our gods to merely survive, but to thrive. So, let's see those turbines whizzing and ideas being thrown off in every quarter.

Imagine what we can achieve when all our turbines are linked together. The power of the universe is at our fingertips and in our thoughts. So, think today what you could do if you had that kind of power.

Chapter 53 – INTERJECTION OF THE GODS

We are going to go in a different direction again today and cover new and different ground, for it is amazing how much diversity there is in this universe. And this book cannot do it justice, but we will try to cover the most salient points and areas, and then it will be for you to go off exploring by yourselves.

Let us cover something I am calling interjection today. This is an interruption where you might interject your views suddenly into someone else's conversation, or you might place yourself in a position where really you might not be wanted or appreciated. So, you are injecting yourself or your views, perhaps at an inopportune time or in an inappropriate manner. You are stopping the flow of what has gone before and making known what you think or what you wish to do.

There are obviously right times and places for interjections, but make sure that you are not interjecting merely to get your own way or your own needs met. The gods learn how to converse and debate respectfully, and take everyone's opinions into the mix for consideration so that a conversation does not become a spiteful fight. Everyone wants to be heard, and when gods converse, they will bide their time until it is the right time, for they know and trust that they will be heard.

Also, gods will not push themselves into the middle of action that is not right for them. They will observe and know their place, and when they have understanding, they will manoeuvre themselves into position where they know they will be of value.

We are interjecting our gods now into the earthly world, and they must find their rightful positions here if they are to play a useful part. They cannot be everywhere at once, for now they are limited by a human body. Their consciousness can be broadcast worldwide, but physically they will be subject to the same limitations as a human.

Some of our more senior gods, it is true, will be able to teleport their bodies around the planet and further afield. But our younger gods, our junior gods, will not have mastered this trick yet, so they are forced to use transport like everyone else. I hear all you junior gods sighing, for I know that this is one tool of consciousness that you would love to master. It is coming, my dear friends, all in good time. Consciousness must learn to travel first, and then the physical body shall follow.

So, where shall we put all these gods that are interjecting your earthly plane? Have we marked out positions for them? Will they slot right in? Will all be smoothed over for them so they can hit the ground running and play their part? To a large extent, this will be true, for there has been much organisation in the higher dimensions over many years. This is not a recent whim that we come down here. This idea has been in the making for centuries, since the plan was first laid. And now it is unfolding, and gods are being revealed.

You know now that they will not be carrying calling cards that say their name and state that they are a god, for we will be, for the most part, undercover. The world will not be aware of this interjection. People will go about their business unaware of who is standing beside them or making their tea.

Humans generally will not know when a god is in their midst. But those who can feel energies and who are partial to love, they will pick up on the presence of these gods. And their minds will become alert, and alarms will be going off to bring to their notice the calibre of the person right beside them. If you are on the same wavelength, then you will definitely pick this up. And if you act at lower frequencies, a god's presence will either warm you or strike you like a thunderbolt to wake you up.

The presence of a god is not always a happy occasion for some, for a god's energies will stir you up, agitate you, and bring all your scum to the top. This probably won't be pleasant, for either you or the god. But be thankful to this teacher for they are helping you on your path.

The gods may hold your hand for a little while and point you to the road that is right. But do not expect them to hang around forever, for as you can appreciate, they have many clients they must get to see.

When a god comes into your remit, open your heart and surrender to their love. You may think this is obvious, but they will unsettle you and make you cry. The joy that you initially feel might turn into indignation, for this god has come to transform you, not just to bring you love and peace. Transformation takes a lot of work, and any god that you meet will drive you hard. They won't have time for resistors or the rebellious amongst you. They will work with their supporters, and once transformed, they will then move on. Do not think to bag yourself a god that you can keep in your pocket to play with every day. They have massive tasks to accomplish, so make your time with them count and then bless them on their way.

Some of you may be lucky and set up home with a god. But then you will need to be a god yourself, for remember, like attracts like, and it can never be any other way. So, if you would like to attract a god, then you must be godly yourself. And you will be expected to have the traits of a god, which I have mentioned in other chapters, and you will be expected to do the job of a god, which is to transform humans in this world. So, if you are not prepared to be like this and act like this, then do not apply for this post. For being a god takes much training, and, to act like a god, all the human must be left behind.

So, whether you are a god or not a god, you are all mingling on this planet. The interjection has already begun. Look around you and feel your way towards these gods. We hope you know them when you find them.

Chapter 54 – THE WEATHER OF YOUR MIND

Let us speak about rainbows today, for they are a beautiful part of our lives. And who is not impressed when they see a rainbow appearing through a rainy sky? So, rainbows can give us a feeling of hope, that even though the skies are grey and rain is pouring down, rays of sunshine are poking through, helping us to believe that a sunnier day is on its way.

Rainbows, of course, are made from light, white light refracted into many colours. And it is light that always gives us hope for better times. For we are made from light at our most basic level, and we resonate with light and it stirs our soul. So, if you are needing to feel a little brighter, then get yourself a picture of a rainbow or conjure one up in the skies.

And you might wonder where the ends are coming down into. Where is the specific place where the ends of the rainbow meet the Earth? Your legends will tell you that these are the places where you shall find pots of gold. Well, the light will always lead you to golden treasure, whether or not it is on the end of a rainbow.

So, think of rainbows when your world is dark and dull, for these skies do not last forever. The sun always breaks through and warms your soul again. The sun is light and it provides the fire for our being. When we are feeling flat and unenthused, we might want to take some of that fiery sun and place it in our hearts. All of us need the spark of life to keep us going. Without it we are dead. So, place the sun within your heart and miracles will happen to boost your energy and verve.

It is the sun that causes rainbows, and they will appear in your heart too. Let the sun drive away your rainy day, and let the rainbow lead you on to new horizons. Follow that rainbow and see what you will find.

There is definitely treasure at the end of that road. But if you just sit there in a puddle with your umbrella up, then the treasure will not be discovered and you will be the poorer for this.

So, when you are in a rainstorm and battling deluges and floods, picture the sun coming out to play, and follow that rainbow that is bridging from your heart. The world is for the taking if you can just get up and explore. You will not discover much sitting in your armchair, or crouching beneath the brolly, hoping you don't get wet.

Rainstorms that hover like a cloud in your life are good opportunities for you to seek the sun. You can do this physically by moving to some tropical locale. But it is even easier to change the climate in your consciousness and bring on those sunny days. You can stir up a thunderstorm or imagine a clear, sunny day. It is up to your choosing, and I know which one I'd plump for, any day.

Thunderstorms are useful, for they sometimes clear the air. All is refreshing afterwards, especially when the sun comes out and glints on the scene. Yet you would not want a thunderstorm day after day. It would be too oppressive and jangle your nerves and make you scream, "Stop!" And even sunshine on a daily basis can become a little tedious, and you might wish for some seasonal change.

You can manage the climate in your consciousness and make the weather of your world as you wish. So, don't just sit there and complain about the rain, not the rain outside your windows but the rain inside your mind. Cut through the gloom and go and find the sun. Install its light within your consciousness and let its brightness reign (rain).

And if there is a drought in your consciousness and no rain to be seen, and the sun is beating down mercilessly and nothing is growing in your fields, then picture the sweet life-giving rain, fertilising your world outside and within. Get planting new ideas and create a better world. What you are experiencing in the land around you is a reflection of what is going on in your mind. So, if you know what will make your fields flourish, then apply this process to the fields within your mind.

I'm all for rain and rainbows, for they are life-giving and directional too. But it is the sun and the light that is needed every day, for there is magic in those sunbeams; there is life in those sun rays.

So, become aware of the weather in your mind, and liken it to what is going on outside your walls. As an individual you may not have that much influence, but as a community your group consciousness creates your climate. So, if you do not like the climate where you live, then perhaps other wavelengths are calling out for you. For every community has its own vibration, and if you no longer fit there then you'll need to be moving on. It is not that you will find the perfect climate, but it will be the perfect climate right for you.

So, think of this next time you complain about the clouds, or the ceaseless heat, or the aridity, or the floods. How are you contributing to the climate of your town? And are you happy with the weather as it plays out in your consciousness every day?

You are the controller of your weather. Climate change is here. How is it working out for you?

Chapter 55 – SET YOURSELF FREE

Let us take a step back, a step back in time, and let us muse on yesteryear. And we can amuse ourselves no end, thinking back on past lives, past relationships, past deeds of valour, and past mistakes. Our consciousness hoards all this information. There is no detail left unstored. And so, at any time we may review this scene or that, even if it is prehistoric or from another world. Consciousness makes no judgement about what it stores away. It is a faithful recorder of history.

And so, we may know that we can access these records at any time and know the truth. But why would you want to swim in these archives, unless you were doing some archaeological research or your genealogical tree? We don't recommend turning over all your old rubbish and bones. For you have lived many lives and, indeed, there are many tales to tell, but these were all just experiences that have made you who you are today.

You might like to know you were Lady this or King that, or that you had a talent in this area or a penchant for that. But apart from being entertaining, where does that get you right now? We would rather that you let go of this storehouse of information and focus on the present and where you are headed to in the future. Just because you had a starring role in one life, does not mean that you will follow on with other starring roles in the future. Of course, we will always want you to be a star. But fame and fortune are not the reason for your mission, but becoming a star of loving ways is.

So, take your head out of the paths that lie behind you and turn around and now look straight ahead. It is what is coming up that is important. So, gauge yourself to see if you are ready, to face your incoming destiny.

Certainly, your path will catch you by the ankles and try to drag you down. You must be willing to kick it away, sever it at the knees, and fly off into the levels of the higher dimensions. Do not let those cords keep you attached to the lower realms. Unhitch those anchors and set yourself free. Open yourself to the brand-new vista, the one that lies ahead. Do not dwell on the past, for in those areas you will all too easily find excuses to stay behind. I am not saying to walk away from your present family and friends, but walk away from all your past ideas and beliefs that hold you. Free yourself from what limits you and keeps you from moving on.

If you were to have your consciousness scraped clean, there would be no fears or inhibitions or procrastination or wondering how. You would merely step forwards into your new world, not knowing of any dangers or wary or hesitant to take your steps.

Often you will find that people who have been successful will say they would never have taken that road if they had foreseen all that that road would hold for them along the way. And so, fearlessly and blindly, they have made their way along their path, conquering challenges as they came up but not being frightened to move their feet forwards. As we become older, we become more cautious, for we know what may face us along the way. And so, we choose to hold back in case we may get hurt, and we never dance towards our destiny for we do not have the nerve.

So, if we can shake out these fears and old beliefs, and make our consciousness like a young person's once again, then life's experiences will not get in our way. We will not say, "Oh, I have been down that path and it was a calamity. I'm not going there again." When we don't remember these calamities, then we are free to choose the road that needs to be taken.

Our life experiences program our consciousness, and this then forces us down a certain set of tracks. And we find we cannot turn off onto new rails because the points are set to the old tracks, and we cannot find the lever that will change them.

It is very rare that you would need to go down only one set of tracks in your life. There are many branch lines to be taken, and your destiny will take you exploring in every direction until you know which tracks are right for you. So, don't lock yourself into one track. Allow the universe to change your points every now and then. Find yourself being shunted in a new direction and enjoying the new vistas and laughing as the landscape goes by.

But if you have put your train into a siding, cossetting it from any harm or eventful journey, then all that will happen will be that you rust up and die. We would have you hurtling down your tracks to freedom, enjoying your ride like a rollercoaster at the fair. Let your spirit sphere take you off those human tracks and onto heavenly ones, then you are not stuck on the ground but can fly through space and other dimensions. Open your heart and let your consciousness fly. There is so much of this universe to yet explore. Do not tie yourself down to an armchair on Earth.

Let go of who you have been and embrace who you are becoming now. There are lands upon lands waiting for your presence (presents). Lift yourself into this new state of being and begin to experience yourself as the god you came here to be.

Chapter 56 – ARE YOU LOST?

Let us be making tracks to our destiny, for it calls to us, it urges us on, and we would be a fool to deny it. Let us sometimes stop in our tracks and take our bearings and check that we are heading in the right direction, for if we are only one degree off we shall certainly miss our target in the end. So, every now and then, check your trajectory. Are you spot on the mark? Are you where you need to be at this time, in exactly the right place and surrounded by the right people?

You will not know this if you keep headlong into the fray, head looking down as if you are entering into some chill wind. Look up, look straight ahead, look all around you. What is going on that you need to be a part of, or need to be set free of? If you are just bustling along in your own little world, regardless of the world around you, then you may be missing some vital signs and clues. For these are set out by your soul to keep you going and guide you on the right road so you'll get Home.

Stop and feel into your heart and use it as a compass and set your sights for there. You will know if you are on the wrong road, for you will not be sitting pretty. There will be an uncomfortableness to your life, a feeling of something not quite right, a feeling of not fitting in. And you may be aware of this edginess to yourself but you suppress it, telling yourself that life is never perfect and you must just strive to keeping on.

Yet, let me tell you, when you are riding the right tracks to your destiny, there is a feeling of buoyancy and eagerness and joy. The road feels like silk and you are happy to keep sliding on. If your road is jarring you and you are upset by all the humps and bumps and inclement weather, then you might like to ponder if this is the right road for you. For, although we gods like to set you challenges, we also want you to feel that this is the true way for you to go. Challenges and obstacles do not mean that you are on the wrong road, but outside of that challenge you will feel strong and sturdy and ready to do what it takes. You are eager to overcome all hurdles. Nothing is going to stop you from reaching that winner's post.

So, if you are not feeling this keenness within you, that determination to succeed at all cost, then perhaps the goal that you are working towards is not the right one. For you will need a dream that carries you through all things, a dream you never let go of, that helps you ride all waves.

Many are those who are doing things half-hearted and then they abandon their cause at the second hurdle. You will need a cause that fires your heart, that will see you sweep away all obstacles, and stand firm on your behalf. If you cannot imagine yourself winning, then it is over before it has begun. So, put aside your doubts and worries, and set off with a clean heart and determined intention to see it through until the end.

If you cannot find a reason to set your heart on fire, then you will need to ponder where you are and where you want to get to. For I have said it a million times: you need to dream up your future. And many have that dream and then put it away again, for it is in the too-hard basket and you cannot imagine the steps to get there.

So, you must train your consciousness to dream the dream, perhaps the secret dream, that you would love to go for. Do not allow your mind to give you a thousand reasons why it should not be. Everything is possible between you and your spirit. Never let the naysayers get you down.

Imagine your dream, imagine it right now. Don't let your focus wander. Imprint it on your mind. Now get your spirit to make you a plan of action. Let your dream tantalise you to get going. Let your spirit fill in the steps to get there. Your dream is not a mirage; it is something that calls you on. Follow that calling with all your heart and soul, and you'll be amazed at what starts springing up in your life that serves your purpose. And before you know it, you'll be halfway there.

But, no dream, then no action. You might as well choose your coffin and take yourself to your grave. For your dreams are what you are meant for. You came here to dream and to make those dreams come true. So, do not fold up those dreams and put them away in some bottom drawer.

Discover your purpose and remember what makes your heart sing. Open your heart fully, where before it's been folded in half. Face up to your future and take action to follow your dream.

Do not discard your dreams as being some kind of folly. This is just an excuse you are using so that you do not have to find a way to go off and chase that dream. No dream is foolish. It is the desire of your soul. It is your clue. So, be the best detective and follow all those clues. You never know what it will lead to—the most interesting discovery of your life.

So, are you on track or are you clueless? Ponder on your route or you'll get lost. Your consciousness has all the answers that you need. So, dig around in your mind and find your map. Your spirit and your soul know the path that you must follow. Tap into their guidance and you will see the signs. You know when you feel lost, so come on and admit it and take advice.

Be brave enough to hold your dream, then your path shall be revealed in all its glory.

Chapter 57 – MANAGING YOUR CREW

This business of consciousness is a complicated thing. It is not all one level and layer. There are many pockets and niches in your consciousness, many pathways and tunnels to explore. And down each pathway you will find a new persona, part of yourself. And you will need to come to know this part of yourself if you are to understand your consciousness wholly.

So, do not be surprised at what you find down these tunnels, for there are very many aspects to yourself and all of them like to play out now and again. So, today you might be like this and tomorrow a completely different person. And you might put it down to the phases of the moon but, in truth, you are merely trying on the different hats in your consciousness.

So, who are you really? Well, you are a combination, a conglomeration, of all these hats and personas. All the many different experiences you have had in this life, and in others, have served to make you who you are today. But you are not a homogenous, one-size-fits-all personality. You have different shades and shadows. And to one person you will show this face, and to another person you will show a different one.

So, you are not the same person every day. You are picking up different threads of yourself, depending on the energies surrounding you and coursing through you. And these energies will come from other people and their consciousnesses, and also from the stars and planets and consciousnesses of the gods. So, you are bombarded daily with different directives and urgings. And you are responding and reacting to these, and, depending on your inner programming, will see you take this action or that.

Some days there is the perfect storm, and all your personas come out in fright and fear, and they clamour for your attention and for all their needs to be met. And on these days you will feel like you are having a nervous breakdown, for managing all the different aspects of yourself can be more than you can cope with.

So, you will need to assuage all your different personas, maybe even one by one, and you will need to calm them and bring them back into harmony. For if any one of your personas is upset, then you will feel unbalanced and not quite right. And what is it that upsets your personas? Well, anything that they have not resolved from their past. And so, speak with this part of yourself and understand their issue, and negotiate a resolution so that you can feel balanced once again.

You can have thousands of different personas, all residing in your consciousness at once. This does not make you schizophrenic, but you need to be aware that you are more than the sum total of all your parts. Just as your human body has many parts that work independently with differing functions, they must also work together to create the being that is you. So, too, does your consciousness consist of many independent parts, but if they do not work together and cooperate for a common cause, then you will get disease and illness if one part decides to take over and play a major role.

Your consciousness needs to be a cooperative, all parts contributing whatever they do that is of value. But when one part has a miasma, then shockwaves will course through your consciousness and shake things up.

So, it is beholden on you to treat all parts of yourself like your employees or your children. You'll need to do the very best for them, listen to their concerns, and resolve them. We cannot have your inner personas causing rebellion, for this is trouble and will lead you into pain. So, let us work with each aspect of ourselves, smooth over those troubled waters, and bring in calm. Sometimes a riot will take place and there is a major upset within your consciousness. Sometimes this is warranted, for transformation is on the cards. And sometimes your personas need to be prised from their positions and sent on their way so better employees can take their place.

You would not credit that all this goes on within your consciousness, but it is just like managing a business or running a school. You have all these different individuals you must take into consideration. You cannot ride roughshod over them and neglect their well-being or their dreams. You are the CEO or the Principal of your consciousness. Are you doing a good job, or is rebellion bubbling up within the ranks? Quell all these disturbances or things might get out of hand. Don't see the offenders as troublemakers but listen to their complaints, for they may have valid issues.

This management of your consciousness stands you in good stead when you become a god. For once you have learnt to manage your own self, then managing others will be a walk in the park. For your own personas within you will be trickier than anyone else you will get to meet. When you have a handle on your own parts, then you will know very well how to handle the personas of others.

You will know those days on which your personas are acting as upstarts, for you will feel this rocking of the boat within and you will know something is not right, even if you do not know the cause. So, take some time to investigate these troubled waters, for with a little bit of love and patience you can often calm ruffled feathers in the shortest space of time. Practise your diplomacy and kindness and trust. Do not be angry with these parts of yourself. They are reacting in the only way they know how, from how they have been programmed. Understand this programming and change it if you can, just as you would change a starter motor in an engine if it was coughing in fits and starts.

You are responsible for the smooth running of your consciousness. Do not blame others when things go awry. You are the captain of your ship and the buck stops with you. Don't let your ship go down for the want of a nail or a Band-Aid. Investigate and interview your troubled crew. Melt dissension in the ranks and show your mercy.

There are many reasons why your personas can come unravelled, for each day you are growing and facing new challenges and paths. Be aware when you are making big transitions that not all your personas will feel on board. You cannot hope to drag all the parts of yourself into new levels without some of them resisting and objecting to this move. So, I say again, work with your crew and get them to be a team. You cannot have insubordination, for you are the captain and you must head your ship towards your destiny.

Sort out your crew and get them all on side, or give them the option to leave and never come back again. What happens to these members who you decide to let go? You will set them free with love and graciousness and melt them back into the greater consciousness where their experiences can play out in other ways. You never need to punish a member of your crew, for they have faithfully done the job that you have allocated to them in times past. Now you are asking of them new skills, new understanding, and sometimes they just cannot cope with this and it is better that they go Home.

In their place you will bring in a new aspect of your consciousness, one more suited to these times. You will set them up with all the right thinking and they will be programmed to serve you well.

So, think upon this and how your consciousness is really working. You are not who you suppose yourself to be. You are a being of many parts and mysteries.

Chapter 58 – EXPLORE YOUR GALAXY

Let us be getting on with more of our adventure into the unknown and the unseen. For there are miles and miles of landscapes to examine and we will never get to the end of them, not in this lifetime or any other. This universe is boundless, and more is being created as we speak. So, how could we hope to ever get around it all?

So, let us be satisfied with our own locale in this universe, our own section that we live in and that we can reach without too much trouble, for there is plenty enough to keep us occupied here. We do not need to go to the other side of the universe and explore those realms. For they are very different from your locality, and you would not understand them even if I tried to explain them to you. Suffice to say that one day you will know more.

But your own neighbourhoods are equally charming and inviting. So, let us stay within our own galactic quarter and then what I tell you will make sense to you, for you will be able to identify with these things. There is more than enough startling cosmos for you to see and get to know without travelling beyond the boundaries of your galaxy.

There are many many stars in your region, countless numbers, and each star hosts civilisations of its own. You did not think that you were the only ones out there, did you? For your galaxy is teeming with races of beings, some like yourselves and the gods, and others quite different, not anything like yourselves. And within your own Earth, you will know the diversity of sentient beings that occupy this land. So, why shouldn't there be a similar diversity of beings in your neighbourhood?

You will not get to meet alien beings in this lifetime except for the forms of us gods. We are the vanguards for your future generations, those who will put out the olive branch and get to meet their neighbours in the planets and the stars. We have spoken about this before, and I have described how you are not yet ready. When this planet is at peace, then can be the time for you to explore beyond your borders.

And yet your consciousness can travel near and far. You are not limited in your journeys. Your spirit sphere can set off and explore. And so, let your spirit do just that. Let it take a turn around this universe. Let it swing over to this galaxy and that. It will put things into perspective for you and help you stop focusing on the minutiae of a tedious life. It will raise you up several levels, for you will become acquainted with what is going on in the background of this universe. And you will see that your petty quarrels on Earth are not significant in the greater scheme of things. And you will stop worrying about the small stuff, for the greater stuff will take over your heart. And there will be much to feel contented about when you understand what is driving the universe and all beings forwards.

You will lose interest in the human way of things. You will want to live above them, out of the firing zone and out of the muck and mire. You will be elevated into a new dimension. And here you will feel like you can fly, such will be the smoothness of your movements.

But you cannot do this from your armchair or even from your car. You must first step into your spirit sphere, take over the controls, and begin to become an ace. Conquer your consciousness and you will conquer all the worlds. You may have a tiny body down on Earth, but you have multiple bodies living in the cosmos and flying through space and time. You are not stuck in this one lower dimension, but you are free to travel at will. So, grab your passport and explore these realms. There is much to discover to your delight and to your benefit.

I could sit here and describe all the worlds that you might see, but it would be like me describing Hawaii or St. Petersburg or Antarctica or the Alps. You have to be there to experience these things first-hand. For this is what fills the soul, and this is what makes you who you are. You cannot educate others if you've never been there yourself.

So, get yourself into all sorts of situations, on this planet and elsewhere. You cannot become a god of the highest order if you don't leave your home and get out into life. So, stir up your heartstrings and play a new tune. Determine to expand your horizons, to grow your consciousness, and fill your heart. Do not go out of this world with little more than what you came in with. Let your consciousness have been given a workout. Let you be a few steps further on than the ones you took as a baby.

Some of you will, of course, have gone backwards, and it's sad to tell that tale, but for many of you it's good to see your progress. Even jumping one level is better than none at all. But you are still on Earth now, and there is time to go exploring. Open your eyes to what has been hidden from you before. Embrace this new knowledge and make it work for you.

This world is spinning into a vortex, and you will want to be there at the upper end. Those in the centre will get shaken until they break. For breaking hearts open is the mandate of us gods.

You choose at which level you wish to live at. It is nothing to do with governments or gods. Your consciousness sets the yardstick, and you attract all at that level to live and work by. So, if your life is not suiting you, then raise your consciousness as early as today. You do not need to sit in the pigswill. You can fly high above it and live your life in light.

When will you understand that you are not just human? Your god self is waiting for you to return. And we don't mean by dying, but by living, living your life to your spirit's standards, raising yourself up to meet their bar.

Are you feeling love and a sparkling in your heart? If not, why not? For now you know what you must do.

Chapter 59 – DEATH

Let us return today to a subject that we have embraced before and elucidate on it in more detail. I am speaking about the subject of death, a subject that is quite taboo in your human world, which is surprising when everyone must face it at some time or another. And you will have faced death thousands of times before in your previous lives, sometimes peacefully and sometimes with great trauma.

So, let us not be afraid to face this subject that will definitely confront us one day. Most of us would like to put it off for a few more years yet. So that you can do what, I ask? Have more fun? Complete a project? Earn more money? Watch your children grow up?

You will be allowed to stay on this planet as long as you are making tracks towards your destiny. And even the worst of sinners do have a destiny to unfold. But if you are denying your destiny and have walked away from it, turned your back on it and have no intention of seeing it out, then you are just taking up space on this beautiful planet and your soul will make plans to bring you back Home, whether you like it or not.

That may seem cruel and unempathetic, but your soul has a job to do, to evolve you to a higher level, and if you go off dancing down a street which is far removed from that desired level, then you will meet with your end sooner rather than later. And even the way that is chosen for you to die will be a lesson for you to ponder on when you get Home.

If you are given a reasonable hiatus in which to dwell upon your upcoming death, then this is a chance for you to get back on your road. And you may be able to beat the odds and undergo a healing, and you will be much changed within your consciousness and take a new track, aligned more to your soul.

Sometimes it has been prearranged that you will leave this planet at this time or another. And this is not so much for your benefit but to provide lessons for those around you. Everyone is affected by the death of a loved one, and this can sometimes be what is needed to crack those hearts wide open.

And then there are times when humans are whisked right off this planet—no warning, no alarm bells. They are suddenly gone and they had no time to prepare. We should not judge that these people are all bad, for sometimes it is the nature of things for souls to recall their creations urgently back Home. Perhaps there is a new mission for them to undertake. Perhaps their reason for being on Earth has changed out of all recognition and a new plan needs to be made.

And some humans are just snatched away before they can do more harm, not only to others but also to themselves. Even a god can get into a downward spiral from which it might take eons to recover if their life wasn't cut short and they were returned back to the sanity of the heavenly realms.

Your planet can be a sinkhole for many beings, humans and gods alike, and we will go in there and save our finest if we see them falling too far and too fast. So, do not think that just because you are a god, roaming the pathways of this planet, that you are exempt from any call-back before your time.

Your soul is under strict instructions to monitor the health of your mission. If you are in danger of falling foul of a productive result, then know you might get that tap on the shoulder at any time—unless, of course, you change your mind.

Your consciousness is capable of turning on a sixpence or a dime. It has all the merits of flexibility if you can only allow it to follow the tracks that it must. When your human ego takes over and dictates the path to your soul, then you are lost and your soul is crying, and all the plans for this lifetime turn to dust.

Your tenure on this Earth is not secured by you and you alone. You are here by the courtesy of your soul. You were placed here through their consciousness, and you will be taken back Home when they feel the time has come. There is nothing you can do to plead your case and get remission, except by turning back to your path and taking the action to complete your destiny. If it is all too much for you, then you will go Home. Your soul is not in favour of dragging part of its consciousness through this world, resistant and rebellious to its calling. This part of consciousness that you are, will be better served in another dimension. Here there are beings that will work with you until you see your truth.

Are you afraid to move on to the hidden worlds? You should not be, for they are places of love and graciousness. You will find succour here and your rebelliousness will just melt away. And you will understand the reasons for your demise back on Earth, and you will probably rue your actions and ask to be given another chance.

You will not be popped straight back onto this planet. There is much learning and preparation to be done. With your soul you will identify your next mission. And perhaps it won't be on Earth, but another planet or star system in a galaxy far beyond.

Know that when you return Home your consciousness remains the same. You won't have a physical body of a human, but your mind will keep thinking many of the same old thoughts. There is a transition period while your consciousness adjusts to your new state. Then, just like on Earth, your consciousness will have new experiences and you will learn how to let go of your old self and prime yourself for a new role.

Then one day in the future you will touch down again in some physical world. And once again you will go through all the motions, of baby to toddler, through childhood, to becoming an adult, all the while making tracks towards your destiny.

And so it has been for many millennia as you have evolved throughout the life of this universe. It is up to you how far and fast you go. Staying trapped in the lower dimensions is your choice every time. So, do not renege on your mission. Understand what you came here to do and get it done. Your soul knows your plan, so tap into their consciousness and share in their wisdom. Work with your soul. You are their child and you are a team. When you go AWOL or give them the finger, your soul will need to rein you in and make plans to bring you Home.

Death is inevitable for you, but you can choose the light way or the dark way, and feel fulfilled when it's time to go.

Chapter 60 – REPROGRAMMING YOUR CONSCIOUSNESS

Let us speak about celebrating the assets of consciousness rather than all those challenges we have been delving into lately.

You will find that once you have killed off all those old segments of your consciousness that no longer serve you or support you, that you feel like you are floating on air, for you will be much lighter without all that baggage. Your consciousness is no longer weighed down. So, now you are free to rise up to higher levels, and it is effortless as you float there, rising it seems as if on thermals. And, of course, from a greater height you are going to see more clearly from your advantageous view.

When you are utilising your consciousness properly then life can begin to feel quite rosy. You will feel like you are on top of things rather than underneath a mallet. And your heart will be wide open and smiling at every face you meet. It is as if you find love in these higher dimensions, which indeed you will do for it is all around you here. But you will feel that special effect that love brings to us when we are in the first bloom of some new romance.

But it won't matter if you have a partner or not, for your soul and spirit are now your partners, and you will never feel a space vacated in your heart again. For when you are in love with your own soul and spirit, then you become in love with your whole world, on Earth and in Heaven. There is a change of attitude within yourself and you are prepared to look kindly upon others, and mercy washes over you and you give of your heart and your wisdom.

So, in your consciousness, one good day can become the timbre of your life. You don't have to wait for a sunny day or for someone to say some kind words. You don't have to have lost weight, or snared a new job, or won the lottery. From within your consciousness you have all the controls to make each moment of your life brim with joy. Sure, there are always tedious mundane jobs to be done, but you can do these with a lightness of heart. You will be filled with motivation for the more important tasks that come your way. You will feel eager to make some progress and be profoundly grateful for the gods and angels and spirits that help you on your way.

You might think that this could never happen to you, that every day there could be sunshine, and your heart will sparkle with joy and fulfillment and inner peace. All those times you have struggled with issues throughout your day, how can it ever be any better unless these issues go away? I am here to tell you that issues are here to stay. The world and the universe will be stuffed full of issues, but that doesn't mean to say that you must let them get you down.

When your consciousness is firing on all cylinders, you will merely look at an issue and say, "Okay, what are the steps to resolve this? Let me get it done without delay." Issues will become grist to your mill. You will power through them like a lawnmower over grass. You will not groan and hide your head and run away. You will feel the power within you to take charge of your life and help issues go away.

We have spoken before about the toolbox of your mind, and how consciousness is your magic wand if only you would use it. And I will reiterate this theme once again here and now; your consciousness contains everything that you need to be a winner in this world and successfully negotiate this universe. It is all the collateral things that you have added into your mind that hold you back and prevent you from seeing clearly the road before you. So, use your consciousness as a road sweeper. Get rid of all this detritus and forge ahead on the path to your destiny.

You will know your thinking that keeps you trapped and stuck. Admit it to yourself and unhinge it and throw it away. Reprogram that space with more supportive thoughts. Who is it that you want to be? Begin to think like that.

Most people rarely think about the thinking in their minds. They flow along on autopilot, never deigning to check if this thought is right for them. You would be up in arms if your computers did not work the way you wanted them to, yet when you yourselves act and react from faulty programming, you rarely do anything to change that basic code. So, if you keep doing things that make your life unpalatable, stop and change that programming and do yourself a favour and give yourself a more productive result.

You cannot blame others for the way your life has turned out. You are the engineer of your world. You have created it from all your previous thinking. If it looks like a dog's breakfast, then isn't it time to get out your spanner and do some maintenance work? The majority of humans never service their consciousness throughout their entire lives. They are like sponges and take all the world's thinking into them, never filtering or rearranging or deleting or throwing out.

So, you must be discerning about what you are letting in. Challenge all the data that comes your way on a daily basis. Is this good stuff to store for later, or is it drivel that you're not letting in? And then, of course, there are the layers and layers of thinking already laid down. This is the programming that runs you. Do you enjoy how you are reacting, or is there something dubious about your programming that you will need to call to task?

I hear many people say, "I wish I could be like this or like that," and yet they do not go into their consciousness to adjust their thinking that would take them onto that path. Most humans accept they are who they are. They would not dream of recalibrating and setting their programming higher. Your consciousness is the core of you, your very source. If you wish to be this or have that, then it is to your consciousness that you go and edit your thinking. It is not as if it costs money to alter your mind. Consciousness is free to everyone, and all updates are free and only require your time.

Your consciousness is a machine that can do anything and go anywhere. How are you driving this superb vehicle? Do you even know what it is capable of? Have you put it through its trials? Many humans just accept their consciousness is like a family sedan. Yet, for some of you, you will have luxury models, or the equivalent of racers and the envy of your world. Any one of you can be the owner of the most fantastic vehicle you could own, for your consciousness is there with you right now. It is the best vehicle you will ever get to drive.

Chapter 61 – WHEELS OF THE UNIVERSE

Let us move into new territory today, for I have a mind to show off some things that we haven't delved into before. So, hold onto your hats and your seats for you might be surprised at these discoveries.

I am going to speak about wheels today. Yes, wheels that go around in a circular motion. The universe is very much into wheels, into cycles, into things that will come around with constancy on a regular basis. For the universe likes to check how it has evolved since the first pass. And as it sweeps around again, in a similar motion and triggering off similar situations, it can gauge how it has risen in consciousness as it works through these same issues once again. It is not that the universe is masochistic and wishes to delve into the same pain time and time again, but really, as you can see, this is the only way to interpret if its consciousness has learnt the things it must during the revolution of this cycle.

Now, some cycles are brief—maybe only 24 hours, and some cycles might be 24 millennia or even more. And there are cycles within cycles, making things a little complicated. But the universe will have its finger on the pulse and will ascertain what has moved forwards and what work there is still yet to do.

Your whole life as a human, and indeed even as a spirit, is about working through cycles within cycles. And some of these are more important than others; they are milestones in your career. So, every now and again you will need to take stock, as one cycle comes to an end and another begins. And this is where astrology plays an important part, for the cycling of your planets will determine where you are.

You will probably feel these cycles affecting you, for they stir up your energies, and your consciousness begins to get new ideas and urges. And if you understand your astrology, you will know where these come from and why it is time to look anew at the life before you. As I have stated before, nothing in this universe can ever stand still. All is in perpetual motion.

And although at times you might think that your life is going nowhere, you are always being rolled forwards and there will come a time when you stand before a gate. And this is the time where you roll from one cycle into another and so you begin a lap again.

Some cycles are so long that you will not complete a circuit in one lifetime. But your consciousness will continue this journey, and your next lifetime, and even others ahead of that, will work through this cycle until you move to higher ground.

So, you are spiralling upwards always, and when you finish a cycle you will be back at the same point as you began but hopefully now at a higher level, and definitely hopefully not at a lower one.

When you come to these bookends that mark the end and the start of a cycle, there will be time for review and reflection on what has gone before. Then you will be shown some opportunities for the future, and it is up to you and your soul to choose which way you go.

Upon your death as a human this same process happens too. So, you could call the cycles within your lifetime mini lives and deaths that you must go through. The end of a cycle is like the death of that phase of your life. So, be appreciative of what has gone before and now look ahead to what is coming in the future. Do not resist and try to hold on to all that is old. The wheels move implacably forwards. You cannot stop them or halt them. You cannot retain everything as it is and expect no changes.

The trees do not seek to hold onto their leaves in winter. The universe is about growth, and you too must grow every year and shake off those old leaves and be prepared to blossom anew in spring. So, as one cycle closes and another opens, open your heart and mind too. Be aware and avidly look forward to those new opportunities for fresh growth. You would not want to stand as a bare tree for this whole cycle, so grab yourself some new clothes and face the sun and develop those new buds.

If you look at your life as a series of cycles, you perhaps won't feel so static and will allow yourself to move forwards with those wheels. There are no brakes to this universe and you cannot stop your progress, for the cogs will keep turning on. Rather, then, align yourself with this machinery of your life. Know that one door is always closing and another opening, that you cannot be a snapshot and keep things from moving on.

Be thankful for each day as you move throughout your cycles. Appreciate what they are giving you and each moment that you are alive. But the next day is always a new adventure, and the cogs click forward and you slide further towards your destiny.

When you are on holiday you always enjoy your journeys. Think of your whole life in this way, that every day is a holiday and you are journeying towards a new destination. Even if you are just going to the same shops that you visit every day, you never know what encounters you might have there. There is space for growth in every moment of your day.

When you step out of your door and think to yourself, "I wonder what could happen while I am away?" then you invite all kinds of adventures into your life, for you are open to these opportunities and your adventurous spirit will invite the universe to play.

So, think not that your life is the same-old, same-old, for no two seconds are alike, if truth be told. You never go over the same ground twice, and it is never Groundhog Day, for the energies are bringing you new situations in every moment. The machinery of the universe is playing out on a great scale. And even though you might think, at the superficial level of your life, that nothing changes, underneath in the waters and in the air above, the vibrations are altering with every minute as wheels go around.

The moon is whizzing through your psyche and bubbling through your moods. Every couple of days the moon has a different focus, and that alone makes your life go up and down. You are bombarded with the wavelengths of the planets and the stars. These are all throwing their energies into your mix, and every day you will find you have a different-tasting stew.

So, give some time to feeling and delighting in these energies. Don't ignore them or deny them. They are part of who you are.

And you will know when you come to a gateway and it's time to ratchet up to some new cycle. Things feel like they are coming to an end and you'll seek closure. And anticipation rises in your heart as you see the new door before you.

Understand the wheels of your life for they are immensely important. And if you wish to understand the cycles that lie ahead, then study your astrology for this is the guide to your wheels.

Chapter 62 – THE WAVES ARE COMING

In all my time as a god I have never seen times a-changing as they are right now. We are feeling the full thrust of the universe's energies coming into our realms in order to transform us. We have been preparing for this for many centuries, but even so, now it is upon us, are we ready, for it seems like we are sorely prepared.

And so, those in the lower dimensions are being yanked out of their positions and they are being forced to sink or swim. For the universe is having no brook with them as they lie about in slothfulness and heathenness.

This is a time for the gods to take control again. They lost it when humans started taking over their own domain. And ever since then the gods have been trying to wrest control back, but the human will has been indomitable.

And the gods have chosen not to wipe them all out and start again. So, the path we gods have taken has been one of trying to bring humans up to scratch, of teaching them the god ways. Instead of fighting humans, we have tried to make them like us. We have tried every method and trick in the book, and whilst we have gained some blessed souls, the majority of humans have not associated with our ways.

So, the universe is bearing down with greater energies than the gods can muster, and the pressure on human consciousness is very strong. And it has to be to break those hearts open, for humans' hearts have been encased in a shell. These shells have been formed after centuries of abuse. It is a protection agent, for if one doesn't feel with one's heart, one cannot feel the pain. And so, we are all for denuding you of your shells, and that in itself will be painful, and you will be vulnerable and open even more to those cosmic rays.

The gods cannot kill off you humans, nor do we wish to do so, for you are the children of our consciousnesses and we would like to grow you into loving gods. It is with heavy heart that we see our children crushed. For if they will not alight on this path to the higher dimensions, then the universe will grind them into dust where they stand. Their consciousness will be reapportioned to more appropriate places for growth. And humans will no longer enjoy their sacred Earth.

You see it all around you now and on your newscasts, the panic and destruction that goes on around your world. Those who have walked through the gateway to their godhood will be saved and safe. But those still floundering in the mire, there is little chance for them if they do not come out soon.

The energies are churning the lower world to dust. We do not wish for these vibrations to exist for very much longer. So, all that has not reached the required bar will be turned away. It is your own wavelength that will save you or sink you. When your vibrations are high you will ride these waves to shore. But those still in the pigswill, they will be swilled away.

For the Earth it is being cleansed now. There comes a new order. There comes a bright new day. We have been prophesying this for a long time. And now it is upon us, what do you say? Your complaints will fall on deaf ears if you have not altered your schedule and rewritten your script and programming, and got yourself out of your hell.

Many have ignored our warnings or denied the fact that we are here. We cannot help but be sorry for you as the waves collide against you, for we have put out our hands and offered numerous ways to escape. But still most humans prefer the old ways. But there will be no celebration in Heaven when all are sunk.

What can you do with a wayward child? There is only so much can be done and then their fate will play out. So, if you have loved ones who are still not coming our way, then brace yourself for some woundings, for the universe will not feel guilty at taking them away. Only those of a higher vibration will be left to tell this tale.

The world will be a very different place, distinguished by its vibrations that will be of a higher order.

I cannot vouch for the safety of all those that you love. So, you must gather them into the higher dimension if you wish to continue your journey with them around. I am not saying that only the gods will survive, but certainly there must be a degree of higher vibration if the waves are to pass you by.

This is not a Judgement Day where the gods call you out. You have marked yourself by the wavelength that you're at, and anything below this standard will not survive these waves. You may wonder what forms these waves will take; watery waves or waves of ash? The waves will take many different forms depending on your climate, but all will serve one purpose—to clear away the muck.

I am sorry that my tone is sombre today but there is no easy way to deliver such bad news. We are at the knife edge now of these changes coming in. Prepare yourself for this blasting, and don't be knocked off your axis but stand firm on higher ground. Your world will change as it has never changed before. You need new leaders and those with mettle to carry on. Do not crumble at the sight that will be before your eyes, but hold onto the goal here, to make this planet rise.

Do not fear all that I have told you, for we are coming into greater love. We are expelling all that has been not-love, and we are starting a new world full of grace.

Chapter 63 – THE UNDERWORLD

Let us be engaged today in a way that we haven't been before. Let us pop down into the Underworld and see what can be seen, if anything at all can be seen in that blackness.

You may be wondering what the Underworld is and where it exists, and how our consciousness interacts with it. Well, because our consciousness is everything, then it means that the Underworld is within our consciousness and part of it. It is a dark world, a shadow world, a polarity to the world of light.

There is nothing wrong with the Underworld, for that would be like saying there was something wrong with the night as opposed to the day. The Underworld exists, and it is a place of darkness, a place without light. But it doesn't mean that it is an awful place, although it does have its secrets and things are hidden from our eyes.

The Underworld is a place that you will come to in your consciousness when you wish to be away from all of creation, when you wish to duck into a world of your own, just you and your consciousness, without any interference from other minds.

Here in this dark cave, like a womb, you will be able to delve into all the aspects of your consciousness, past, present, and future, and there will be no hindrance from the human part of yourself. Within this dark space you will be able to be in touch with all aspects of yourself. And you will feel into things rather than think them, and knowings will come to you like osmosis from the universe.

So, it is necessary to be in touch with this dark, underworld part of yourself at certain times throughout your year, for within these confines you will start to birth ideas. For this is a place of conception, not only for women but for males too. In this darkness all can swirl around you, and you can feel into things in a way that you haven't done before. For your eyes generally keep you fixed on targets and everything else becomes lost along the way.

But in this cave of the Underworld within your mind, there are no targets, there are no goals or rules. All is let loose for you to experience. There are no boundaries, no fences, no limitations, and no glass ceilings. The Underworld is a place of pure potential. Everything is there in the mix. You are free to latch onto whatever you please. Here you can mix any colours and there is no one to tell you that it can't be done.

The Underworld of your consciousness is interlaced with the Underworlds of others. And so there is a grand sweeping flow through the universe as consciousnesses experience a complete letting go.

So, far from being a place of horror and sinister characters and fear, the Underworld is a place of complete relaxation. All forms and structures are dissolved, and the only substance is that of ideas. All of creation starts right here, in the darkness, in the night-time of our souls. It is a beautiful and wondrous place to be. And it is from here that all becomes manifest. But creation takes place in the light, while pre-creation takes place in the dark.

So, understand now these polarities of light and dark. One is not good and the other evil. They are both essential elements of all that is created in this universe. It is the yin and yang of life. But I would prefer that you don't label them as the masculine and feminine elements, for there is no gender aspect to any of this. There is the dark womb where things are conceptualised and conceived. And then there is the light world where things are given the spark of fire to become manifest physically in your worlds. Every man and woman has both these elements within their consciousness, and they must learn to use both aspects if they are to create a whole and happy world.

There are some who will prefer the dark world and some who will prefer the light. Do not judge them for their preferences, for some were designed more to conceive and some were designed more to manifest. But everyone has both aspects within themselves.

You cannot manifest until you have conceived. And if you only conceive, then you will never get to create anything at all. So, practise going into both the dark world and the light world and experiencing the flavours there. The dark world is still and serene and meditative. The light world is lively and buzzing with activity and fire.

And you will know those in your human world who are aligned more to one than to another. The world of your oceans is more aligned to the dark world, and so is the area of outer space. And on the surface of your planet, is evidence of the light world, all that has been created from consciousness and the minds of man.

Understand how these two worlds interplay and then you will understand how the universe came into being. And now you will be able to understand how to create your own personal universe around you.

Appreciate this dark world and take some time to retreat there. Get to know its nooks and crannies. Get to know how to rest there, and make use of these energies for all they're worth. Abide in the Underworld and your consciousness will never be the same, for it will be infiltrated by the ideas of this universe. And what you choose to bring through into the light world is up to you.

Don't look a gift horse in the mouth but dive into this deep world and discover all its riches. Access is not limited. All have a pass at any time. So, come, do some deep-sea diving and float in this dark world and soak up its potential.

Once you are aligned with the beauty of this night, there will be more wholeness in your life, more harmony and balance too. Drift into this space and open your heart to this fascinating world. The darkness is like a velvet cloak around your mind. Feel safe and protected as you dream within its folds.

Chapter 64 – GHOST STORY

Let us up the ante today and let us speak about spooky things, those things that humans rarely give voice to. Let us speak about ghosts and the antics that they get up to. For, yes, ghosts certainly do exist, and if you see one you are not going out of your mind.

"What is a ghost?" you may well be asking. Well, it is an imprint from the hidden dimensions, a footprint you might say, of where a spirit has been or is residing right now, for remember there is no time in these dimensions, and what you are seeing is like a photograph of that spirit's electronic identity.

You are seeing through into another dimension where the veil is very thin, and where the spirit or ghost has come down to your vibrations, or you have raised yours to connect with this entity. There will be a link between you, that's for sure, for as I have stated in the past, like attracts like, so you have attracted this ghost or spirit to you.

A ghost is one of the physical forms of the consciousness of a spirit. I have told you that consciousness and spirit can take on many different forms. And often they like to revert to appearing as the physical body of some persona that they have been in the past. They are play-acting, as it were, and putting on this hat or that hat and working through the issues that they had when that consciousness was held in that body.

Now, most spirits or ghosts do not choose to linger around the low vibrations of this earthly planet. They choose to dwell in higher vibrations, and they choose to be in and out of physical form and float around as their spirit sphere. But now and again, a spirit has the urge to visit old haunts, excuse my pun. And so you might catch a glimpse of it as it floats through the ethers, a mass of pulsing light, if truth be told.

There is a difference between the glimpsing of a spirit or a ghost and the visitation of a god or angel. For gods and angels will take on the semblance of a solid physical body, whereas ghosts will come with but the electronic signature of themselves.

It is said by humans that ghosts are spirits or entities that are trapped between the two worlds. They have not been able to leave the earthly dimension and make it to the hidden world of spirits. There is some truth in this, in that ghosts have an urge to come back to places where they feel their destiny came undone. Yet all ghosts will have arrived in the spirit world and taken on their new form before they have been allowed to swan back to their old locales. Nothing stops the process between death and arriving in the spirit world, you can be assured of that. There are no lost souls, only those who are pining to be given another chance.

Some spirits like to come back and give comfort to their loved ones. Other spirits come back for vengeance or to give fright to those who have done them wrong. But for the most part, spirits do not care to re-enter this earthly world, for there are far greater amusements in Heaven and a far lovelier world that brings them peace. Coming back to Earth is not denied them but it is discouraged, for we prefer our spirits to be moving on.

So, if you do see a spirit, stand your ground and send them love, for this is what is needed to help them rise to the higher vibrations. If a spirit has been rattling sabres at you, then ask for forgiveness and forgive them too. Do not seek to take a spirit on, for although it is monitored and cannot win, it does you no good to enter the fighting fray. The angels will be watching out for wayward spirits. They cannot run amok or create death and destruction upon this Earth. Only the gods have that kind of power to create or destroy upon your planet.

"So, what of poltergeists?" you might ask. "Don't these cause a lot of panic and destruction?" Well, by now you will have realised how powerful is your consciousness, and your consciousness can manifest quite powerfully upon this Earth. The evidence of a so-called poltergeist is truthfully the out-picturing of a person's manifestations in their own consciousness. They are causing these things to happen, but they are not aware that it is coming from themselves.

We have spoken before of the many personas within your consciousness. A poltergeist will be one of these personas playing out. Yes, you did not realise you could be so powerful or destructive. This is why you must work with all and each of your personas and bring them into line.

You will already understand how one or other of your inner personas can sabotage your plans at times. Poltergeists are merely extreme versions of this. There is no wild spirit or ghost that has got out of hand. So, while we would like to blame others for this spiteful state of affairs, we must know that it is coming from a hidden part of ourselves, and the more troubled we are, the more troubling will be the circumstances that we create.

So, you can rest assured if a ghost or spirit passes you by, that they are really quite benign and will not be allowed to cause you issues. But they really are visitors from our hidden worlds. You yourself have been in this state in the past, and one day in the future you will be in this state once again.

So, marvel at the interaction of our separate worlds, how one can pass through into another, and you as your spirit self are doing this all the time. Marvel at the ingenuity of gods who have created this so. It is a magical universe that we live in. Laugh and adore it and play along with all you find.

I hope you have enjoyed my ghost story today. It is not a tale of horror, but a tale of who we are.

Chapter 65 – PURSUE YOUR DREAMS

Let us speak about an irregular subject today, and by that I mean, one that does not have smooth edges, that is a bit jagged, that is difficult to hold, especially within our consciousness. I am speaking of the subject of pursuing our dream.

It is something most people find very hard to do. Of course, there are exceptions, and some humans know exactly what they want and go after it with single-mindedness. But, for the rest of you, you have these dreams swirling in your consciousness, the big dreams that is, and you are too afraid to go after them, and so they sit there like some nebulous cloud, unreachable and untouchable, or so you imagine.

It is not a smooth and easy path to manifest your dreams. And that zigzag nature of the path puts many people off and they retire all too early from pursuing what is meant to be their destiny. They give up and go for easier goals. But there is always a niggling and a nagging within them in the background of their mind, that if only things could have been different they could have fulfilled that dream.

I am here to tell you that *you* are the one to make things different in your life, that will get you on track towards that destiny. Don't throw up your hands in regret and tell me it can't be done, for 'where there's a will, there's a way', is an old saying amongst you humans, and us gods agree. Don't give up on your dreams, for these are the purpose why you came down to Earth. You would not have these dreams if they weren't important to you. But you will need courage and you will need persistence, and you will need to hold that dream firm in your consciousness, like a target before you that keeps you running true.

Don't be so weak to let your dreams dissipate and crumble into dust. You will forever feel unfulfilled, knowing that there was something you had to do, and that you weren't achieving it, that you had put it aside so that it won't get done. It is the measure of your personality if you can raise yourself up and go for gold. No one will be more ashamed than you if you return Home with your mission incomplete.

So, haul out those dreams from the darkness where they lie hidden. Put them back on a pedestal and walk around them and take them in. You now know that whatever is in your consciousness gets created upon the ground, so fill your consciousness with all the details of your dreams, and watch as doorways open and paths unfold before you. Your dreams will remain in their cloud if you do not give them any thought.

Perhaps, in the past, it hasn't been the right time for successful navigation towards these dreams. But try it out again and see if you can get further this time around. Don't give up on the first pass. Keep returning to your dreams and make a plan. Sometimes *you* are not ready for the dream to unfold in your life. And so, it may take a while for you to get up to scratch. Then will come the window, the opportunity for your dream to come true.

So, spend some time dancing with your dream and get to know every aspect. And make all the calls that you need to bring it into creation and bedded in this world. Your dreams will not just magically manifest before you. You will need to invest some effort, and there will be jagged challenges along the way. For your destiny provides a course of lessons; what would you learn if we just placed it in your hands?

So, dig out those dreams and picture them with all your senses. Create a world in your mind where those dreams were already made. Step into those dreams and live your role and check what needs tweaking, for nothing can be manifest upon Earth until you've birthed it in your consciousness in the higher and hidden dimensions.

Examine your dreams and ask your soul if they are right for you, for it is no use making for the wrong destiny. Be sure you are on track and your goal is solid. Your soul may suggest some alterations here and there, and they will advise you on the path to take, and the next and immediate steps to get there.

You don't want to be procrastinating and waiting for a brighter day, for who knows how many days that you have left, and you don't want to find yourself back Home and wishing you'd acted sooner.

So, come, chivvy yourself and get some motivation. Remind yourself why these dreams won't go away. They are pestering you in the background of your mind. They are saying, "Follow me!" What will you say?

Be aware of the emotions that are triggered by my call to action. Are you lazy or are you fearful? What excuses are you making to not be running towards your dream? There is all the help in the universe available to speed you on, but it is you that must move your body and your mind. It is not our dream but your dream that needs to urge you on.

Your dreams may be in tatters, but your thoughts can mend any tears. Sew together your destined goal, embroider it with details, and put it on and wear it with great pride.

Do away with the hindrances that make you baulk and hesitate and fear. You now know how to let these segments go. Speak with all your inner personas and get them all on board. Have all your ducks moving in the same direction. Align all parts of yourself to the same cause.

On your deathbed you do not want to be crying because you had not finished your tasks. Let your heart go to the next world, knowing that you have dreamed and that you got the job done.

There are so many dreams floating around your Earth. It is a cause of all the cloudiness. So, let us fulfil dreams and bring in bright new days.

Chapter 66 – A STORM IN YOUR CONSCIOUSNESS

So, as it is very much in the news today, let us discuss storm season. There are hurricanes, tornadoes, and wild weather playing out all around this globe, and if you haven't been hit by it yet, you soon will be, for there will be no part of this planet left untouched. All are being given a severe shaking up to see what they are made of, to see how close they are to the gaining of godhood, or if they are already gods, they are being tested to see if they are still suitable material. For you cannot hold the badge of godhood without continually working for it and being fit to hold this office. So, periodically you will be challenged to see if you can hold your mettle.

There is nothing that a god can avoid, so you might as well accept all that comes your way and deal with it with alacrity and a smile on your face, and bring yourself up to brighter climes again. There is nothing will be too much for a god to handle, and if it looks like being so, then resources will be funnelled your way. Gods support other gods, and the angels are always on hand too.

You might be asking, "What of us who are not yet gods? Can things get too much for us? Will the gods and angels help us too?" Well, it will depend on what is in your consciousness at the time. If your heart is open and you are praying for help, then we gods are not so uncompassionate as to ignore your pleas and abandon you to your fate.

But be aware that if it is your fate to meet your demise, then this is the time, this is the hour, and you may as well make peace with your maker and float to the other side. When it is time for you to go Home, there is nothing us gods can do to interfere with that process. So, accept that you must die sometime, and this is that time and you must say goodbye.

When you understand that it is just your body that is dying and that your consciousness lives on, then you will not receive this news so traumatically. For we live and die thousands upon thousands of times. You have done it before and you will do it again in the future. So, rally yourself to become your spirit. Surrender to this journey and be pleased that you are going Home.

Now, for those of us who are left on the ground, picking up the pieces after some great wilful storm, it may be hard going but this is your lot. It is time to be creative and to manifest from your mind. Don't sit there all woeful and doleful and whingeing that life is unfair, but get up and do your darnedest and recreate your life and improve it as you go. This is a time to take stock of all you hold dear, to evaluate your priorities, and to move on if necessary if the damage has been too dear.

I have said before that consciousnesses need to be woken up from their staleness, and a big storm is a big clearer of the air. Suddenly you might see the path before you with greater clarity, once all the old debris has been cleared away and you are resetting your foundations for the future.

Storms have the capacity to shift things like nothing else. And it is not just physicality that gets moved, but your whole consciousness becomes adjusted and you are open to innovations that you would not have seen before.

So, although it is irritating to have your life thus affected, a storm does a great job for us gods. We can reach many people who would otherwise have remained untouched. I'm not saying that we gods are the creators of these storms, but we do utilise their pathways to benefit our work. We can shift a storm a little to left or right. We can reduce or increase its intensity. We can make it skip over some homes and demolish others right next door.

So, by now you will know what will save you, for we have spoken about this before. Your vibrational level is so important here, for the higher you are, the less a storm will affect you. Your planet will see a marked increase in massive storms, for your climate is definitely changing, and you will need to be prepared to ride these out. The best way that you will cope is to be above them, not flying in some plane but flying with your consciousness.

I know many of you still cannot appreciate how your consciousness can save you from these fates. But when you understand that you are dealing with two worlds here, your higher vibrations move you out of the lower world and into the one above. So, things can smash into the lower dimensions and you will not feel their brunt, for your higher vibrations move you into a higher dimension that floats above the crises that are played out on lower Earth.

Storms are a great leveller in more ways than one. They might level buildings but they affect all social strata whether you are wealthy or poor. In the aftermath of a disaster, consciousnesses will want to pull together in support. So, a crisis is a great teacher for humanity. It brings out the best in many when they are able to offer their help. There are always those, of course, who tend to suck everyone dry. They may soon become victims of these storm scenes, for we are removing those of lower vibrations from this Earth.

So, think about storms in a new light now. Get your vibrations to their highest levels and have no fear and ride it out. Certainly, there may be plenty of work for you to do in the ensuing days and weeks, but understand the opportunities that this is offering you, a time to break with the past and build anew.

So, approaching storms should not be viewed with panic or dismay. Accept that things are about to change and open your heart and move forwards into the fray. A storm in your consciousness will show you some new way.

Chapter 67 – PLAYING WITH MOTHER NATURE

Let us speak about rain today and how that equates with consciousness, for we have already spoken about how consciousness affects your weather and your climate.

So, what does rain mean for you, if you are experiencing too much of it or too little? Is your consciousness the culprit behind this? Well, your consciousness will be one of many that is forming the climate for your area, and even more locally than that, for your neighbourhood.

So, be aware of what is going on in that group consciousness, of you and your neighbours, and how you are creating that mini weather system around you. Obviously, there will be some unstable consciousnesses in that mix if your weather isn't perfect, if it is extreme or all over the place, when good balance would be sunshine accompanied by regular rain.

Can you, a lone pioneer of your neighbourhood, make a difference to that weather system and change it or tweak it so that you are living in the land of Nirvana? Well, yes, I have to say that you can. And it is not essentially that you will have your own personal rain cloud over your little patch of ground while others all around you may be parched, or that the sun will shine only on your garden and everyone else will be in shadow under a great big cloud.

No, to all intents and purposes, the weather will seem the same throughout your region. But it is you that will react differently to it. And if there is a drought then you will find great ways to cope, and if there is a deluge you will not be so affected and may even find it a blessing for your crops and your plants.

So, it is not the actual weather itself that you will change if you are pouring your harmonious energies and intentions into the atmospheric conditions around you. Rather it is your circumstances that you will change. You will make the most of whatever is being doled out by the universe. You will find ways to be bright and happy, no matter what the state of the sky. You will roll with the winds and make hay in the sunshine. You will be grateful for whatever is given and you will find ways to thrive. Remember that saying of humans, "When given lemons, just make lemonade."

This is the consciousness of a god, not to sit there complaining and wailing, "Woe is me!", but to raise yourself up with innovative action, rise to the challenge, and see how you can work with Mother Nature. When you do not resist all that is going on around you, you will find yourself in the flow of the universe's energies. And when you have an open heart and open mind, you will be imbued with many new ideas to make a difference.

We have stated before that the universe is ever-changing. That means your world, your personal world, can never remain the same. The cog wheels are always moving you on. And you might attempt to do some fancy footwork to keep things idling the same, but it would be like running on the blades of a waterwheel; it won't be long before you are spun off and dunked in the water again.

So, welcome the weather, be it sunshine, snow, or rain, and use the tools of your consciousness to make the most of whatever is presented. This means being awake and alert and open to opportunities. If you plod off to your same old work and never look around, then you will miss all those doorways and portals and will wonder why everything just stays the same.

So, the vagaries of weather are opportunities for you to see and to feel things from different perspectives; the moods of the universe and how they will affect you today.

Watch for extreme climatic conditions, for then the group consciousness has sent things too far. The desire of the group has been too intense. There is no mid-point or balance, as if a pendulum has been swung to the opposite side of the scale.

So, if you are in drought, then the drought will persist if that is all that fills people's minds. Then there comes a turning to desperately wanting rain, so intentions turn on the rain taps, but too fully and downpours ensue. The right way is to focus on balance; mid-range sunshine and mid-range rain. Picture your world as perfectly catered for. You'll soon get the hang of it and happiness will reign (rain).

When you are the victim of some planetary natural disaster, think not that you have been abandoned by the universe or the gods. For you will have been protected to the degree that is necessary, and you will have been exposed according to the trials that you must take. Everything that you experience is a challenge to foster your mind. If you are weak in some areas then the weather will reach right in. It will show you the lessons you are learning, so be grateful and don't shake your fist.

These can be very convoluted scenarios with many of you learning lessons, bouncing off one another and finding strength. You are here to work with your fellow man and gods. Come together with your consciousnesses and make this world a more harmonious and balanced place.

There is richness in the diversity of weather. Breathe it and soak it in. Dance with the antics of this universe and don't let yourself be thwarted by an inclement day. There are jewels in every moment. Open your heart and let them in. Fly with whatever is on the agenda today from Mother Nature, for she is wise in her powers and she loves it when you play.

Chapter 68 – YOUR SOURCE AND HEALING

Thank you, Sophia, thank you. I see you are incapacitated today, so let us speak about the healing arts again, for this is a major tool of your consciousness and one that is very handy for gods and humans alike. For there is no end of healing that needs to be done with your consciousness, bodies, and the world.

Let us take a different spin on healing today than what we have covered before, for I am all for improving your information and capabilities.

We have said before that you must focus on seeing yourself whole, or the situation harmonised, if you are to heal anything that you desire. But there is a little more to it than that if you wish to be extremely effective and take no time at all to heal the wounds before you.

If you can bring your source energy into the situation, then this is you as a creator god, and your creator god self can manifest anything, for all of creation has come from their hands and their hearts. So, if you can reach back into the depths of yourself and reach the part of yourself that is your kernel that sits at your very core, the energy that is available at this point can override anything and bring it back into fullness and harmony once again.

Now, you might be asking, "How do I reach my source?" Well, this is a journey you will have to undertake in consciousness. It cannot be forced by the human mind, and yet you will need the will of the human to get you through every barrier that will stand in your way. For your source is at the highest of vibrations. It is the part of your consciousness that sits at the very top. And it is possible to get yourself there for brief visitations, but you will need to raise your vibrations to that level, and that can be very hard. There are many humans who have done this, so it is not an impossible task. But you will need to be pure in your intentions, for the power of your source cannot be used for unwise situations.

First of all, have the intention to meet with the source of yourself, and in quiet meditation raise yourself up with all the loving and purest thoughts that you can muster. Sometimes your source will make it easier for you and come down lower and meet you half way. And the day you meet your source for the first time, you will cry with ecstasy that this is who you really are.

Your source can imbue you with power which you can direct to the issue at hand. And miraculous things can occur in a moment. Believe it and try it, and you will never look back again. This is how miracles happen, when your source gets involved with your game. It is the most powerful aspect of your entire consciousness.

Treat your source as you would a monarch, for they are your king and queen, and all power lies with them. That is not to say that gods and angels and souls are not powerful in themselves, but ultimate power lies with your source. When you can bring your source online into your daily life, then you will be a generator of power, the likes of which the world has hardly seen.

The power of the gods lies with their contact with their source. So, I advise you to start searching for this connection, for it will take a while to harness your vibrations and get them to reach that high.

We are not asking for the whole of your consciousness to reach your creator god source, for that would mean you could become a creator god yourself, and patently that is not going to happen while you are in human form on Earth. What is needed is for the human part of your consciousness to rise to the levels at the top. But even then, you will still have parts of your consciousness that reside at the very bottom of the valleys. So, you must know that your consciousness is like a ribbon that stretches from bottom to top. And each horizontal thread of your ribbon is a vibrational level that you must get to. And yet you are the whole ribbon at the same time, so parts of you can be at the top, parts of you in the middle, and parts of you at the bottom, floundering in the mud.

All these different personas that you are, they are all living at different levels of vibration along your ribbon within your one consciousness. And your source sits at the very head and monitors all below. So, you are a complicated consciousness, are you not?

So, trying to heal yourself or others when you are wearing the hat of a persona at the bottom of your ribbon, is not going to be as effective as wearing the persona of your very source. The higher up the ribbon that you can travel, the greater your power for healing your world. You are like a dial on an old-fashioned radio. You need to dial yourself to the higher frequencies to bring in the riches of the higher dimensions.

Most of your healing will need to be done on your personas that exist at the lower end of your ribbon. There will be thousands of these, so don't think it an overnight job. Every persona is an experience that you have had, a role that you have played. There will be many of these characters for you to work through. You are not schizophrenic, just a multi-faceted consciousness that has worn many faces and different hats.

You will know what I mean; there is probably a party you, a glum and moody you, a radiant you, an excited you, and a dispirited you that asks, "What's the point?" You are not just one homogenous personality that presents the same face every day to every kind of situation. If you were like that, wouldn't you be some kind of zombie?

No, on a daily basis, you are wearing multiple hats and playing several different roles. So, now we are adding a new one to your collection—the source of all you are, the true power behind the throne. You will be unstoppable once you get this power entrenched within you, for you will be a king or queen of creation, of healing, of putting this world to rights.

Allow the power of your source to flow from every pore. Be like a star, be radiant. You cannot imagine the good that you will do and the benefits that will follow. You think a star is bright; my goodness you should see your source! For the stars were created by these creator gods, and *you* are nothing short of miraculous as well.

Chapter 69 – DESIGN YOUR DEATH

Let us speak about something abstract today that you will need to give some thought to. And I wish to highlight this subject before we come to the conclusion of this book, for you will need to get to grips with it, for you cannot deny it for it will definitely affect you one day. And this is the subject of death.

We have spoken about this before in previous chapters, for you are coming and going over many lifetimes and you will experience multiple deaths during the time of your existence as a consciousness. So, it is best to be prepared for this to happen once again, is it not? And you'd think with all the practice that you've had, that you'd be able to take it in your stride and with aplomb, and face your death with dignity and with good grace.

But, no, most of you are wailing like banshees at the thought of your demise. And you are putting it off for as long as possible and holding on, often, to miserable and miserly lives at the expense of letting go and jumping back into the higher dimensions and going Home.

We already know now that whatever is in your consciousness plays out for you as your reality down on this Earth. So, if you are fixated with fear on the possibility of experiencing a horrible or painful death, then you know what is going to eventuate, for whatever you are thinking about you will attract.

So, all those who fear death by cancer are bringing it towards them day by day. And if you fear being smashed up in some accident, then it is only a matter of time before that accident will visit upon you.

Therefore, why don't we ponder on good deaths, deaths which are delightful and peaceful and a good letting go? We might elect to die peacefully in our sleep. We might elect to have a heart attack; one swift moment and we are gone. We might elect to go out in a blaze of glory, and whatever that glory is is up to you. We might wish to be surrounded by family and those we love, or we might prefer to go it alone and not be pulled back by those shedding tears.

So, begin to create the scene that you wish for your death. You cannot put it off forever. It will arrive one day, and sometimes sooner than you think. It is not a wise thing for humans to deny the existence of their death. As a society this is mostly shunned, and people tiptoe around this subject, not liking to mention it even though it is obviously on the table.

And if you'd like a nice funeral, why not arrange it before you go? For you might be miffed, once you are in your spirit sphere, to see people giving you a send-off in ways you don't appreciate and which don't bring you joy.

So, although you might think this a gloomy thing to do, approach this task with delightfulness. Make it a celebration of your lifetime this time around. Acclaim your achievements and all the value you have added. Don't ponder on the grim bits but seek out all that went well. Write yourself a eulogy, congratulating yourself for a life well spent. And if you haven't spent it well, well then, there's still time to get your house in order.

Do not take a single day for granted, for it might be your last one on this planet. So, fill every moment with the joy of being alive, focusing on what you came here to accomplish and being well-pleased with those things that you've achieved.

Next time you come here, if this option is open for you, you might have a completely different set of rules and roles to play out and hats for you to wear. So, try to tie up all this lifetime's loose ends and mess. Don't leave it to others to untangle the legacy you've left behind. Leave everything in order and don't leave secrets never told.

Be transparent and display your life before you, that others may benefit from all that you have learnt. Why would you want to spend a lifetime attaining knowledge if you haven't shared it as wisdom in some useful shape or form? This is what I mean by adding value, that the world is richer in some way from you having been placed on its ground. Don't let people be saying at your funeral, "Well, they were a waste of space and a waste of a lifetime as a human being on this Earth."

You yourself, when you study your inventory of accomplishments when you return Home, may be saddened or embarrassed if your list is not very long. Don't think that we are just speaking of world-changing innovations. Just being a good father or mother, or daughter or son, is a great achievement in itself, and will not go unrewarded. Have you been kind? Have you been loving? Have you done the jobs necessary to make life work for you and all around you. Have you completed your mission? Have you supported others along the way? Have you worked with your spirit and your soul to improve on your consciousness that you came with when you entered this world?

There is no hell that you will be banished to if you haven't done any of these things. Your hell will be in your own misery, that you didn't make the most of your time in human form.

So, while you are still up and about and still living, ponder on how you can contribute to a life well-spent. Ponder on the way that you would like to be transported back Home. And get all your affairs in order by living a disciplined life day by day. Sometimes you'll be given notice, and sometimes you will not. So, face up to these facts and arrange your consciousness in line with your desires.

Do not be sad if your time is coming to an end. It is but a phase in the lifetime of your consciousness. You are moving out of one form and into another which you will like. There is hardly a soul who doesn't enjoy being in Heaven, for it is a paradise of love-liness, and you will be glad when you go Home.

Chapter 70 – SPRINGTIME IN YOUR MIND

Let us speak about an entirely different subject today, rather than the death that we have been occupied with of late. Let us speak about spring, as in the season. For spring is a wonderful time in most people's lives. It represents new birth, new life, things coming into their fullness and potential. Who doesn't love a beautiful spring day, burgeoning with the possibilities of summer and all that ripeness and sunniness, good times and fun?

So, spring is a preparation period for the bountifulness of the coming summer. In spring we plant our seeds, prepare the soil. We are filled with excitement at what could grow this year. It is an optimistic time, filled with anticipation, for we do not know how our seeds will turn out, and we are eager to give them all the love and nurturing that they will need to bring them into fruit, that they will nourish us even further.

Know that your consciousness rides in cycles just like this, that there are seasons for you to be doing this or that. And if you try to delay the process of this cycle, you will find your results disappointing or that they even come to naught.

So, be aware when it is spring in your consciousness, that this is the time to lay your plans. And do not try to plant in your winter, for this is time to lay fallow and catch up on other tasks. And do not expect to be harvesting moments after you have laid out your seeds. For you know how it is in the fields and gardens; so too in your consciousness will things take time to mature.

When was the last time you had springtime in your mind? When were you excited with brand-new ideas and eager to take action?

If it has been a while since you have seen a spring, think about how it is in the garden and apply these concepts to your thoughts. Let there be freshness and new colour. Let there be designs and the dreaming of what you will reap. Foster that feeling of anticipation of the summer. Put away your wintry thoughts and come in out of the cold. Let yourself warm towards innovation.

Spread your eye around the inside of your mind. What can be hoicked out and jettisoned, and what can be put back in its place? Feel the new energies and the sparkle as your mind comes alive with the beauty of this new season. Dream of how you want your summer to play out, then make your plans ready so your dreams will eventuate.

Remember how you felt as a child, as excitement gained momentum with summer holidays looming large. This is the timbre of spring, a welling up of energy and expectation, an eagerness to get busy, thinking and with your hands.

It won't be springtime forever, so get out there while the energies last. If you miss these opportunities which these days offer, you will sit there in the summer staring at barren soil. So, take a leaf out of my book and plant up while you can. Set up the pathways that you will stroll down in summer, and open your heart to the expanding sunshine and its rays.

You are moving towards the peak of your year, so support this springtime cycle and give it all you've got. Whatever you put in now will reward you in coming months and years. So, think to the long term and how you want to shape your dreams.

It's not enough for you to look at other's gardens and nod and say, "How pretty!" and admire all their work. You too must produce a bountiful mind. It can be quite simple, and everyone will have their style, but your mind cannot remain as just a patch of mud. You must work your soil and nourish it, fertilise it and care for it, and plant appropriate things for your climate and your life.

If you can be self-sufficient and depend on just yourself, then that is a useful asset of your consciousness, that you won't be reliant on others and you'll be able to support yourself.

There are no limits to the area of your garden or your field. You can take as much space as you want and can cope with. Resources are available to seed your Earth and feed your mind. Try not to be a one-crop person, but diversify your plantings so that you'll have something all year round. Interact with other people and get cuttings from their minds. Swap ideas and processes and you'll have a jewel of a garden in no time.

There is nothing so satisfying as harvesting your crop, but first it must get planted and be nurtured and watched over if it's not to fail.

So, dream of how it will be at the end of this summer. What is lying in your arms that brings a smile to your face and love to your heart? Spring is the springboard to that summer of your dreams.

Chapter 71 – LOVE AND NOT-LOVE

My reason for speaking today is all about love. They say love makes the world go around. Well, love certainly makes the universe go around, for the universe *is* love.

Now, there may be many things in the universe that are not love, but I can tell you that all these things are pure love underneath at their basic core. They have merely been covered over with not-love thinking that comes from fear. Essentially, we could split everything into two camps, that of love and that of fear. But even fear has an underlying basis of love. It is the fear of not having love that is the underlying basis of fear.

So, if the universe is love and the universe is consciousness, therefore consciousness is love too. And as consciousness is who we are, then we must be love as well.

So, if you were to take away all your fear, lift it up and look underneath, then what you would see lying there is pure love. Take a moment to think of yourself as pure love, as this sparkling diamond of consciousness without any flaws or fear. Imagine what that would feel like and what you would be able to do. For it is only fear that keeps you constrained and inhibited. Without those fears you'd be willing to take on the world.

So, our task is to dig down deep and find that pure love within us. It has been covered over by the thoughts and emotions from multitudes of lives. We are working in every lifetime to free ourselves of some of these layers, but unfortunately in every lifetime we are creating new layers of not-love and setting them down. So, do we ever get ahead? Well, that will depend on you. If you take two steps forwards and one back, then you will eventually make some headway. And we know it is difficult to be perfect, so making some headway is better than none.

You can speed up this process by daily getting rid of your layers, and at the same time raising your vibrations so that your pure love rises up and comes to the fore. It is like magma rising up within the chamber of a volcano and eventually, with enough pressure, your pure love can rise to the top and explode with magnificence into this world. So, yes, be a volcano of pure love. Spread your loving lava on all around you. Cover the ground and your surroundings with your fertile ash. Perhaps you will never think of volcanoes in quite the same way again.

Love comes in many varied tones and colours. It is not just romantic love but it is love in every thought and nuance and event. You could instil love in every second of your day, but how many choose to do so? They rather let their day be grey.

Love can cure all animosity and is the remedy for all fear. If you are focused on love then you cannot be not-love. You are one or the other; make up your mind which you will be.

Love can be breezy but also damn hard work. It is not the love that is difficult but keeping all the not-love at bay. For rising up in your consciousness will be the layers closest to the surface and these are usually your triggers and any unloving thoughts. So, you will need to get past these layers in order to find your love. And most people fall at the first hurdle and trip up into that first layer and get enmeshed in all the not-love.

Can you be determined to force your way through the layers of not-love? Can you deny them air and acknowledgement? Can you push on through like some tank? It is better if you rid yourself of these layers altogether, then the going will be made easier if your loving layers are close to the top.

Almost everyone has experienced their love layer at some time, so don't tell me that you don't have one. It is there but may lie hidden, buried beneath all your gunk. Your love is your treasure. It's been within you all this time. Most go looking for it out there, but love is stored at your core and has been since your birth. So, if you want to know what love is like, go exploring the depths of your being. Unplug the chamber of your volcano. Set your love free and let it explode.

Most people only experience this when they meet a partner and fall in love. Then those stars of love are exploding around their ears. But you can have this experience in many more ways than this. Your whole life can be a series of love explosions; even minor ones will fill your day with joy.

So, know that love is definitely within your reach. It sits in your core in your consciousness, awaiting its revealing so that it may show its brilliant face to this world. Do not deny this exposure, for your consciousness exists to be love. Be determined to be rid of all that stands in its way. For the glory of love is the most beautiful thing in this universe.

You are a diamond of love and so is everyone else around you. The universe is a vast network of diamonds. How beauteous is this web, like a spider's web after the rain.

When will you see yourself as this walking, talking, breathing entity of pure love? Shake off the mud that has covered you and let us see the real you, this consciousness filled with love.

Chapter 72 – THE JUMP INTO GODHOOD

Let us speak about dirges today, those sad songs we sing when we have lost someone or something. It commemorates the passing of something.

So, what sad songs are you singing in these days, when all that has gone on in your world is coming to a termination so that you may move on into the new world?[1] Will you look over your life and your possessions with sadness, or will you be satisfied that they have served their purpose? You have done your best with them, and now you are turning your back on the old life and the old ways, and you are moving into a new paradigm and dimension.

We do not look upon this step lightly, in that I mean, we take this transition very seriously where you are moving into a more light-filled world. We understand that it is a terribly difficult step for you, to let go of all that it means to be human and to step into the shoes of a god. Nothing will ever be the same again. Your community will change. Your friends will probably fall away. Your family may not understand you. And there may be bitterness inside yourself for all that you are required to leave behind. And yet we must not face backwards and hold onto the way that we have come. Now we must face forwards and look to our future and what needs to be done.

If you knew without a shadow of a doubt that you were moving into a world where love sparkles and all is delight, then you would not hesitate to come this way. But you do have doubts and plenty of fears. For you cannot imagine that things could be so perfect, for the old world

---

[1] Chiron is speaking here, not of physical death but moving from human consciousness into god consciousness and godhood.

had challenges aplenty every day. But you must have faith that Heaven is appearing to you now. It certainly has been a long hard winter, but spring is here and summer is on the rise. So, let us have some optimism and vigour in your veins. Let us expect to see some changes, but changes for the better and the benefits will be all yours.

You have been waiting for these times all this lifetime and many more. Now they have come upon you, do not deny them or run away. When it is time to step up into the realm of the gods, it is a victory for the whole of humanity, for now you have proved that humans can indeed aspire to the godhood. Many are the ones who are now knocking at our door. We welcome them with open arms, and we'll show you around for there is so much more. So, wear your badge of honour with great pride. It is difficult to make the jump to godhood, and those that do will be rewarded in ways you cannot imagine when you are sitting back on Earth.

Let me assure you, you are not dying and passing over, losing your physical body and requiring a funeral for loved ones to say goodbye. No, it is your consciousness that has attained its godhood. And so, you will be a god in your human body and that will take some getting used to and we will understand your pain. But once you have adjusted to being your spirit and walking this Earth, there are all manner of new things you will encounter, new ways of seeing, and perspectives broaden so you'll understand more. You will still need to sleep and eat and clean your teeth and bathe. You will be just like a regular human being but not so regular within your mind.

Now, your consciousness will shine with your godhood. It puts a sparkle on everything and everyone. The air has a frisson of freshness and adventure. You will not want to wait in the starting stalls. You'll take off running and your beating heart will set a pace.

And so, as you're packing up your boxes, tying up loose ends, and saying your goodbyes, do not weep for all you have collected or have experienced. Feel satisfied that it's made you what you are. But now you are turning a new page; in fact, you are starting a new book. So, let us be elated at this progress and be excited by the coming years and what there is left to achieve.

You have been victorious and we celebrate you for that. Yet we cannot rest on our laurels, for the universe is always moving forwards and we must roll with it too if we are to keep up. But, by all means, take some time to reflect on all that's gone by, of how you have completed your journey, from baby human into godhood, a journey that has defined you, stripped you bare, and made you shine.

So, these are not days to wallow in self-pity and grief. You are rising into a new world; new challenges, yes, but also much more peace. So, sing no sad songs or focus on what you are losing. You are gaining so much more and you'll be working in your new position as a god. You didn't go through all these travails to stay sitting in your little corner at home. As a god you will be facing this world with all your talents. They will get to see your glory and your heart will be filled with your success.

Don't be so humble and feel you are not worthy of these gongs. You have worked your little human hide off. You have shed your human skin to reveal the god that lay beneath. It may take a while for this victory to sink in, although you have known for a long time that this is the path you've been following. But when it comes the day for the ceremony and the accolades, there can be some overwhelm, and you look around you and ask, "Who, me? Am I ready?", and we say, yes. This is your time to come into your Sun.

If you have read the previous chapters, you will understand the meaning of this tale. Your whole lifetime as a human on this planet is a journey towards godhood and moving beyond the Veil. Fortunate are those who make it to their dream, for, standing as a god on your planet, you will get to taste stardom and radiate who you are.

So, sing no sad dirges, but hear the trumpets and their fanfare.

Chapter 73 – CHANGE THOSE HUMAN MINDS

I am wondering what next to speak about, as we wind up these musings and try to give this book a good conclusion. For I am not shutting the door on consciousness, for there is so much to delve into and explore, but we need to draw a line under things somewhere, so in the next few days we shall begin to wrap things up. It has been a pleasure to be part of your journey with you, as you have discovered more about consciousness and the way that you work and who you are.

My hope is that you have learnt to expand yourself, that you no longer think of yourself as a person with just a brain. Now you know that you are the arms and legs of something much more powerful and exciting. And one day you will tuck back in those arms and legs and return to your spirit sphere, and you will reflect back on all that this life had to offer.

So, while you are in this human form, what more is there that you could do? Well, there are many things that you could be working on; making sure you are on track to your destiny, opening your heart in all directions, and letting go of those segments of fear. In truth, the one thing you are aiming for is the attainment of your godhood. That is the crowning glory for any human. Some of you may get there in this lifetime, and some of you may have a few rounds yet to go.

Do not give up, but work with all the tools in your toolbox and you'll do just fine. Even if you progress only a millimetre every day, that will be some milestone by the end of your year.

You will be noticing the flux that this world is in. And you may be noticing those who are doing the work with their consciousness and those who are closed in heart and mind. Try not to judge and, even less, to preach. Just be the best role model that you can be, then you will attract those that need your attention. I will say it for the last time in these chapters, that like attracts like, and so you will attract whatever is residing in your consciousness. If you don't like what you are attracting, then now you know what to do.

Raising your vibrations will get you to new levels, and in those new levels you will find your life will change. New friends, new family, new jobs, new homes; everything is placed on the table to be appraised as to whether it serves you best or it must go. So, we are forever wheedling out the lower consciousness and all those bad vibes, snipping off the end of your ribbon so that you can better fly.

So, what will you do when you put these pages down? Will you close the cover and go on with your life, saying, "That was interesting" and give it no more thought? Eighty per cent of you will do exactly that. Will you be one of the top percentiles who will take my words to heart? Applying all you've learnt here will not come from one reading and one pass. To truly transform your consciousness you will need to work at it daily until these things become habitual and you begin to *feel* the change.

You have been trained by society to be a puppy dog of Earth. We gods are simply trying to retrain you, and not to be a dog but a god. And you may notice that if you reverse 'dog' you end up with 'god'.

We wish you not to be slaves of those who would captain this Earth. We wish for each one of you to be captains of your own ship. Can you take control and move out to the shining waters? Many of you think there is no option but to stay. Well, I hope now that by my words I have shown you another solution, and you will begin to track down your destiny that will lead you to the higher worlds.

One day the planet shall be filled with gods and peace. We are a long way off that day coming, but this is our destiny, the destiny of the gods. We have created humans; now we must fashion them again. We must build them into magnificent beings, for patently we cannot allow them to remain as they are right now.

All would agree, I hope, that this planet is ripe for transformation. We have seen terrors and horrors aplenty. Let us put this past behind us and generate a loving world. Man must forgive man, and ultimately must forgive himself. They must discover the source of their consciousness, that diamond fire that is truly who they are. There cannot be one piece or thread of consciousness that is left to ride wild across this beautiful planet. All consciousnesses must be joined to our common purpose, which is to live safely and peacefully in love and joy.

So, get yourself up through those gates to your godhood. Train as a Master and come back down again. Spread your wisdom and your ethics. Teach the people of this planet what they don't yet know. You were once a dull and unwise human. Now you have opened this book and it has opened your mind. Feed your consciousness with this great knowledge, and take it out into the world that others may feed from it too.

Do not allow this world to pull you backwards into its clutches and into its hell. You now know that your spirit can fly higher at any time. So, prepare your escape routes and make sure you are strong. Know who you are now and believe in all I have told you. It is time for your consciousness to use its magical powers. Heal yourself and this world, and step out and take your wand.

We gods congratulate you, those who have stepped into their power. Remember to cloak yourself in the mantle of love, and go spread your wisdom and change those human minds.

Chapter 74 – OUR SUN

We are entering into our swan song, so let us pull together all the pieces and let us make sure we have not forgotten any threads. I am mindful that this is but Stage One in these teachings and that there is so much more unsaid. But we will build upon these foundations at some future date. So, if your questions have not yet been answered, hold onto them, for all will be revealed by the end.

These are the building blocks by which you shall know the basics of your consciousness. When you understand all that we have spoken about here, then you will be well on the way to understand the more advanced mechanics. Be sure that you have put these foundation stones in place first. As the gods feel that you have adopted these capabilities, then more doors will open for you and more hidden things revealed. Do not try to run before you can walk, but do indeed learn to fly.

I would like to speak about the sun today and its solar rays. The sun is our magnificent star of our solar system. It is at the heart of our life force. And each one of us has some of its consciousness within our own. We will one day become a star like this too. And we are pre-programmed to love this entity, this consciousness that monitors us from high above.

Without the sun our whole solar system would be doomed. Without the sun in your heart, you would be doomed too. The sun is vital to your existence on this Earth, so appreciate its sunniness and its divine and pulsing rays.

You might think that the sun is just light, but it is much more than that, as your scientists are beginning to appreciate. It sends out its magnetic waves which can severely disturb our planet. It also holds our planet in orbit. Without it we would spin off into outer space. But there are other hidden energies that emanate from our sun. These cosmic rays affect us too, and it is the consciousness of our star finding its way into our heart.

The sun's consciousness is the wisest in our realm, not as wise as the gods beyond it, but the controller of all within its space. Everything in this solar system is subordinate to our sun. So, we can appreciate why the ancient ones venerated the sun and placed it as their highest god.

Link your consciousness in your heart to that of our own blazing star and you will be vivified and made alert, for the sun's rays are stimulating and it is these that give you life.

You might think that the sun just sits there in the sky and does nothing more than shine. But our star is the central hub of our solar system. It is mission control, and from here all is monitored and destinies created.

So, if you are not feeling like a star yourself, look to your idol and take upon you some of its rays. Fill yourself up with the glory of its brilliance, and connect with its consciousness and listen to what our star has to say. For this star is not just some inanimate object, hanging in the heavens. The sun itself is the physical body of a god. This is how this god has chosen to manifest itself, and one day you will get to try this yourself.

So, be more aware now of the sun looking over your shoulder. Do not run from it and into the shadows, but embrace this father-mother god and know that you are one of its children. You have come to Earth to shine like the sun itself, to be a star of brilliance and radiate your love and light. Are you still under the covers and no one is able to see who you are? Pull back those shades and shrouds and blankets and give us your light and do not be afraid.

The sun will not last forever, but its consciousness will live on. And there will be other stars that we will cluster around until the day comes when we make it to stardom ourselves.

You can make a journey into the sun at any time. You are welcome to share its hotspots. You are welcome to dissolve and blend your consciousness with theirs. This will not be the end of you, but the birth of someone new, for the sun is marvellous at bleaching out old stains and reinvigorating you with extra life blood and motivation to step down upon the Earth once again.

So, do take your consciousness for a sun bath every now and again. It sloughs off all the old and the useless, just as fire does for you back on Earth. So, do not be afraid of the sun's heat and its storms. It may seem like a fiery, hellish place but, in truth, it is a kind of Heaven where you can be reborn.

You might be wondering if any of the other stars will do the same job as our own. Well, they are not your direct father-mother sun, so although you will feel brightened it is our sun that will benefit you most. The other stars all have their own particular rays. Each star is unique and different, just as each consciousness on Earth has its own remarkable traits. You may visit any star in the universe as you please, but come home to our own star, for family is important and you will gain harmony from visiting here.

The stars of this universe are all gods who have made it near the top. So, next time you look out at the night sky, gaze with wonderment at how many great gods there are. But it is the star that shines in our daytime that is the greatest god for us. Savour the benefits of our sun, then, for without it our Earth would be done.

Chapter 75 – LATE FOR YOUR DESTINY

I am going to speak about tardiness today, the fact of being late for something, of dragging your heels and procrastinating over taking action. You might think this chapter comes a little late in the day in this book, but better said now than later.

We all have a preponderance for being late for things at some time or other in our lives. And it is usually when we don't want to get there, when we are holding ourselves back, when we are resisting moving forwards. And so, we may be late for school or late for our job, late in catching the train or plane, and, worst of all, late in meeting our destiny.

It has many repercussions and consequences when we are late or tardy. For the universe runs with many cogwheels, and when it is time for your cog to fit within another, then if you miss this opportune moment, the cog will keep on turning without having linked you to it. And so, you will miss your date within this cycle, and who knows how long it will be before this cogwheel comes around once again.

So, look lively when it is time for you to jump on board. The universe waits for no one, and you are either in its slipstream or you are left behind. And there is no worse feeling than being left behind and abandoned, especially when you might see loved ones forging ahead and being whisked smoothly into higher climes.

So, you will not want to be late when the step up is offered to you. Grab hold with both hands and jump on up. There will be no worse feeling than regret if you watch the opportunity slip away. Be aware of any resistance to moving forwards on your path and your climb. Undo these blockages and speak with your lower selves, for if you let your inner children rule you, you might never get to see what you are destined for. You must take a stand and be determined to make your dreams come true. The universe has certain synch points where you must meet it. Don't drag your heels, but get there on time.

You will need to open your heart and unfold your love if you are to allow the universe to work its magic in and through you. Take down your defences and imagined protection. Let yourself be vulnerable and open to the gods. If you are hiding yourself from us, then how can we put you in our team? So, joyfully present yourselves to us. Report for duty with smiles all around.

You pull yourself back and make yourself late when you are scared of what the future holds for you. You may be dwelling on all the impossibilities or negative vibes, so drop this kind of thinking and dream your dreams and let good things abide.

If you knew you had a date to attend a wonderful celebration, you would don your fine clothes and you would pitch up at the door with time to spare. So, foster these kinds of feelings for your destiny, then you will be raring to get out of the door. In every moment, drop all your fears and insecurities that your day will be bad, but anticipate great things happening, for in any moment magic can occur.

There are many who procrastinate and pretend they don't have time. They will look to put other things first in their life, when their sights should be set on their vision and making like an express train towards their goal. But, no, you just need to do this or do that, and before you know it the day has already ended. So, we would like you to prioritise the things that must get done first. And these are the things to do with your mission. Whatever is taking you on the path to godhood, that is what should be claiming your time. You can make all the excuses under the sun, and we have heard them all before, but in truth you are here to complete your destiny and everything else is merely a supporting act.

So, come, get your priorities in order. Don't be wasting time there and putting your destiny on hold. Grab your soul and ask them what you need to do right now. And they will get you on the right track, making sure that you get there on time. Even if you are vague as to the details of your destiny and where and when, just ask for your soul's help to get you where you need to be, and follow your urgings and any signs that you are shown.

Make straight for your destination. Do not tarry and wobble about. Put all your eggs into this basket, and show up for your date as the cogwheel comes around. Unhitch your anchors and anything holding you back. Be like the racehorse out of the starting stalls. The gun has gone off; let's see you run. Of course, this is not all running. There will be times to sit back and rest, but only once you've made your date with destiny. You have interlocked your wheels and been moved on.

There is no sorrier sight to watch than those who've been left behind. The weeping and gnashing of teeth will last for ages, and there is nothing we gods can do until the cogwheel comes around again. So, please be aware now that time is of the essence. You cannot afford to dilly-dally, not when destiny is waiting for your presence. So, arm yourself with good high vibes and expect the best to happen in every way, and move yourself towards the door and destiny, and run to your assignation in good time before the wheel moves on.

There is no such thing as time in our universe, not in our higher dimensional worlds, yet the universe runs like clockwork with its cycles. So, when it is time for something to happen, you will need to be there.

Chapter 76 – IN SUMMARY

Let us hold a mirror up today on all that we have looked at in these pages and all that we are becoming through the use of our marvellous consciousness. And where do we go from here? Well, I shall reveal that in a moment, once we have seen where we have been.

It has been a winding route, has it not, from the first chapter to the last? And we have gone this way and that way in every one of the ten directions. And I hope I haven't bored you, but that you have taken it all on board.

We are a rambunctious lot here in Heaven and we do not always play by the rules. And so, not for us a code that you must stick to rigidly and religiously. We are all for finding innovative and flexible ways. And so, my lessons have been rambling but I hope that they've made sense, for I don't like to be a fusty old fuddy-duddy, teaching you by rote. I want you to absorb the meaning of things through experiencing them as I speak.

But you may well have to ponder on these words for longer than the seconds it takes to read them. For our consciousness would become overwhelmed if we tried to take in all these themes at once. So, go with those topics that attract you the most, and start there until you gain some mastery in that area. And pick up these chapters every now and again to refresh your memory and your consciousness, and be led down the right road towards your rightful destiny.

We are not finished here, oh mark my words. In truth we have only just got started. Your consciousness stretches to infinity, and therefore so will my teachings. I'll be learning along the way just like you.

So, we have spoken about how consciousness came to be, and how we ourselves came to be from that first mind. We know how we have been created from the consciousnesses of the gods, and how, as humans, we are returning on a journey to find the god in us again. We have delved into aliens, exoplanets, and the stars. We have met up with the angels and studied who they are. We have been acquainted with our toolbox that contains our magic wand. We now know many methods for our evolvement, and discovered the jewels that will get us going and keep us calm.

We have taken a trip down into the underworld and soared high above to meet with creator gods. We have delved into the past and the future. We now know what is coming to us and how we need to jump up into the higher Earth. We have examined ways of all and every kind, and we are aware now of vibrational levels and what it takes to raise ourselves up. We understand now how our consciousness is like a ribbon of wavelengths that we can dial into. And we know now what our spirit is, and what our soul does to guide us through our lives.

We have looked into the structure of water and man-made things, and we have discovered that all is not how it was deemed to be, and that we must look further with our inner eye to see the things that have been hidden from humanity. We have spoken of portals and bridges to the higher worlds, and how it is imperative for you to get here, for things on the lower Earth are going to go gravely askew. You now know how to let go of the darkness and fears that imbue your mind, and how the universe contains a recycling depot to bring everything back into purity once again.

Your consciousness must be nurtured, just as if you were growing a crop. You cannot just let it lie stagnant or fallow, for if you serve no purpose then you'll be in for the chop. We described the death process, and all that goes before and after. And we introduced you to the gods and godhood, who you'll be meeting now and in the hereafter.

There will be many questions spawned by all my chats. Write them down and send them to me, and I will try to answer them in future books. But even if I don't receive your letters I will pick up on your thoughts and include these in my work. So, know that I am monitoring you, all who read this book, for I'm interested in how you will fare from here on.

And if you like what you have read here, I will be interested in taking you on, for my role is as a teacher and I have students far and wide. Come join my happy family of metaphysicians. There is much to discuss and much to be done to spread the word world-wide. I am excited that you have made it all the way through until the end. Your perseverance is to be applauded; a good trait to have as a god.

Dive back into this book as often as you can, for there will be much that will be forgotten. Refresh your consciousness with all that it can do. You will have begun to know now what a remarkable person you are. Perhaps as a physical human you are no great shakes, but as a consciousness you are glorious and the world awaits your light.

So, start to think of yourself more as a spirit that can fly. Your consciousness provides all the magic that you need. You are a god, no doubt about it, so don your boots and cape. And believe it, believe it now. There has been so much hidden from you but now the door is opening wide. The universe is showing us her wares. Let us be kids in a sweet shop and avail ourselves of her joys.

It has been my pleasure to describe these things that are close to my heart. My wish for you now is that they affect your heart too. Fly with your consciousness and discover our hidden dimensions.

With blessings and great love,
Chiron, teacher and healer

***Because this book contains much metaphysical knowledge that many people may find requires some extra explanation, Sophia has written a companion book, *Guide to Consciousness and the Unseen Universe*, to describe these concepts in further detail and with many analogies from her own experiences and teachings.

APPENDIX 1 - About Sophia Ovidne

Sophia has been channelling the Ascended Masters (the gods) for decades, not only Chiron but many other Masters such as El Morya, Lady Sedna, Jesus, Kuthumi, Quan Yin, St.Germain, Djwhal Khul, Hilarion, Thoth, and Pallas Athena. There is no particular god or Master that she is affiliated with; she works with whomever requires her to be their messenger. She is a teacher of spirituality and metaphysics and has published many books containing the gods' and angels' messages to humans, as well as spiritually-based novels.

Passionate about the metaphysical world and astrology, Sophia is helping, through her books, articles, and workshops, to educate people in a sensible and rational way as to what exactly exists out there in the universe, unseen by human eyes. She is dedicated to assisting humans with their connection to their spirit and soul, and with their emotional and spiritual issues, and in finding their way to Ascension and their own godhood.

Born in London to an English mother and Polish father, Sophia is the eldest of five sisters. She has travelled the world extensively, and lived in England for twenty-two years, in South Africa for thirteen years, and has been in Australia for over thirty years and currently lives near Brisbane, in Queensland. She spent the first thirty years of her working life in the IT industry, as a programmer, analyst, and management consultant, before stepping onto her spiritual path and eventually embracing it full time.

Sophia is also a novelist, artist, spiritual astrologer, and has a diploma in hypnosis and NLP. She loves to garden, and growing flowers and her own fruit and vegetables are one of her happiest pastimes.

A quarterly Message from the Masters is written/channelled by Sophia, which can be accessed for free on her website www.earthwithspirit.com. The website also contains information about the Masters/gods that Sophia works with, gives information about any workshops she is presenting, and details how people can receive a personal counselling session or astrology reading with her. It also has free meditations and extensive information about the healing properties of flower essences. She can be contacted through this website.

www.ingramcontent.com/pod-product-compliance
Lightning Source LLC
Chambersburg PA
CBHW032038150426
43194CB00006B/332